ETHNIC NATIONALISM

D0911069

PRESS
CARD
HERE

Former Yugoslavia

ETHNIC NATIONALISM

THE TRAGIC DEATH OF YUGOSLAVIA

Bogdan Denitch

UNIVERSITY OF MINNESOTA PRESS

MINNEAPOLIS

LONDON

Published by the University of Minnesota Press
2037 University Avenue Southeast, Minneapolis, MN 55455-3092
Printed in the United States of America on acid-free paper

Library of Congress Cataloging-in-Publication Data

Denitch, Bogdan Denis.
    Ethnic nationalism : the tragic death of Yugoslavia / Bogdan
Denitch.
        p.   cm.
    Includes bibliographical references and index.
    ISBN 0-8166-2458-5 (alk. paper). — ISBN 0-8166-2459-3 (pbk.)
    1. Yugoslavia—History—1980–1992. 2. Yugoslav War, 1991–
3. Nationalism—Yugoslavia. 4. Yugoslavia—Ethnic relations.
I. Title.
DR1307.D46 1994
949.702'4—dc20   93-23710
                                                                  CIP

CONTENTS

ABBREVIATIONS

EFTA	European Free Trade Association
HDZ	Croatian Democratic Union
IMF	International Monetary Fund
IMRO	Internal Macedonian Revolutionary Organization
LCY	League of Communists of Yugoslavia
SDP	Party of Democratic Change (Former League of Communists of Croatia)
SDU	Social Democratic Union
SKOJ	Communist Youth Organization of Yugoslavia
UJDI	Union for a Democratic Yugoslav Initiative

Introduction

THE RELEVANCE OF
THE DEATH OF YUGOSLAVIA

Why Former Yugoslavia Matters

This book is about the rise and political uses of ethnic nationalism at the end of the twentieth century. Its specific focus is the destruction of Yugoslavia, but it uses that case to attempt to generalize about the interaction of nationalism and democracy, particularly in post-Communist countries. I will try to use the tragic death of Yugoslavia as a prism through which to examine several far wider sets of problems. The central problem for which the destruction of Yugoslavia provides useful insights is that of the relationship of the politics of identity, of nationalism, to democracy. (I could go on to specify the politics of national identity in multiethnic states, but then *most* states are multiethnic to one degree or another, although only a few recognize and even fewer celebrate this reality.) Beyond this central problem, the tragedy of Yugoslavia contains many other and more specific useful lessons for the post-Communist states of Eastern Europe and especially for Russia, which is itself a multiethnic state, and for the other states that have emerged out of the Soviet Union.

Yugoslavia had been arguably the most successful experiment in building a multinational federation in Europe since the Second World War. Its gradual and painful disintegration and the increasingly bitter and confused combination of civil war and war of aggression by the

1

largest successor state that has emerged out of Yugoslavia — the state that also inherited the lion's share of the old armed forces — leave a legacy of destruction and intercommunal hatreds that will take decades to overcome. Some kind of a solution, however, will have to be found because a war on the threshold of the European Community profoundly destabilizes the chances of further European unification. If the carnage in Bosnia goes on and even spreads, not only will Western Europe be forced to deal with an ever-larger number of desperate refugees, but stability in the whole area will be threatened by the signal the war in Bosnia gives to all other nationalist would-be bullies.

If the leaders of Serbia[1] and Croatia, the two most powerful states that have emerged out of the wreckage of Yugoslavia, can get away with tearing apart and partitioning Bosnia-Herzegovina, a sovereign member of the United Nations, with no effective penalty, what is to stop military elites in other former Soviet and East European states from proposing similar solutions to their own national grievances and aspirations? There is hardly a border in the entire region that is immune to challenge on the ground that it commits an injustice to the ethnic or historical claims of a neighboring state.

This is why a solution for the Bosnian conflict is so important for both the region and the UN. A solution to the Bosnian conflict, however, is not possible without involving, on the one hand, the authoritarian regimes in Belgrade and Zagreb, and, on the other hand, the support of the United States and Russia. Otherwise the peace settlement will be exposed to endless mischief and challenges. These various factors make a peace settlement a tall order, and they also make the conflict in former Yugoslavia a matter of world significance.

The success or failure of the UN armed peace mission in the Serbian Kraina enclaves in Croatia and even more in Bosnia-Herzegovina will contain a large number of lessons and precedents, and not only for Eastern Europe and the states of the former Soviet Union. Yugoslavia in its death agony may be giving birth to a more effective and muscular international order enforced by a UN that goes far beyond its traditional hand-wringing statements when faced with communal wars, rebellions, secessions from multiethnic states, or civil wars against unpopular regimes. That would be an enormous step forward toward international peacekeeping and would require substantial armed forces under the direct command and control of the UN. The danger in this is that the task before the UN would be so huge as to overwhelm it.

Potentially, given today's world, a role for the UN as a world police force is a bottomless pit. After all, if the Security Council can guarantee the safety of the Muslim majority and all other citizens who do not want to live in ethnic ghettos in Bosnia; and if it can guarantee the safety of the Serbian minority in Croatia, even (one could say *especially*) against the legal, internationally recognized government of that state, then why should it not do so for the imperiled Armenians in *their* own enclave in Nagorno-Karabakh within Azerbaijan, or for the minorities in Moldavia, or Ukraine, or the Baltic countries? Then there is the general problem of the Romanies (Gypsies), who are massively denied citizenship rights and persecuted in much of Eastern Europe. The number of potentially equally compelling cases around the post-Communist world is enormous. And then, of course, the nasty question comes up: Why only the post-Communist world? Based on the sheer number of casualties, Burma, Sudan, and Kashmir require the attention of any world organization, as do the endless problems of Israel and the Palestinians. These present-day injustices in turn pale in comparison with the drawn-out agony of the Kurds, split as they are among five states. In point of fact the UN mission to Cambodia was undertaken at roughly the same time as the one to former Yugoslavia.

That Third World nations like India were most uneasy about sending the blue helmets to former Yugoslavia — and also most insistent on trying to limit the mandate of the UN — calls to mind further implications of the situation there. Too many obvious and nasty parallels to places like Kashmir and the Punjab suggest themselves. If Croatia, Slovenia, and Bosnia had the right to secede unilaterally from a multiethnic federal state and to receive international recognition, why not, let us say, the Punjab and Kashmir or even Tibet? To pursue one parallel further, both Punjab and Kashmir have minorities that would be violently opposed to a secession from India, and in both cases, like those in Croatia and Bosnia with their Serb minorities, the "ethnic or national differences" are, at least in their origin, based on religion. These kinds of parallels suggest the scope of the implications of the death of Yugoslavia. To further illuminate those implications, it may be helpful to briefly examine four related issues: the UN-protected zones in Croatia; peace proposals for Bosnia; the role of the army; and the role of economics in the crisis.

UN-Protected Zones in Croatia: Problems and Precedents

The Serbian minority in Croatia lives mainly in the cities. These Serbs differ from their Croat fellow citizens only in religion — they are Serbian Orthodox while the Croats are Roman Catholic. However, a substantial number of the Serbs live in compact majorities along the old Croatian frontier. That frontier had been organized as a military enclave directly run by the old imperial Austro-Hungarian army, which for centuries used the area as a major recruiting ground for soldiers and gendarmerie.

This area, known as the Kraina,[2] was integrated into Croatia only at the end of the nineteenth century. It is poor and has always produced a totally disproportionate number of officers, soldiers, and policemen. It produced a major proportion of the Communist-led partisans in the Second World War; it also produced a large number of officers in the Yugoslav army. It was certainly a very bad idea for the Croatian nationalists after their electoral triumph in 1990 to pick a fight with these notoriously quarrelsome and generally well-armed frontiersmen by trying to humble them and by proposing to purge and "Croatize" the police and judiciary in their enclaves. Remembering wartime massacres by Croatian fascists who were allies of Nazi Germany, the Serbs in Croatia were oversensitive to excessive flaunting of Croat nationalist symbols. The immediate change in the constitution so that it now asserted that the new state was the state of Croats — rather than, as it had been, the state of Croatians, which included the Serbian people in Croatia and others — made the Serbs overnight into a minority in the country their ancestors had lived in for at least four hundred years. These provocations, combined with vast manipulation by the Serbian government in Belgrade as well as by the political police and military intelligence, led to revolt by the Serbs in the Kraina region. Unsurprisingly they were backed by the Yugoslav army after a brief period of neutrality.

The six-month war in Croatia was immensely destructive of property, cultural monuments, and, in the case of Vukovar, a whole city; it created huge numbers of refugees, roughly three to four hundred thousand fleeing within Croatia and one-quarter million going to

Serbia. In effect the first "ethnic cleansing" was taking place. The war in Croatia was stopped in the early spring of 1992 by a cease-fire that included the so-called Vance plan. This plan left the Serbian rebels in control of just under one-third of Croatian territory; that area was designated a UN-protected zone, and its borders were to be controlled by UN forces. However, most provisions of the Vance agreement in Croatia were never carried out. The UN proved unable to enforce them.

As a condition for obtaining a withdrawal of the Yugoslav army from Croatia, including the Kraina, and the disarming of the Serbian militias in that region, the UN guaranteed that its forces would not withdraw for the first year of its mandate, even if asked to do so by the government on whose soil they were stationed. A more convincing guarantee for the UN-protected areas lies in the fact that a major assault against them, in contrast to the limited attempts to change the borders that took place in January 1993, would almost surely involve a renewed war with the Yugoslav army and this time a declared war with the present rump Yugoslavia. But that means that until there is a stable peace agreement among the states of former Yugoslavia, Croatia *has* effectively lost a substantial amount of its sovereignty over a fairly wide stretch of its territory.

This has led to a number of problems, not the least of which has been the inability of the UN to carry out the other provisions of the Vance plan that created the UN-protected areas. For example, the provisions that the Serbian militias would be disarmed, that the quarter million or so Croatian refugees would be enabled to return to their homes, that civilian authority would be restored, and that ethnically mixed police forces would replace the present all-Serb police have all been blocked. More to the point, the Serbian military authorities in the UN-protected areas had continued blocking the main communication arteries connecting Dalmatia with Croatia as well as playing cat-and-mouse games involving the hydroelectric dam that supplied the bulk of electricity to Dalmatia. Such a situation predictably led to further fighting as the Croatian armed forces attempted to correct the most intolerable features of the stalemate created by the Vance plan in Croatia in January 1993 and again twice during the summer of 1993. More armed conflict in Croatia is all but guaranteed unless the UN develops sufficient muscle to enforce the agreements it brokers.

Vance Plan in Croatia: A Bad Precedent for Bosnia

If the Vance agreement does not work in Croatia, where it addresses a far simpler set of problems, how can it, or some variation of it, be expected to work in the far more complicated situation in Bosnia-Herzegovina? The real problem is not as it has been posed for over a year in the Western press: military intervention or no intervention to stop the Bosnian war.[3] The real problem is what kind of an internationally sanctioned and UN-brokered political settlement will emerge out of that war.

For any remotely acceptable political settlement to begin working, far more massive and sustained use of international forces, including international courts and police, will be required. The costs will be huge. The cost of not doing this, however, will be continued carnage and a delegitimation of the UN — it will be marked as an impotent body unable to carry out the resolutions of the Security Council even when a relatively high degree of consensus exists. Therefore, the fate of the UN as an effective peacemaking and peacekeeping mechanism may be at stake in the aftermath of the bloody breakup of Yugoslavia, not to speak of the fate of the grandiloquently and prematurely named "New World Order."

That is only one of the lesser costs that are being paid for the destruction of Yugoslavia. Far greater costs have been paid and wait to be paid. Bosnia's existence as an independent state has become a sham, and the Vance-Owen agreement has become a mechanism through which the demise of a genuine Bosnian government would be legally legitimated. Both the Serbian aggressors and the Croatian "allies" have seized control of vast territories where the Bosnian government has no authority whatsoever. Both Serbs and Croats have set up "independent" ministates based on the principle of ethnic homogeneity. The Vance-Owen agreement in its original form proposed to legitimate this de facto reality by insisting that the only real players are the ethno-religious communities. Thus it recognizes the existence of only Muslims, Serbs, and Croats. In the original plan these ethnic entities, which are assumed to be represented by certain present leaders who claim to speak in their names, receive an equal number of "provinces," presumably a more polite term for "cantons," three each to be exact. No provisions are made for the more than 26 percent of the population that is intermarried; for the substantial numbers of urban dwellers who refused to describe themselves as either Serbs, Muslims, or Croats in the last census; or for the Serbs and Croats who support and have fought for the Bosnian government against their ethnic fellow nations that are trying to destroy Bosnia. All of that has been buried under the assumption that the *only* civic links that remain in Bosnia are those of the ethnic community. That, of course, is what the Serbian and Croatian nationalists have claimed from the very beginning.

The original plan has been modified somewhat, but the modifications hardly bode well for Bosnia. The "final" simplified version proposed in the summer of 1993 reduced the above-mentioned nine provinces to three ethnic units, which would have a right to leave the Bosnian state and join any other state. That virtually guarantees that the Serb and Croat units would join their mother republics and that Bosnia would be reduced to a predominantly Muslim rump. Further, because Serbs and Croats in Bosnia will remain armed with heavy weapons and in any case can easily be supplied by the bordering states of their fellow nationals, the plan leaves the Muslims and the urban nonnationalists to the tender mercies of precisely the present tribal leaders and war criminals who have rent Bosnia apart. The problem here is that to prevent all of this from happening a massive UN presence would be necessary to stabilize and maintain balance in the situation; further, the UN would need a peace-enforcing mandate with real teeth. Without such a massive presence and without such a mandate, these "provinces" will rapidly move toward becoming ethnically homogeneous or, at least, toward being safe only for the dominant ethnic group. To support the formation of ethnically homogeneous "provinces" or ministates in highly mixed areas is to promote "ethnic cleansing" — that is, the forcible expulsion of nondominant ethnic groups in a given canton. Because peasants and many people in small towns will not desert the land on which their ancestors have lived for centuries, forcible expulsion can be effective only when it is carried out with great and visible brutality.

Thus all those who support the creation of ethnic or national states, instead of states that will embrace all their citizens, support, consciously or unconsciously, policies of ethnic cleansing that lead to near-genocidal brutalities like the ones seen in the Bosnian war of 1992–93. This means that romantic nationalist poets, historians, intellectuals, and their foreign sympathizers share the guilt of those who carry out ethnic cleansing.

The brutality with which the ethnic cleansing has been carried out made the central claim of the xenophobic nationalists a self-fulfilling prophecy. Their central claim was that different ethnic and religious communities cannot coexist in peace. The brutality of the Bosnian war may well set off a cycle of revenge and counterrevenge that will make this claim de facto true. That is why the claims of the nationalists to ethnically exclusivist states must be rejected, and that is why the international community will have to hold war-crime trials to provide for some kind of legal catharsis through the punishment of at least some of the major war criminals. Instead it now proposes to treat some of these criminals as legitimate heads of states. Ideally, for real civic life to be possible again in a postwar Bosnia-Herzegovina, there will have to be both war-crime trials and something resembling the de-Nazification processes in Germany and Italy after the Second World War. That may be an unattainable ideal, but legitimating the results of a murderous war of aggression by the Serbian leadership, legitimating a land-grab by the Croat extremists, and betraying all those *non-Muslims* who backed the Bosnian government would be a moral and political disaster that would guarantee continued conflict. It would be a tragedy if the international community and the UN legitimated this new barbarism by supporting the creation of states that are the national homes of a dominant ethnic group.

The Role of the Yugoslav Army: A General Warning

The Yugoslav army — which from the death of Tito to the demise of the federation was completely free of any effective civilian control — has been the major aggressor in alliance with the leadership of Serbia, first in the unsuccessful war against the Slovenian unilateral secession and then in the messy undeclared war against Croatian secession. It has also even more clearly been the aggressor in Bosnia-Herzegovina. The army began to cut loose from its institutional moorings with its unsuccessful armed intervention in Slovenia in the spring of 1991. The process through which the army became a rogue elephant began when the nationalist quarrels, provoked by the increased assertiveness of the leadership of the largest republic, Serbia, paralyzed the federal government.

The malign development of the Yugoslav army should worry the leaders and opposition of all post-Communist states; it sets a very bad example. After all, the Yugoslav army had not been unique in its tight interrelation of the top army, party, and state leadership. The army never pretended to be merely professional; it was also the guardian of the established new order. That was the pattern in all ruling Communist regimes.

Nor was the Yugoslav army unique in that it faced a bleak and financially insecure future under the new post-Communist arrangements. Even the presumably inviolable army pensions and officers' housing were no longer secure. One can say that this is equitable, given that most other social and professional groups also suffer privation and insecurity as post-Communist societies attempt the hard transition toward democracy and productive economies, while also trying to satisfy new nationalist appetites.

That may well be the case, but questions of equity aside, armies are different. They have arms and can defend what they perceive to be their legitimate interests through violence and threat of violence. In the case of the Yugoslav army, those interests have recently had little or nothing to do with meaningful, legitimate political ends. This was revealed first through the army's unsuccessful invasion of Slovenia in the spring of 1991 and more decidedly when it took the side of the Serbian leadership in the criminal war in Croatia by the summer of the same year. That war was waged with great destructiveness and was directed primarily against civilian targets. It was accompanied by wholesale looting of civilian property and atrocities against both civilians and combatants by both sides. The army enabled the more vicious Serbian volunteer paramilitary units to commit a great deal of criminal looting and killing. It did so by disarming Croat villagers and then standing by when the volunteers moved in to do their killing. This was later repeated in Bosnia on a far vaster scale. It was a grimly appropriate symbol of the army's impotence to achieve meaningful political goals through military action that it moved on to attack the town of Dubrovnik, a major cultural treasure, thereby consolidating the outrage of world political opinion and greatly speeding up the recognition of the secessionist republics.

The Yugoslav army was not only unsuccessful; it also contributed mightily to accelerating the demise of Yugoslavia. Even when unsuccessful, it proved capable of causing a great deal of long-lasting damage. Once the state began to disintegrate, the Yugoslav army's existence, salaries, status, and privileges were effectively guaranteed only by its own military power and activities. That is a very dangerous example and lesson for other former Communist-led armies. The war in Croatia and to an even greater extent the war in Bosnia have also on all sides generated volunteer informal armed forces that — operating alongside the regular armies and police — fight, loot, and kill civilians. These freebooters have been recruited from the previously unemployed or marginal young. These forces are often composed of the same alienated groups from which xenophobic skinheads and soccer gangs have been recruited in Western Europe. In the ruins of Yugoslavia, however, these groups are both numerous and armed. They will not willingly fade into unarmed irrelevance and obscurity after some kind of a peaceful settlement has been reached.

The question is what forces will be willing *and* capable to disarm these militias *by force if necessary.* Their kind are all over Eastern Europe and in the states that have emerged from the former Soviet Union. They represent the material from which a general pattern of more or less political banditry may arise throughout the region. There are no firm structures or accepted limits that can rein in people with guns anymore. The new post-Communist governments are weak in their ability to exercise authority and increasingly low in popularity and legitimacy.

Dismal Economies Threaten Democracy

The catastrophic free fall and collapse of what had been a relatively prosperous Yugoslav economy and the end of one of the more successful economic reform programs in Eastern Europe provide grim warnings that the transition to pluralist democracy and a less-centralized and noncommand economy is extraordinarily difficult. This was even the case under the almost optimal Yugoslav condition where the economy had already been partially opened to decentralization and market competition for decades in the peculiar hybrid called "market self-managed socialism." Yugoslavia and the Independent Commonwealth that had temporarily replaced the Soviet Union had a similar problem in managing their overall economies: there were no effective institutional mechanisms to arbitrate and settle differences between republics that had become in all but name independent states. There was therefore no way of coordinating economic policies; there was no real control of currency. In short the "normal" mechanisms at the disposal of modern capitalist states to regulate the economy were absent. The transition to a full market economy demanded by the international financial and credit-granting communities involves stresses and sacrifices that are probably too much for new, fragile, pluralist states to manage.

The costs of a rapid leap into a market economy, under the conditions that the international financial institutions insist on, may include democratization itself. The tasks involved are difficult under the best of circumstances and are all but impossible in an era of the awakening and gathering of the tribes — an era of rising exclusivist nationalism and politics that place a primacy on national identity. In that setting, otherwise normal economic disputes about priorities are all too often transformed into national disputes.

In the past this dynamic has been borne out in arguments about, for example, whether Scotland had the right to keep all of "its" oil. The Lombard Leagues in Italy do not want to keep helping the poor in the south of Italy. How much of the contemporary Catalan unhappiness with a unified and today quite decentralized Spain is based on the Catalans' better economic situation and their desire to keep their earnings?

Local economic nationalism, then, was by no means a peculiar Yugoslav disease. What should terrify all who think about politics and the future are the similarities between the path traveled by Yugoslavia and the destruction of a unified Czechoslovakia and even the future relations among the nationalist states emerging out of the ruins of the former Soviet Union. Yugoslavia's prognosis had not been worse than theirs. To the contrary, it was far more favorable.

There is a general consensus among economists in the Yugoslav states that when the dust settles and a peace settlement is reached, the independent new states that emerge out of the ruins of the Yugoslav federation will have, at best, on average, a gross national product (GNP) and a living standard of roughly half what they had before the disintegrational processes began around 1987 or 1988. All the advice sold for whatever the market could bear by economic wunderkinder from Harvard and other centers of expertise to eager and naive buyers — advice on how to manage everything under the sun, including societies and economies these experts knew near to nothing about — did not help. The advice was both very costly and quite predictable. It was just as rigid an alchemist's formula as the one that had been exported by the Soviet Union in its own heyday of certainty in the universal benefit of central planning. The current product being exported to each and every country on the globe is market capitalism and private ownership. For some incomprehensible reason private ownership and an unrestricted market economy are supposed to be *the new* and even novel paradigm. Shades of Hayek and Friedman and others who had long labored thanklessly in the vineyards of that particular faith. It took a Reaganite and Thatcherite counterrevolution in the Anglo-Saxon countries for that particular faith to be revived. Looking at the world economy today it is hard to see why it remains popular, but then ideologies and faiths have never needed empirical verification.

There is some reason to hope that the Clinton administration will permit a cold, skeptical eye to be cast on these dogmas and that a more realistic and flexible approach will be pushed by the world financial community, the World Bank, and the International Monetary Fund (IMF) — all of which are exquisitely sensitive to the momentary ideological prejudices of whatever administration rules in Washington. The new kids on the block include some very knowledgeable people — for example, Professor Laura Tyson from Berkeley, the new Chair of the Council of Economic Advisors, who has major expertise in Yugoslav and East European economies and does not appear to suffer from excess respect for untrammeled laissez-faire economic dogmas. The problem is that a great deal of economic damage has already been done by a rigid insistence on prescribing shock therapies for everything that ailed centrally planned economies.

Grim economic shortages are only one price that the peoples of former Yugoslavia will have to pay for a catastrophe that has been visited on them, primarily by their own, more or less popularly elected, political leaders. To be sure these leaders had abundant help from abroad in destroying the economy. When massive and above all timely aid would have stabilized a reforming federal government of former Prime Minister Ante Marković, forces abroad responded with inaction. Other help in destroying Yugoslavia was provided by the clumsy and crude meddling and bullying by Germany and Austria, which showed their absolute devotion to self-determination in a region where their past record surely calls for at least some caution and modesty.

The European Community did not help when it decided that avoiding a dispute with a newly assertive Germany was more important than sticking to its initial view (proposed by its mediator, Lord Carrington) that the recognition of unilateral secessions of Slovenia and Croatia without guarantees for minorities and human rights and without settling outstanding disputes about properties was hasty and dangerous and would widen the conflict. If nothing else the fate of Bosnia-Herzegovina shows that those who urged caution were right. The least that should have been done, given the bloody warning in Croatia, was to provide for a UN military presence in the major cities, to establish safe havens, and to establish a UN screen on the frontiers of Bosnia *before* recognition.

The New Independent Yugoslav States: A Grim Future

The post-Communist democratic regimes that will develop in the new independent republics of Yugoslavia under the circumstances described above will necessarily be stunted. They will have more than a few similarities to the decaying authoritarian Titoist Communism in its declining years, which the new nationalist regimes have replaced. The similarities will be mostly with the *negative* heritage of Titoism. With the exception of Slovenia and Macedonia, the new states will have strong, excessively strong, presidential systems. They will, again with the same exception, have weak parliaments and even weaker opposition parties and movements. The mass media will continue to be more or less controlled, sometimes through direct censorship, at other times informally.

Narrow self-satisfied and provincial nationalism and shallow clericalism will probably be the fate of most of the independent states that succeed Yugoslavia. Conservative and religiously based nationalism will replace an admittedly shallow Yugoslav cosmopolitanism. Everything associated with modernity will be suspect, partially because of association with the past Communist era. This will explicitly include the formal and informal gains made by women over the past four decades. All of the new, independent Yugoslav states will be culturally more provincial and economically much poorer.

All citizens will also individually be culturally much poorer as they lose a multicultural as well as multinational Yugoslavia that had, perhaps exaggeratedly, a high reputation abroad for its own national republics. Yugoslavia, despite all nationalist propaganda to the contrary, had made it possible for at least four decades for its individual citizens to be Slovene, Croat, Serb, Montenegrin, Muslim, or Macedonian (even if it did not do so for the Albanians), and it also made it possible for these people both to be proud of their own specific national heritage and to feel at home throughout Yugoslavia. That will now be lost for a considerable time. It will be hard to reconstruct the brutally torn intellectual, institutional, personal, and economic ties — cutting across the republic boundaries — that made up the real fabric of Yugoslavia for over seventy years. Once the war is over and a genuine peace is at hand, some of these networks may be reconstructed through voluntary cooperation of the democrats, democratic socialists, new trade unions, feminists, and social-movement activists. In time some institutional and economic cooperation may become possible again.

The new, independent states will be narrower: their citizens will not be able to also have a broader Yugoslav identity, and they will be the poorer for that. Specifically, in former Yugoslavia one could *also* have been a Croat, Serb, Slovene, or whatever. In new, independent Slovenia, Serbia, and Croatia, as well as the other new republics, one will not be able to be a Yugoslav. This will be so even if the Serbian and army leaders insist on calling the rump state that they inherit "Yugoslavia." That state clearly will not be a multinational federation of equal nations; it is Greater Serbia, in all but name.

For many — for the children of the more than one and one-half million mixed marriages, and for all those who had identified only as Yugoslavs and not as members of the constituting nations — the death of Yugoslavia is a great personal loss. They no longer have a country of their own. Those who identified as Yugoslavs in censuses, not to speak of those who might have chosen to do so if the choice was that identity or a narrower national one, were more numerous than at least two nations, the Macedonians and Slovenes, which did acquire separate national states. Their national rights have been totally overlooked in the gathering of the tribes because, according to the nationalist gospel, there is no such thing as a "Yugoslav," and all who identify as such either are suffering from false consciousness (i.e., do know not what they really are) or are hidden Serbian hegemonists.

Therefore, those who consider themselves to be "Yugoslavs" are not even granted minority rights in the new democratic national states. They are simply supposed to vanish or identify with one of the new states. That is a very high price to pay for an experiment in trying to combine transition from authoritarianism with the building of national states. Yugoslavia was not an ignoble experiment, and it engaged the best minds of generations of its peoples for over seventy years. On the whole it made more sense than the alternative that was realistically available at the time. The practical alternative in both 1918 and 1945, given the relations of power domestically and internationally, had been a Greater Serbia. Croatia had been on the losing side in both world wars, and until a few years ago no one took an independent Slovenia or Macedonia very seriously, certainly not seriously as a factor in international politics. That might have been unfair, but it was the case. Without Yugoslavia many South Slavs, mostly Croats and Slovenes, would have remained under alien rule.

If useful lessons are drawn from the Yugoslav experiences that prevent all of the mistakes made from being repeated by others setting out on the difficult road of democratization, there will at least be some small benefit from the agonies the various peoples of Yugoslavia are going through. This will, however, be but a small consolation for the victims of the experiment. Regrettably, the new Independent Commonwealth that replaced the Soviet Union seemed to repeat the organic errors of Yugoslavia. The agreements among its members resemble the Yugoslav quasi-confederal constitution of 1974, without Tito, or a democratic equivalent of Tito. In many ways it is even weaker when it comes to coordination, and for practical purposes it ceased to exist after the abortive military coup against Gorbachev in the summer of 1992. The largest nation, Russia, was very much stronger in comparison with its potential commonwealth partners than Serbia was in relationship to other Yugoslav republics. Great asymmetries of power among the partners make it difficult to maintain associations of equal states. The Independent Commonwealth did not even have years of past joint struggles, analogous to Yugoslavia's struggle to maintain its independence against the Soviet Union, which could have acted to build some trust among the leaders of the new commonwealth states. But then these ties did not prevent the breakdown of Yugoslavia.

The misfortune of the peoples of Yugoslavia is that their former nation has been used as a laboratory for working out a number of general political and economic problems — problems that are in fact almost five decades old — that now haunt the post-Communist states in their region. Yugoslavia's specific road to disintegration and war is one that no other European nation has, thankfully, tried yet. However, the Transcaucasian republics of the former Soviet Union seem to be doing their level best to repeat the Yugoslav experience.

One of the great dangers in all this is that these processes of disintegration will negate certain gains made over the last centuries. The major historical gain in expanding democratic rights, from the French Revolution on — that is, the idea of a secular democratic state of all of its citizens, of the *entire* demos — should not have to be redefended in every new generation. Clearly that particular concept is in peril throughout Eastern Europe and the former Soviet Union. To be sure, the concept, standing by itself, is sparse and inadequate, but it is nevertheless indispensable. Without it any richer and more substantive approaches to democracy are not possible. It is the place where one must begin, and it is that which new national states deny.

The Importance of History and Facts: Notes on the Audience and Scope of This Book

As stated earlier, this book attempts to draw some lessons from the fate of Yugoslavia that are relevant to the rise of populist and traditionalist nationalism in Eastern Europe and the former Soviet Union. Some of these lessons, however, have an even more general relevance — indeed, they have meaning for the politics of the Third and even the First World because the rise of the politics of national identity is by no means limited to former Communist-ruled countries. For that matter neither are the issues of democracy and social justice that I also try to examine in this book. This work, however, is also specifically about Yugoslavia. I hope it will prove to be useful both to specialized readers with a background in the politics of Eastern Europe and to that increasingly rare bird, the intelligent and educated general reader. I will attempt to avoid academic jargon and will be modest in the use of endnotes, merely providing suggestions for further directions that can be explored by a reader or providing minimal sources for some more controversial assertions. In order for the nonspecialized reader to be able to get into some of the specifics of the Yugoslav situation, some minimal background and facts about Yugoslavia are provided. Chapter 1 is largely historical and can be skipped by those primarily interested in contemporary politics. They will do so at some peril, however, since so much of the language and substance of the disputes in Yugoslavia, and in the whole of Eastern Europe and the former Soviet Union, are permeated with history. It is often a very bad and one-sided history, but it is history nevertheless.

History unfortunately involves dull and specific facts, sometimes even dates. History and facts are unfashionable in advanced academic circles nowadays. Popular culture in the United States has long accepted the vulgar statement that history is bunk; currently that know-nothing prejudice is confirmed by the latest trends in the academy. Deconstructionism and postmodernism have apparently convinced an entire generation that it is sufficient to be acquainted with a powerful and, above all, fashionable and contemporary general theory. The important thing is that the theory seem to be new. These overarching abstract theories enable their adherents to generalize glibly about most everything, including politics in lands they know nothing about.

Facts can be relativized to fit any pet theory. History is further trivialized by the pernicious concept that texts "speak" for themselves. They do not. In order to be properly understood they must be placed in their general and historical context. But that in turn requires knowing at least something about history and culture. Americans and Europeans have had little patience to learn about peoples who for whatever reason they considered "peripheral." That was the fate of most colonized peoples as well as the East Europeans. This ignorance of facts about other cultures and histories, of course, has never stopped U.S. policy makers from prescribing or supporting detailed solutions for countries they knew little or nothing about. When this was done by conservative theorists and political scientists, it used to be called intellectual colonialism.

This is a parallel to the invincible ignorance with which the United States tried to impose its prescription for the ills of much of the Third World. Unfortunately people on the progressive and left side of the political spectrum suffer from a similar disease of cultural arrogance. They are continually shocked and surprised when it turns out that the enemies of their enemy are not necessarily their friends. The enemies of American imperialism in Vietnam did not end up being popular and democratic governments. The enemies of Communist authoritarianism in Eastern Europe and the Soviet Union did not necessarily end up being decent and tolerant democrats. Those who fail to learn indispensable details about the histories of the countries that they have strong feeling about are doomed to constant surprise and disappointment.

The failure to learn about other cultures and histories has led to bloody errors and failures all over the globe almost as often as politically malignant aims or the pursuit of narrow economic interests. It is not possible to understand the post-Communist societies without some history. Come to think of it, it is not really possible for Americans to understand their own society without knowing some history. It is a devastating comment on our arrogance and pride that as the United States turned to an imperial role after the Second World War, becoming the sole superpower by 1990, the teaching of history, particularly of other cultures and nations, has steadily declined. It is now quite possible to obtain a college education in the United States without having been exposed to any history whatsoever. This may be a triumph of postmodern curriculum revision, but I fail to see how it can produce a political public capable of making choices about foreign policy. Everything politically relevant cannot be reduced to television sound bites, or expressed in the language of popular media and culture.

A Personal Note: A Fair Label Warning

In chapter 7, I offer some rather extensive autobiographical reflections. Here it may be appropriate — at the risk of being repetitious — for me to state a few bare autobiographical facts and some biases that affect the analysis that follows.

By ethnic origin I am a Serb. I spent some of my childhood in Yugoslavia, but most of it outside that country. I moved to the United States when I was seventeen. I spent two decades as a trade unionist, a socialist, and a civil rights activist in the United States before returning to academia to get a late Ph.D. I have been a professor of political sociology for almost two decades. I am a citizen of both the United States and the Republic of Croatia in former Yugoslavia. For more than two decades I have spent roughly four months a year in Croatia, living in the town of Supetar on the island of Brač.

Although I am a Serb by origin, by choice I am a secular Yugoslav (as if that choice were still possible) and an egalitarian democrat. In other words, I am a democratic socialist, a rare but not quite extinct breed. I have been an active participant in and commentator on Yugoslav politics, mostly in the Republic of Croatia, for many years.

When the present crisis began I was among the founders of UJDI (Union for a Democratic Yugoslav Initiative), which was directed against all nationalist politics of the republics' leaders but primarily against Slobodan Milošević in Serbia and Franjo Tudjman in Croatia. We, a group of activists in the Croatian UJDI, went on to organize the League of Social Democrats of Croatia in 1990, which is a regrettably small social-democratic party similar to the parties in the Socialist International.

Major efforts of my political friends have gone into building new democratic trade unions controlled by their members. They have met with considerable success even in the teeth of enormous nationalist propaganda demanding social peace and national unity. In 1991 the democratic opposition in Croatia organized the Democratic Oppositional Forum to fight for democratic rights within that republic. Similar groups, parties, trade unions, human rights groups, feminist circles, journals, and organizations exist in all republics of former Yugoslavia.

Democratic nonnationalist opposition groups are most often led by people who have known each other from decades of democratic and reformist activism under the old regime. Mostly they see eye to eye and agree that the most urgent priorities are to achieve peace and to fight for genuine democracy and human rights. They differ on details but — and this is important — continue maintaining contacts and communicating. Maintaining networks and communications across warring lines is an important investment in future relations among the republics that emerge from Yugoslavia. It is the best guarantee that a genuine peace will one day be possible, a peace that does not lock the present combatants behind impenetrable walls.

The oppositional circles in Serbia and Croatia, as well as their friends and allies in the other republics of former Yugoslavia, represent the best hope that something will remain of a common politics and cooperation among the new Yugoslav states. But decent people and their activities are hardly ever news; nationalist demagogues are. Gatherings of peace and human rights activists are rarely covered by the media, domestic or foreign. Massacres and brutal communal fighting are always news. There have been ten interviews with marginal fascist psychopaths in Serbia and Croatia for every interview with a human rights or peace activist. Thus the media have helped the bad guys. At least they have certainly helped them in Yugoslavia.

I should add that I terribly miss that very imperfect Yugoslavia that I had felt to be my genuine and irreplaceable homeland. Those feelings had led me in the past to be more optimistic than turned out to have been justified about its prospects for survival. That was an honest mistake, shared with most non-Yugoslav and Yugoslav analysts up to the mid-1980s. However, I had never supported the preservation of just any kind of Yugoslavia — certainly not one that could be preserved only by a cruel war in Croatia and a siege of Dubrovnik, a baroque city where I went to elementary school and that, at least since 1964, I have revisited every single year. If a loose, democratic, federal Yugoslavia, one acceptable to the majority of each of its peoples, is no longer possible, then it is better that it cease to exist. By the same token, however, I could personally not support the replacement of an imperfect Yugoslavia by anything except a genuinely democratic Croatia, a Croatia that can be the homeland of all of its citizens — Croats, Serbs, Hungarians, Italians, Roms, and all others who want to live in a modern and democratic state of equal citizens. Yugoslavia should, for the time being, be replaced by independent sovereign republics that will be democratic secular states of all of their citizens.

Such democratic, egalitarian republics might well at a future date, starting from ground zero, move to reconstructing some kind of a loose, and above all voluntary, association or confederation of equal Yugoslav states. After all, there was a powerful logic at work behind the creation of Yugoslavia in 1918 and its restoration in 1945. That same logic, which drove disparate leaders of South Slav nations together, is still present, even though it is on hold for the time being. As things stand, the best long-range chances for such an association to succeed would be inside a European Community, where boundaries have become increasingly irrelevant. In politics, however, it is sometimes necessary to attempt solutions that are not optimal. Nevertheless, one thing is clear: only that kind of a completely voluntary association of essentially sovereign states, whatever it calls itself, could constitute a *third* Yugoslavia that would have a better long-range prognosis than the first and second Yugoslavias did. But that is just hopeful speculation.

The present is grim and offers all too little prospect for a genuine solution to the Serbo–Croatian, Serbo–Muslim, and Serbo–Albanian conflicts; the only solution in sight is a surly peace of exhausted combatants. The better alternative is a peace imposed by the international community, in this case the UN, but even a grudging and surly peace, with which no one is basically satisfied and which leaves the widespread desire for retribution by both sides unfulfilled, is better than war. Still hope does heal, and the peoples of the states of Yugoslavia badly need healing today.

The best of all alternatives, of course, would be the effective self-mobilization of democratic, egalitarian, and nonnationalist forces in Croatia, Serbia, and Bosnia. These forces would get rid of the present nationalist regimes that are doomed to ethnic conflict and warfare. These democrats alone can get rid of the authoritarian regimes and the constant national mobilization against imagined external and internal enemies.

Only decent democratic governments that respect and protect both collective rights — that is to say, ethnic and class rights — as well as individual human rights can make a lasting peace. That peace will have to include two fundamental dimensions: absolute respect for the existing borders and the will and means to make those borders basically irrelevant in the lives of the peoples and in the workings of the economies of the newly independent states of former Yugoslavia.

Chapter 1

ESSENTIAL BACKGROUND
ON YUGOSLAVIA

The Formation of Yugoslavia

Yugoslavia was originally created as an independent state after the First World War by the unification of two small independent kingdoms, Serbia and Montenegro, with the South Slav provinces that had been parts of the Austrian Empire for centuries. The extraordinarily multiethnic Austrian Empire had been transformed into the joint state of its two dominant national groups under the name Austria-Hungary in 1866. Although it was a modern, bureaucratic, legal state that granted considerable cultural autonomy to its subjects, Austria-Hungary treated most of its Slav subjects at best as backward provincials, at worst as subject peoples. The South Slav provinces had thus long struggled against the empire. Likewise, Serbia and Montenegro had fought long and bloody wars of liberation against the Turkish Empire, which had ruled more or less repressively over its subject non-Muslim peoples for four centuries. Thus Yugoslavia emerged as a state as a result of long, although inconsistent, nationalist struggles for liberation against two multinational empires.

The struggles of the small Balkan nations for independence were very inconvenient to the European powers in the nineteenth century because they disturbed the existing balance of power on which general European peace rested. Even more destabilizing for the European order, their claims were based not on historical continuity or dynastic legitimacy but on popular will. Further, the Balkan revolutionaries raised the general issue of nationalism, which was dangerous to the bordering multinational states like the Turkish, Austro-Hungarian, and Russian empires. They were also indirectly nuisances to the European colonial empires where the principle of nationalism, not to speak of popular will, was profoundly, even fatally, subversive. Like many of the present-day "inconvenient" national liberation movements (such as those by the Kurds, the Basques, the Palestinians, and the Kashmiris), the Balkan nationalists placed a priority on the national independence of their own suppressed, and sometimes oppressed, nation above all other political considerations. Like the Italian national revolutionary conspirators, the *carbonari,* and the Polish and Irish national revolutionaries, they were explicit revolutionary opponents of the international status quo throughout the nineteenth century. Inspired by radical democratic ideas, often by Giuseppe Mazzini and even Mikhail Bakunin, they were, like their intellectual teachers, prone to building underground conspiracies. They were mortally hostile to the status quo and to the then-existing world order, which required their continued subordination to ramshackle multinational empires.

The actual commitment of the nineteenth-century national liberation movements to democracy in any recognizable form was dubious at best. Nevertheless, the language of repressed nationalism in the nineteenth century was generally radical and democratic, just as such language was often fascist in the period between the two world wars and Marxist-Leninist after the Second World War. The Balkan revolutionary nationalists thus were precursors of the anticolonial movements after the Second World War. They were premature, if unconscious, Third Worlders. Like other former oppressed and colonial peoples, the Balkan peoples had, in very differing degrees, adopted some of the culture, language, and institutions of their conquerors. The relationship between the conquerors and the subject peoples was, as it is almost always, an ambivalent love-hate relationship.

Travelers and scholars had long commented on the imprint that the Ottoman Empire had left on Macedonia, Kosovo, and Bosnia, and that imprint was only somewhat less on Montenegro and Serbia. Strong Italian influence, left by years of Venetian rule, is still evident in Dalmatia, Istria, and the town of Rijeka. An even stronger imprint was left by Austria-Hungary on Vojvodina, Croatia, and, above all, Slovenia. Central European Germanic culture was imprinted through centuries of rule and institution building; further — with the partial exception of the Orthodox Serbs in Vojvodina and in the Croatian military frontier, or the Kraina — a common and well-organized religion, Roman Catholicism, had united the ruling and subject peoples. In the case of the Serbs, like that of the Catholic Irish in Great Britain, a separate religion was both grounds for discrimination and a basis for maintaining a distinct national identity. It is very unlikely that the Serbs would have maintained a separate national identity from the Croats in the Austrian Empire if it had not been for the Serbian Orthodox church.[1]

The unification of the South Slavs into a new state was possible only as a result of the defeat and disintegration of Austria-Hungary at the end of the First World War. Peace proposals by the United States, known as President Wilson's Fourteen Points, emphasized that self-determination and ethnic criteria be used to determine new frontiers, but there was much ambiguity in the plan. Italy claimed strategic frontiers that had been offered to it by the allies in the secret clauses of the Treaty of London of 1915 as an inducement to join in the war against Austria-Hungary and Germany. This included Slav-inhabited parts of Istria, the city of Fiume (Rijeka), parts of Dalmatia, and some islands. The pressure was therefore great for the temporary state of Slovenes, Croats, and Serbs, representing the Austro-Hungarian South Slavs, to merge quickly, and without too much negotiating, with Serbia and Montenegro, which were among the victorious powers and could offer some minimal protection against very visible and real Italian nationalist rapacity. The South Slav provinces of Austria-Hungary, which had never been united before, thus merged with Montenegro and Serbia to create the Kingdom of Serbs, Croats, and Slovenes in 1918. The new state was renamed the Kingdom of Yugoslavia in 1929.

The lack of thorough negotiations about unification meant that major differences on how the new state was to be organized were hastily papered over. This haste was to prove a serious mistake that would haunt the new state in the years that followed. The Serbs as victors in war and with an established state basically regarded the new state as an extension of Serbia, which had, in their view, liberated its Croat and Slovene brothers and sisters from foreign

Austro-Hungarian rule. The Croats, Slovenes, and Bosnian Muslims, in contrast, for the most part considered that the new arrangement was — or at least should be — a voluntary federation of equal peoples who would jointly construct a new state with new a constitution, laws, and civil service. In those two opposing views were found the roots of the conflicts that in turn destroyed both Yugoslavias. Nevertheless, there was wide support for the new state at its birth.

Yugoslav Historic Internal and External Borders

The internal borders of Yugoslavia in 1918 are still of some relevance because they closely resemble the present controversial or "administrative" borders that were adopted by the victorious Communists in 1945 for "second" Yugoslavia at the end of the Second World War. In brief, the areas defined by the borders established in 1918 included the Slovene-inhabited Austrian province of Carniola and the southern parts of the Austrian provinces of Styria and Carinthia — these being united for the first time since the early Middle Ages; Croatia and Slavonia, including the old military frontier, the Kraina, which had been an autonomous part of Hungary; Dalmatia (which had been a part of the Austrian lands), less the city of Zadar and a few islands that were kept by Italy despite bitter protests; Bosnia-Herzegovina, which had been jointly administered by Hungary and Austria since 1878; and Vojvodina, an ethnic mosaic with a Serbian plurality, carved out of the southern parts of Hungary. To this legal and administrative potpourri were added the kingdoms of Montenegro and Serbia, both much enlarged by the Balkan Wars of 1912–13 with administratively as yet unabsorbed territories gained from Turkey. Macedonian distinct national identity was not recognized in the new state.

While Serbia and Montenegro already had a hard-won independence, at the time of unification Croatia alone among the South Slavs in Austria-Hungary had a vestigial statehood and a national parliament with considerable autonomy. Slovenians gained their distinct existence as a national state in first Yugoslavia, while the long-suffering Macedonians received their recognition only in second Yugoslavia after the Second World War and the victory of the Communists. The second Yugoslav state, which was the legal successor of the first, bolstered its territorial gains at the expense of Italy. This expansion involved Istria, Rijeka (Fiume), Zadar, and some islands. These gains directly enlarged and benefited Croatia and Slovenia.

The new Yugoslav internal borders after the Second World War and the victory of the Communist-led partisans in the civil war basically followed the earlier historical and administrative guidelines wherever practical. Thus the uncontroversial old Slovenian frontier with Croatia was continued through Istria. Croatia, united with Dalmatia, followed its old Austro-Hungarian boundaries with the following changes: it added its part of Istria and Fiume; it added Baranja, which had been a part of Hungary; it did not include the compactly Serbian eastern province of Srem, which was attached to Vojvodina; and it did not include the Bay of Kotor, which became a part of Montenegro. Bosnia-Herzegovina kept its old Austro-Hungarian boundaries of 1878–1918, with some very minor concessions to Montenegro around Kotor. Macedonia had a new, more or less ethnic boundary separating it from Serbia. Vojvodina, except for some minor areas around Belgrade, simply encompassed the autonomous province of the Republic of Serbia north of the Danube and Sava rivers, an area that had belonged to Austria-Hungary. The Province of Kosovo was carved more or less to follow the areas with an Albanian majority. Therefore, it is clear that these "administrative" borders are not merely arbitrary and unhistorical, as claimed by Serbian nationalists today. However, it is also clear that, except in the case of Slovenia and Macedonia, these borders were never meant to be ethnic boundaries. They left some 650,000 to 700,000 Serbs in Croatia and roughly twice as many in Bosnia; they left almost 800,000 Croats in Bosnia, 200,000 in Serbia, and some in Montenegro; and they also left a huge number (around 2,000,000) of Albanians divided between Kosovo, Serbia proper, Macedonia, and Montenegro.

It is all but impossible to imagine any new "fairer" boundaries that would not require endless bloodshed to establish. The only reasonably clear case for a change in frontiers might be that of the Albanians, who urgently need attention to their grievances. A major national grievance has been the arbitrary separation of Albanians between three republics and the Province of Kosovo, which lost all of its autonomy, including its elected legislature, in 1990. For practical purposes Kosovo has been occupied by Serbia at least since the dissolution of its legislature.

For the rest, it seems to me, the relatively minor injustice of keeping the present admittedly messy borders was always far preferable to opening up what could only be a general bloodbath that would probably lead to even more unjust borders and massive voluntary and involuntary shifts of population. However, it is clear that that is precisely what the Serbian government and nationalists threaten. Their demand that all Serbs live in one state could be fulfilled in only two ways: either by maintaining some kind of Yugoslav state, which is no longer possible (in good part because of the actions of the Serbian regime), or by a bloody war to partition Bosnia-Herzegovina and Croatia, which would be criminal. It also sets Serbia into conflict with all of Europe and most of the world. The only temporary solution possible is that the former Yugoslav republics become independent within their present boundaries, with extensive human rights[2] as well as minority rights and autonomy guaranteed by the European Community or the UN. I regard human rights as having priority over minority rights because without human rights that permit the majority to organize alternate and nonnationalist parties and media, minority rights will at best be rights in a ghetto. Most minorities in Croatia do not live in ethnically compact areas where minority rights or autonomy could offer much protection. Also I believe that human rights necessarily include the right to defend those rights collectively, that is, to organize parties, media, and trade unions, all of which are essential for a democratic society. Without democracy, minority rights are a sham.

The irony of all this is that the Balkans now find themselves back where they were more than a hundred years ago, when — at the Treaty of Berlin in 1878 — the international community drew and guaranteed the borders and minority rights. The European powers tried to assure both peace and some measure of decent government by policing Macedonia while keeping it under Turkish rule. They met with very modest success. One can only hope that the second time around, the UN — with the backing of the European Community, the United States, and Russia — will do better. Yugoslavia as a geographic area is today just as "inconvenient" to the European states as the Balkans then were, and prospects for peace and stability in the region are similar to what they were in the earlier period. Yugoslavia is just as dangerous now, when it no longer exists as a state, as it was earlier, and it is just as prone to provoke quarrels among would-be patrons of different sides. Rather than Yugoslavia becoming a part of a unified Europe, it has become a part of the historical Balkans. The potential patrons of the individual Yugoslav states are also just as self-interested as the patrons of the Balkan states were in the nineteenth century.

The new rival states, despite all logic to the contrary, will not cooperate economically in a legal and organized way; this is to the detriment of all, except smugglers and black-marketeers. Nationalist quarrels between the new states will strengthen nationalist and chauvinist politics within the states. The disintegration of Yugoslavia is a giant step backward from an independent and nonaligned country to squabbling and even warring petty states scrambling for foreign patrons and support. Regrettably, that is only one obvious cost of dismembering the federal Yugoslav state; there are many others, including the lives of tens of thousands and the creation of an enormous refugee problem.

The National (Ethnic) Makeup of Former Yugoslavia

Yugoslav census statistics have been reasonably accurate. Table 1 gives the national breakdown of the population in 1981 (the last full census).

Serbs, Croats, Muslims, Montenegrins, and the overwhelming majority of the "Yugoslavs" — that is, at least 83 percent of the population of Yugoslavia — speak one language. That language is Serbo-Croatian or Croato-Serbian. Narrow sectarian nationalists have tried to invent sufficient differences between the Croat version of the language and the others to be able to call it a different language. That is absolute nonsense. Since the language was standardized in the mid–nineteenth century around the Herzegovinian dialect, it has clearly been one language. It is written in the Latin alphabet in Croatia and the Latin and Cyrillic alphabets in Serbia, Vojvodina, Montenegro, and Bosnia-Herzegovina. The differences between the literary versions are of an order resembling the differences between British and American versions of the English language.

There are clearly distinct *regional* dialects of Serbo-Croatian.

Table 1
BREAKDOWN OF YUGOSLAV POPULATION IN 1981
ACCORDING TO PRINCIPAL GROUPS

Group	Population	Percentage of Total Population
Serbs	8,140,000	36.3
Croats	4,428,000	19.8
Muslims*	2,000,000	8.9
Slovenes	1,754,000	7.8
Albanians	1,730,000	7.7
Macedonians	1,340,000	6.0
"Yugoslavs"	1,219,000	5.4
Montenegrins	579,000	2.6
Hungarians	427,000	1.9

*Muslims in this case are "Muslim as an ethnic group," which means Slavs who are Muslim and speak Serbo-Croatian. Most of these people live in Bosnia. As used in the census, the category excluded Muslims who are Albanian, Turkish, or Gypsy.[3]

However, Serbs *and* Croats, and Muslims for that matter, of a given region tend to speak the same dialect. Some minor differences may exist, but they are mostly a function of education and class. The only firm, identifiable difference between Serbs and Croats is religious — Croats are Catholic, and Serbs are members of the Serbian Orthodox church. The tiny numbers of Protestant converts barely affect this reality. Muslims "by nationality" are unsurprisingly mostly Muslim by confession or if nonbelievers are descendants of Muslims.

Religion is the most commonly used ethnic identifier, just as in Northern Ireland. This was brought home to me years ago when I was pretesting a survey questionnaire that included the question, "What is your religion?" The first respondent immediately asked me, "And what is yours?" I replied, "I am an atheist." To which he shot back, "I know all you damn intellectuals are atheists, but are you a Catholic, Orthodox, or Muslim atheist? I want to know your nationality!"

This neat division of groups along religious lines was not always so. There were Catholic Serbs around Dubrovnik at the beginning of the century and some Orthodox Croats. There were Muslims who identified themselves as Croats or Serbs. There were even some Yugoslavs once. However, by and large that is, regrettably, the past. Both the churches and the nationalists have labored mightily to get close to a 100 percent fit between religion and ethnic identity among Serbo-Croatian speakers and have tended to reinforce nationalism rather than any sort of "catholic" universalism. The churches are indeed both militant and national in former Yugoslav lands. The two identities thus reinforce each other.

Slovenes and Macedonians speak distinctly different South Slav languages with Macedonian being somewhat closer to Bulgarian than to Serbo-Croatian. The other two major languages are Hungarian, spoken by roughly one-quarter million people, mostly in Vojvodina and eastern Croatia; and Albanian, spoken by two million people in Kosovo, southern Serbia, and western Macedonia. These are the official languages of Yugoslavia and its various republics and provinces. There are also minorities who speak Turkish, Rom, Bulgarian, Slovak, Italian, Rumanian, and a few other languages.

The Romanies (Gypsies) are heavily undercounted or underreported in studies and censuses. Given Yugoslav demographic projections, the Albanians probably numbered, in 1991, over two million. That would make them more numerous than three national groups that have their own national republics: Montenegrins, Slovenes, and Macedonians. This makes their status as an oppressed group within the Republic of Serbia — they have a huge majority in the Province of Kosovo — even more intolerable.[4]

Wartime Massacres: The Present Burden of History

In addition to the heavy losses from the civil war and resistance in 1941–45, dreadful massacres of civilians took place throughout Yugoslavia. The worst were conducted by the Ustaše against the Serbian population in Croatia and Bosnia. They also murdered left-wing Croats and the Jews and Gypsies who came within their jurisdiction. One of the more notorious death camps in Nazi-occupied Europe was run by the Croat fascist Ustaše at Jasenovac.

Lesser in number, if for no other reason than that the perpetrators did not hold state power under the Nazis, were the brutal massacres committed by the Serbian Chetniks (of all varieties) against Muslim civilians in Bosnia, Montenegro, and the Sanjak area of Serbia, as well as against Croat villagers. To these must be added the Hungarian massacres of Serbs in Vojvodina; Albanian and Bulgarian brutality against the Serbs; and the burning of villages by Italians. Germans massacred tens of thousands of civilians, mostly in Serbia, in reprisal for the resistance and deported large numbers to forced labor camps. Most Jews in Yugoslavia were exterminated. The few who survived either were in the Italian occupation zone and managed to get to Italy or were in the resistance or the liberated territories.

The victorious partisans and the Yugoslav National Army — their acts inspired by ideology rather than nationalism — added their own brutal revenge to the totals of war dead by inexcusable, massive executions of tens of thousands of the surrendered die-hard remnants of the Ustaše, the Croat Domobran (Home Guard) army, and Serbian Chetniks. These were mostly captured in the last days of the war in Austria and returned by the British to Yugoslavia. The Communists also executed large numbers of real or imagined internal enemies during and immediately after the war. Huge proportions of the total wartime casualties were slaughtered because of national and communal hatreds and massacres and countermassacres, rather than because of the side they had taken in the war.

The massacres committed during the Second World War have not become merely historical facts. They are part of the present-day political scene. They are politically almost as powerful as the history of the Holocaust is in Israeli politics today. They are also just as often misused for narrow political and partisan ends. They represent the basis for what appear to be wild charges and countercharges of past attempts at genocide, charges that can then be used in the present or future to justify new rounds of killing.

For example, grossly exaggerated numbers for wartime massacres of Serbs in Croatia have been used by nationalist publicists to justify the revolt of the Serbs in Croatia against a government that, through insensitivity if nothing else, seems to identify with the Nazi-sponsored Independent State of Croatia, which had perpetrated the massacres. The Yugoslav army and the Serbian government cite the wartime massacres as justification for their present murderous war against Croatia. The fact that *Germany and Austria* have been the most active and aggressive defenders of a separate Croatia confirms

the fears of many that history may be repeating itself. Croatian nationalists cite equally exaggerated numbers for partisan executions
and massacres at the end of the war to justify *their* hatred of Yugoslavia and of the Serbs who played a major role in the partisan
movement.

The Political Manipulation of Wartime Massacres

Dreadful as the real massacres were, the facts and numbers about
them have been distorted and politicized beyond all resemblance of
reality by revenge-seekers, nationalist yellow journalists, and pseudohistorians. A number of factors were involved in how the numbers
were calculated. It is clear, however, that the official Yugoslav figures
submitted right after the war were exaggerated in order to maxi-
mize the war reparation from Germany. Then there are different *valid*
ways to calculate losses. For example, the following are some valid
statistics that can be combined and used for various purposes:

1. Gross demographic losses, including potential births: 2,022,000

2. Real demographic losses: 1,696,000

3. Emigration caused by the war (this involved mostly the German minority and some collaborationists and their families):
   669,000

4. Total wartime casualties: 1,027,000

5. Losses abroad (concentration camps, etc.): 80,000

6. Casualties *in* the country: 947,000[5]

The real losses were thus around one million, for *all* wartime
casualties. These are quite dreadful losses for a country whose population numbered just under sixteen million in 1941. No exaggeration
of the real should be necessary to make the point that the massacres
were a terrible crime against humanity and must not be allowed to
occur again. However, in the poisoned nationalist polemics of the
present, all sides try to exaggerate their own losses. Roughly 530,000
of the civilian and combatant casualties were Serbs and Montenegrins. The breakdown illustrates to what extend the partisan war was
both a civil war and a revolution:

1. Combatants (partisans and Yugoslav army): 237,000

2. Collaborationist troops: 209,000(!)

3. Civilian victims (*all nationalities, all causes*): 501,000

Some things logically follow from these grim statistics. To begin with, if they are even roughly accurate, it is clear that it was not possible for the Serbs to have had two million wartime casualties, as their more extreme nationalists claim. The *total number* of all war casualties — Serbs, Croats, Muslims, and the Jewish and Gypsy dead — is slightly over one million. By the same token it is not possible for the notorious Croatian death camp in Jasenovac to have accounted for more than one hundred thousand casualties. That would be a terrible figure but still not the one million or seven hundred thousand cited by the Serbian nationalists.

There are the victims from other camps and places to be accounted for — those dumped in numberless caves and pits; those murdered and massacred in the villages throughout the Kraina and Slavonia. That is where the war is now raging, in no small part because of these massacres fifty years ago. Then there were the massacres of the Muslims, Croats, and leftist Serbs in Serbia by the Serbian nationalist Chetniks. Further, it is necessary to account for the reprisals throughout Serbia by the Germans and for all of the rest of the wartime victims of the occupation. There were also the massacres of the collaborationists, or those thought to have been collaborationists by the victorious Communists during and after the war.

There were, in short, far too many dead and far too many killers and people who had collaborated with the killers. The memory of the victims is not honored by gross exaggerations of their numbers in the name of a vengeance toward the fellow nationals of those who carried out the massacres and who were not even born at the time. Democracy and a law-abiding society require that people be responsible only for their own personal guilt, not that of their family, tribe, or nation. In any case, those most obviously guilty were the Nazi Germans (and let us not forget the Austrians!) who made the whole murderous tragedy possible.[6]

The Role of the Yugoslav Communists
in the Partisan War

When the war broke out in 1941, the Communist party had twelve thousand members, and there were roughly eighteen thousand members of the Communist Youth Organization of Yugoslavia (SKOJ). Because the party and youth organization mistakenly and dogmatically attempted to continue resistance activities in the cities, where the workers were, their ranks in the urban centers were devastated during the first year of occupation. That devastation was accelerated by the fact that the prewar Yugoslav police generally turned the records and personnel of their large and experienced anti-Communist section over to the Nazis and their allies. As a consequence of these factors, the mortality rate of the early partisan commanders and political commissars was very high — less than three thousand of the original party members survived the war and revolution. The party was re-created during the resistance and revolutionary war. The war was fought in the backward, rural parts of the country, for the most part in Bosnia, Montenegro, and Croatia, and it was mostly fought by the young, as guerrilla wars usually are.

The partisans, led by the Communist party of Yugoslavia, began their armed resistance against the Axis occupiers not long after the invasion in April 1941 — the struggle began as soon as the Soviet Union was attacked in June 1941. Despite the occupation and partition of Yugoslavia by Germany, Italy, and their allies, the partisans carried out this struggle not only *against* the Axis occupiers, but also *for* power and a new social order. This is what differentiated the Yugoslav resistance from all others in Europe during the Second World War. The pursuit of revolution, however, led to the failure to build any kind of a genuine united antifascist front, if one had been possible at all. It also produced early political tensions with the Soviets, who were for a policy of waging a patriotic war first, and postponing the question of political power until later, if ever. Only a small number of left-wing parties cooperated with the partisans in the war of liberation. The exception was in Slovenia, where leftist Catholics and other leftist democrats did cooperate with the resistance. This explains the greater survival of non-Communists in the political life of Slovenia after the Communists took power.

At the time of consolidation of power in 1945, there were roughly

150,000 members of the Yugoslav Communist party, most recruited from the time of the surrender of Italy in the fall of 1943 through the end of the war in June 1945. Membership, in what was now the ruling party, grew quickly: 253,000 in 1946; 482,000 in 1948; 607,000 in 1952. By 1962 the membership passed 1,000,000. This was now a party very different from that at the beginning of the war. Roughly one-third of the members were now workers, including former workers who had moved up into political functions.

Unlike the case of the other Communist parties in Eastern Europe, the Yugoslav Communist cadres had mostly joined the party *before* it took power. They joined a party when membership meant risking death or concentration camp. And above all they already had a powerful party and army in place when the Soviet army arrived. Therefore, they viewed themselves as allies, junior allies if necessary, but not satellites or dependents of the Soviet Union. Despite repeated requests for Soviet aid — which was urgently needed for symbolic reasons, to counter the politically undesirable effect of the aid that was received from the "Western imperialists" — no such aid was received until the Soviet and partisan armies met in northeast Serbia in the fall of 1944. From that time to the end of the war, very large quantities of Soviet arms arrived, including tanks and planes, and the Soviet troops participated in the bitter, bloody battles to liberate Belgrade. A central part of the national liberation legend is that the bulk of Yugoslavia was liberated by the units of the Yugoslav National Liberation Army. That legend is essentially true.

The Yugoslav revolution in many ways resembled the Chinese revolution more closely than it did the Bolshevik revolution. Unlike the Bolshevik case, the backward, rural areas were taken over first; the cities were conquered later. But above all the Yugoslav party had the self-confidence of a party that had defeated its internal class and political enemies by itself, without Soviet help or advice. In that historical fact were imbedded the seeds of the future break with the Soviets and the Communist Information Bureau (Cominform) in 1948. That break made possible an independent Yugoslav path of development, a distinct Yugoslav model.

The Yugoslav model of socialism was a newly improvised, very different, nonstandard, nationally specific Communist model that began to disintegrate only in 1988 under the pressure of newly invented or reinvented nationalisms. At that point similarities with other Communist and post-Communist states were probably greater than at any time since the Communist takeover at the end of the Second World War. Yugoslavia's republics have painfully rejoined Eastern Europe. They had set out, of course, in a direction quite different from that taken by the other countries of Eastern Europe — they had set out toward the European Community. They have, however, ended further from their aim than they could have possibly imagined. The nationalist bypass has proved to be very long and rocky. I very much doubt that it can lead the newly independent republics of former Yugoslavia to a democratic European home, in any near future. The pity is that as late as 1988, the republics joined in Yugoslavia were ahead of all East European countries in their prospects for entry into Europe.

Growing nationalist conflicts; repression of Albanians by Serbia; the murderous and destructive war led by the federal army and the Serbian forces in Croatia and even more so in Bosnia[7] — all these have contributed to placing the newly independent Yugoslav republics in a position worse than that in which federal Yugoslavia had been. It was an illusion that breaking up Yugoslavia would speed up the entry of the former republics into Europe. The death of Yugoslavia has thus not benefited those responsible and has injured the far more numerous passive accomplices, who thought it would be harmless to indulge in a little national assertiveness and triumphalism. They certainly did not expect the consequences.

An Ethnically Balanced Distribution of Power

Before its destruction Yugoslavia had an important advantage over other multinational states in that its most numerous national group, the Serbs, were no more than 40 percent of the population. For historical reasons they were also scattered throughout a number of what later became republics and provinces. In any case, the Serbs themselves had developed under different political cultures: some had lived in the small independent states of Serbia and Montenegro; others had lived in the relatively modern, bureaucratic, multinational Austro-Hungarian Empire; and still others had lived under the decaying and arbitrary rule of the Ottoman Empire as late as 1912. They were all united for the first time in their history in "first" Yugoslavia as a result of the collapse of the Austro-Hungarian Empire at the end of the First World War, in which Serbia was among the victorious powers.

"First" Yugoslavia more or less used the historical pre-Yugoslav state and provincial boundaries. As noted above, when the Communists formed "second" Yugoslavia at the end of the Second World War, they consciously followed that pattern. The result was that it was possible to restrain the domination of the federation by the Serbs for most of the duration of postwar Yugoslavia — from 1944 to 1988, to be precise. The largest national group, despite claims to the contrary by rival nationalists, did not dominate the federation, at least not the top federal offices.

The second asset of the Yugoslav federation was that it had many national centers of autonomous power. In federations with only two major national players, like Belgium and Canada, at least as far as national questions are concerned, there tends to develop a zero-sum approach. That is, the gains of one national side are seen as being necessarily at the expense of the other.

However, in the Yugoslav federation at least six or eight republics and provinces were, in political terms, increasingly autonomous players as the years went by. In addition to these players were the institutional centers like the army, the political police, the federal government, and, most importantly, the presidency. Up to his death in 1980, Marshal Josip Broz Tito personified the presidency and was the ultimate arbiter among the various elements of the nation. Tito might not have been a nationally oriented Croat, but he was a Croat and not a Serb. This helped make the federal center appear more neutral. This meant that shifting dominant combinations and alliances in the federal center were possible around different issues over the years. No republic's leadership was necessarily in either a permanent majority or a permanent opposition. All could hope to become a part of the ascendant or dominant group and win the marshal's favor.

On the one had, during most of the 1960s and 1970s a disproportionately influential role in the federal center was played by the cadres from the smaller republics of Macedonia and Slovenia. The same was the case with economic policy. On the other hand, as discussed above, Serbs, particularly Serbs from the Kraina, and their closely related Montenegrin cousins dominated the officer corps. Up to 1966, when Tito removed Alexander Ranković as head of the political police, the Serbs were dominant in that organization as well.

This power arrangement was the result of Tito's deliberate policy of trying to keep the center from being dominated by one national group and giving all a stake.

Generally speaking, then, the leaders of the two largest republics, Serbia and Croatia, were for the most part kept from dominating the major federal posts. This is still worth mentioning today because the current nationalist fairy tales repeatedly mention the supposed Serbian domination of the federal Yugoslav states as a major grievance of the Slovenes and Croats during the years of Communist rule. It was simply not the case; the perfectly *legitimate* complaint was against the authoritarian Communist rule as such, but that rule was essentially equally hostile to all nationalism.

Rigid use of an affirmative-action ethnic "key" assured a near-equal distribution of cabinet posts, ambassadorships, and other important federal appointments between cadres from the republics and provinces. The parliament and other federal institutions made major efforts to be multilingual, and in this respect comparisons between the policies of Switzerland and Yugoslavia were quite appropriate. To be sure, the exact doses of equality were measured by those in the genuine power center of Yugoslavia, the federal and republic leadership of the League of Communists, with Marshal Tito as a final arbiter in case things got out of hand.

Until the second half of the 1980s these complex arrangements had produced a stable multinational federation where, whatever else was wrong (and a great many things *were* wrong), the national question seemed to be settled. It was certainly *more* settled in Yugoslavia than in the other multinational states in the region, and in most of the world for that matter. This is not to say that the issue of nationalism was ignored before the mid-1980s; it is only to say that, for the most part, the issue was dealt with in rather complex and subtle ways.

Up to the late 1980s, then, other issues *appeared* to be more urgent than the national question — democratization, strengthening the economy, and above all entry into the European Community or at the very least the EFTA.[8] The national question retained a burning and urgent importance mostly to the more marginal and romantic nationalists, the bitter losers of the civil war of 1941–45, and the novelists, essayists, and poets with populist leanings. Serious politically minded and modern people had other more urgent and important concerns for years, until they were rudely awakened in the late 1980s.

By roughly 1986, the revived and in some cases newly invented national questions either drove all other issues from the political arena or distorted them. The revived and newly aroused nationalisms in Yugoslavia led to bitter conflicts between the leadership of Serbia, the largest of the republics, and all other republics; to the destruction and delegitimation of all federal institutions; and to the devolution of the Yugoslav National Army into an institution that has independently conducted a murderous and destructive war against the republics of Croatia and Bosnia-Herzegovina.

The national question blasted apart the already decaying one-party monopoly of the League of Communists, reducing it to mutually hostile leagues of their own respective republics, to be joined later by a hard-core "military" Communist party committed to a unified Yugoslavia. It also led to an armed confrontation and rebellion by a substantial part of the Serbian minority in Croatia against the first government (albeit narrowly and clumsily nationalist) freely elected in that republic in multiparty elections since the Communist victory in the civil war in 1945.[9] However, it is simply wrong to claim that Titoist Yugoslavia did not pay much attention to the national question and to the preservation of the rights of the republics from domination by the federal center, and especially from domination by the most numerous national group, the Serbs. Titoism suffered from many other weaknesses and committed many other sins. If anything, it paid far too much attention to the issue of multinationalism and thus kept the fact of national identity central in determining career paths of at least two generations of politicians and civil servants. One unanticipated but in retrospect predictable result was that loyalties to the republics, which for the most part meant *national* loyalties, were kept high, while loyalties to a federal Yugoslavia were kept low. Even during Tito's lifetime it used to be said that he was the only real Yugoslav. That turned out to have been a bad mistake for which the present generations are paying.

Yugoslavia had pursued a broadly and culturally tolerant policy toward the non–South Slav minorities, which in line with the Soviet practice were renamed "nationalities." To be sure, this cultural national autonomy was accompanied by a hard-boiled authoritarian Communist party regime, which soon repressed all other parties and independent organizations, including nationalist parties. In practice the autonomy was that of the Communist political elites of the

various national groups. One very large minority, the Germans, numbering over one-half million, were removed from the national scene
through forcible deportation and flight. The Yugoslav Communists
had constituted postrevolutionary Yugoslavia, at least in theory, as
a federation of equal, sovereign South Slav nations. Croats, Serbs,
Slovenes, Macedonians, Montenegrins, and Bosnian Muslims all received federal republics with considerable cultural and later political
autonomy.

In order to gain further understanding of both the general and
specific ways in which nationalism was handled in former Yugoslavia, it is necessary to delve a bit more into both the recent and
more distant past. That past is sometimes historical, at other times
mythical.

National Makeup and the Role of the Yugoslav National Army

The Yugoslav National Army was the only institution for which
the case *could* be reasonably made that the carefully crafted ethnic
balance did not operate. There for decades the Serbs did have a pre-
ponderance among the professional cadre of officers and generals.
This was the result of three specific historical factors.

The first was that certain underdeveloped areas — specifically, the
Kraina region in Croatia, Montenegro, and Bosnia — contained significant numbers of Serbs who needed work and careers. They thus
went from those underdeveloped areas and joined the military in
large numbers for exactly the same reasons that Gascons and Corsicans in France, Highlanders in Great Britain, and Southerners in the
United States have been overrepresented in their respective armies.
As mentioned above, the predominantly Serbian Kraina region had
provided a grossly disproportionate number of officers and generals
in the old imperial Austro-Hungarian armies as well. For centuries
it was almost the only career open to ambitious and educated young
men in that backward frontier march of the empire. A second factor was that the Kraina and Montenegro had contributed greatly to
the partisan forces during the Second World War. This had led to the
devastation of those regions, but it also meant that the children of the
veterans had an advantage in getting access to the military academies,

and thus professional military careers. The third reason is that alternate careers that opened up as a consequence of higher industrial and postindustrial development in Slovenia, Croatia, and Vojvodina made military careers relatively unattractive to the ambitious young in those regions.

One unfortunate result of the national makeup of the army officer cadres was that the army was largely commanded by persons who were unusually, one could even say excessively, sensitive about the policies of the new anti-Communist nationalist government in Croatia toward the Serbian minority, which happened to be concentrated in the Kraina region, the very region from which many of the officers came. This sensitivity was greatly exacerbated by the fact that, as noted earlier, horrible, huge massacres of Serbian villagers by Nazi-supported Croatian Ustaše had taken place in that same region during the Second World War. Again, these had occurred often in the villages from which a substantial part of the military cadre came. There was clearly no chance that they were going to be neutral, whatever their clear duty or pretenses. They would certainly not be neutral in a struggle between their kith and kin from the Serbian villages in the Kraina region and the new, aggressively nationalist Croatian state. This was predictable even if that state's government was the result of free elections, and even if that conflict was clearly manipulated and greatly exaggerated by cynical national politicians sitting securely in Belgrade. The federal army would necessarily, and tragically, end up in alliance with the nationalist leadership of the Republic of Serbia, which continued to relentlessly play on and exaggerate the already existing fears of their fellow Serbs in Croatia. Clearly the Serbs in Croatia were being used by Milošević in Belgrade. Equally clearly they were already predisposed to be so used, and therefore intolerant, maximalist, Croat nationalist oratory played right into Milošević's hands.

The Croat nationalist leadership had been insensitive to an extreme in celebrating their ambivalent electoral triumph. It did not help matters that the new Croat authorities did little or nothing to protect law-abiding Serbian citizens as they were "disappeared" in Gospic, Zagreb, Zadar, and other cities. The perpetrators of a massive "crystal night" in Zadar in the spring of 1991 and other outrages against the Serbian minority were never brought to justice. It helped even less that the new Croatian authorities proceeded on a vast level to purge the Serbs from the judiciary, the police, and other positions of authority in the Ministry of Justice.

One thing this action made sure was that the dispute between the new nationalist Croatian government and its Serbian minority could not be settled through courts, which were no longer considered even theoretically impartial by the minority. Instead — in a way similar to the 1848 dispute between the Kossuth-led, intolerant Hungarian nationalists and the Serbian and Croat minorities — this conflict was going to be settled by the sword. In that conflict, unfortunately and quite predictably, the Yugoslav National Army, for a number of reasons, including the ones named here, could not and would not be neutral. It would side with the Serbian minority in Croatia. By so doing it would help destroy what little legitimacy Yugoslav federal institutions had left in Croatia and in the other non-Serbian republics. Thus the major federal institution that had been counted on to be the ultimate guardian of Yugoslavia effectively sealed its doom. The army had by 1991 become an institution primarily defending its own corporate privileges.

The Ambiguous Lessons of the First Free Elections

By 1990 Yugoslavia was irreversibly on the road to multiparty pluralism as the framework within which both the fate of democracy and the future of the Yugoslav federation itself would be determined. Neither the fate of democracy nor the future of Yugoslavia was certain by that time. Multiparty contests began in Slovenia and Croatia in the spring of 1990 and for the rest of the federation by the end of the year.

The results of the first free elections in Yugoslavia since the Second World War were ambivalent. In Slovenia, Milan Kučan, the leader of the reform Communists, won a large majority, over 58 percent, making him the first freely elected reform-Communist head of state in Eastern Europe. Overall, the reform Communists and their allies received 22 percent of the votes. The rest of the votes were mostly distributed among parties that were centrist or left of center, and clearly committed to further democratic development, including the former Communist Youth Organization reborn as the Liberal party. It was also the case that a high degree of consensus existed in Slovenia in favor of independence from Yugoslavia.

Thus if Yugoslavia was to have a chance to survive as a state after the Slovenian elections, it would have had to do so as a loose confederation — there was no other way to keep Slovenia in the federation voluntarily. To use force in the matter would have required a military coup. In the end there was an unsuccessful military invasion in the spring of 1991. This abortive invasion of Slovenia and the continued war in Croatia made it certain that by the summer of 1991 no acceptable terms could be formulated that would hold together even a loose federation.

The Slovenian electorate demonstrated both their moderation and maturity. They remained moderate in the face of the invasion by the Yugoslav National Army, provocations and conflicts that accompanied further democratization, and the difficult withdrawal of the League of Communists from state power on all levels. Since their defeat in the elections, the former Communists have evolved smoothly into an effective social-democratic opposition, and they have excellent prospects to win in future elections in an independent Slovenia. By 1992 they were the largest party in Slovenia and a part of the governing coalition. The prospects for democracy are excellent in Slovenia despite the quite grim economic situation.

In some not-too-distant future Slovenia might, just might, consider membership in some kind of loose (mostly economic) association of independent Yugoslav states. This would be an enormous help to the Slovene economy, whose markets and sources of raw materials are in the eastern parts of former Yugoslavia. That depends primarily on a civilized conclusion of the war being waged by the federal army and its Serbian allies in Croatia and Bosnia and on a settlement of the conflicting claims to the succession and division of property of the old federal state. In any case, that sensible option has been put off into the indefinite future by the barbaric behavior of the Serbian aggressors in Bosnia and Croatia. The present Croatian tendencies toward creating a narrow, nationalist, authoritarian state where the Serbian minority is discriminated against and treated as bearing a collective guilt for the behavior of the Serbian regime and militias are also very unhelpful to any normalization of relations among the states emerging out of former Yugoslavia, states that are doomed by geography and history to have some kind of relationship.

Nationalist Right-Wing Populists: Restructuring Croatian Politics

While Slovenia emerged from its first free elections with a center or center-right ruling coalition accompanied by a strong and competent democratic leftist opposition, Croatia was not so fortunate. This was partially due to an electoral system that was picked by the Communist-controlled outgoing legislature, a two-round system much like that of France. As a result a sharply polarized electorate has emerged. The election system in Croatia maximized the probability of polarization, unlike the system in Slovenia that used proportional representation and that thus naturally pushed toward compromise and coalition. Picking this system was yet another of the numerous strategic errors made by the Croatian Communist reformers; they wanted to monopolize the political space on the left; they delayed the legalization of alternate parties to the last possible moment; and they entered the election with the burden of the local, unpopular, county *nomenklatura* on their backs.

It was not possible to vote for the left without voting for the Communists in that first free election. Many voters saw the election not as a choice between competing programs but as a referendum on the past performance of the League of Communists. Delaying the legalization of the new political parties maximized the advantages of those who would play on the familiar themes of ethnic xenophobia and exclusivism and old national real or imagined grievances. That and very large funds (millions of dollars were involved) from émigrés abroad, many very right-wing and passionately nationalist, guaranteed that "hot" populist and nationalist themes would drown out "cool" rational and moderate themes in the campaign. The political terrain had been all too well prepared by two years of relentless raising of nationalist issues and bullying from the Serbian leadership, which kept playing the self-appointed role of the guardian of all Serbs everywhere, including Croatia.

A double referendum took place in Croatia in 1990, one on the League of Communists and the other on the politics of the Serbian leadership of Slobodan Milošević. Even under these maximally unfavorable circumstances the League of Communists did reasonably well, getting around 32 percent of the vote. The Croatian reform Communists did particularly well in the less provincial regions of the port city of Rijeka and Istria, as well as in the areas where the Serbian minority was strong. This electoral base was soon lost to Serbian nationalist parties after the national disputes heated up. The Croatian Communists' electoral results reflected the special "difference" that distinguished the Yugoslav Communists from their East European counterparts. Unlike the others, they had been the obstacle to Soviet domination over their country, rather than the instrument of such domination. Nevertheless, the victory of the nationalist right-wing populists of the HDZ (Croatian Democratic Union), led by Former-General Franjo Tudjman, has been an extremely serious setback to the orderly evolution of a democratic post-Communist Yugoslavia.

General Tudjman's party received roughly 42 percent of the vote. The electoral law gave the party two-thirds of the parliament. The nationalist legislative majority rammed through a presidential system that has reduced the parliament to impotence, changed the constitution by a simple majority in a way that helped provoke a revolt by the Serbian minority, and proceeded to purge the civil service, judiciary, and police. Under the guise of preparing the economy for privatization the new Croat nationalist government also purged Serb and Communist managers and seized direct control of radio, television, and the main press. It also proceeded to carry out a ruthless centralization of Croatia, abolishing the wide county and city autonomy that had existed under the old regime. The school system and universities were also centralized in the name of efficiency. A rigid "Croatizing" of language standards was imposed by linguistic nationalist sectarians in schools, government agencies, and publications.

The immediate casualties were moderate politics of transition toward democracy with the ability to compromise, tolerance of differences and of minorities, and a willingness to settle historical ethnic grievances peacefully. The already difficult transition toward democracy had been made much harder. The Serbian minority in the Kraina region took up arms and seized large parts, around 25 percent, of Croatia. That worsened the national tensions in Yugoslavia and in Croatia, solving nothing. This was the harbinger of the open bloody war and facilitated the armed aggression of Serbia and the federal army against Croatia.

The First Serbian Elections: No Change

In 1990, the first free elections in Serbia made no real changes. Slobodan Milošević's party, renamed the Serbian Socialist party, inherited the property and local assets of the League of Communists of Serbia and its fronts. Complete control of the most important media, especially the all-important television and radio, combined with control of the local administration and police, assured an easy victory for Milošević's party. It got *both* the old Communist vote *and* most of the nationalist vote. The largest opposition party was the anti-Communist nationalists led by a fiery, bearded, romantic writer. Milošević's party undermined his appeal within a year by engineering a by-election victory for the most notorious semifascist Chetnik demagogue, Vojislav Šešelj, who essentially took over one extreme of the political spectrum. The full corruption of the Serbian "Socialist party" becomes evident when one considers that this demagogue is ever present on the government-controlled media, inspects the armed forces, and publicly boasts that his paramilitary troops murder prisoners and commit atrocities. He is obviously tolerated by the ruling party because he has proved useful.

By 1990 the ruling party was busily attacking Tito's legend and widened its anti-Communist nationalist support. Tito was denounced for his "anti-Serbian" policies of maintaining some balance inside the federation. Tito's pictures, which had been universally present, were removed from public display, and ghoulish proposals were debated in the Serbian parliament — one being to dig up his body from its monument in Belgrade and exile it to Croatia. The worst of the jackals attacking the dead lion had been his most repulsively servile poltroons when he was alive. But then this is not uncommon throughout the region. It is just that in Serbia the leadership of Milošević had been particularly servile and obnoxious in the past with its adherence to the cult of the dead Tito. Tito deserved better after his death.

The Milošević government retained an authoritarian control of the media, provoking protests from intellectuals and even a nostalgic student demonstration in the spring of 1991 that was repressed by the police and that brought out army tanks to the streets of Belgrade. Unfortunately this was a false spring because the Serbian opposition is almost as firmly nationalist as the regime. When it is not uncompromising about Croatia, demanding new borders and protection of Serbs, it is uncompromising about Kosovo. This is the case with the large, nationalist, conservative anti-Communist opposition; it has also been the case with the smaller, more liberal Democratic party.

Therefore, democratic change in Serbia, without which no real peace is possible, will have to come from persons who are not present players in the political system — that is, from massive upheavals from below, bringing as yet unknown political players to the fore. Such a development is possible given the increasingly desperate economic situation. In short, the hope, and it is admittedly a slim hope, is that something a little like Solidarity in Poland in 1980 will emerge in Serbia. That development will be accelerated when it becomes clear that a multinational Yugoslavia is dead and when the European and world blockade of Serbia begins to have an effect. The process will be accelerated when the new independent unions, the broad democratic public, and the real opposition come to understand fully that the present government is a great misfortune for Serbia; that it, and not the Croats, or Albanians, or Slovenes, or the European Community, is responsible for the economic catastrophe; and that it has to be fought tooth and nail. Initially this will mean waging economic strikes and the growth of the peace movement.

When the peace movement and economic strikes begin to combine, those involved will face repression and will have to turn to mass agitation and mass political strikes. That implies a very rough path indeed for peace and democracy. New players brought to the fore by new trade unions and popular movements can be would-be Perons or would-be Walesas or even democratic popular tribunes of the people. It is hard, as history has shown, to institutionalize such popular movements and create stable, decent, law-abiding democracies. But then, the path to democratization is nowhere smooth. The Yugoslav situation should be observed with great attention by the reformers in the Independent Commonwealth arising in the former Soviet Union. After all, the developments in Croatia and Serbia reflect forces and strains not terribly different from those at work in Ukraine, in Russia, or, for that matter, in Hungary and Slovakia. Given that the economic situation in Yugoslavia was more favorable than in those other areas, the lessons from Yugoslavia become all the more urgent.

The nationalist genie is out of the bottle. How it is managed will affect the fate of democracy. That is why those who first raised the ghosts of historical populist nationalism — for whatever reasons, no matter what their democratic protestations, or how much could have been gained in the short run — have a serious political responsibility.

The Yugoslav elections in 1990, which put the nationalists in power, were, at least in part, the bitter fruit of democratization too long delayed and too reluctantly embraced and of the reckless games that the Serbian Communist leadership has played with Serbian nationalism over the Province of Kosovo and with the fate of Serbs in Croatia. All this is all too depressingly familiar when we look at the stormy prospects of social, economic, and political reforms in Eastern Europe and the Independent Commonwealth.

Developments after the Elections: The Present and Future Role of the UN

Conditioned reflexes reflecting the old authoritarian ways permeated many federal institutions, even after the elections. For example, in the spring of 1990, Yugoslav diplomatic representatives joined a handful of hard-line Third World authoritarian regimes in voting against condemning human rights violations in Cuba and China. This, perhaps prophetically, was done in the name of opposing foreign intervention in the internal affairs of independent countries. Those who voted in that way could hardly have predicted that within a year and a half there would be ever-louder calls for intervention by the UN in Yugoslavia against the brutal war being waged by the Yugoslav federal army, in alliance with Serbian irregular troops, against Croatia and Bosnia. And they could hardly have predicted that newly independent Bosnia would be desperately calling for UN troops to be stationed in that republic to prevent an extension of the Croatian bloodbath.

UN troops were deployed by the spring of 1992 throughout those parts of Croatia that were effectively controlled by the local Serbian militias or the remnants of the army. This, however, was the result of an agreement between the Croat government, the local Serbian authorities, and the federal army. The UN-occupied areas effectively freeze the status quo and are supposed to lead to a general demilitarization of the area combined with a protection of the local, mostly Serb population from the Croat government. This is a de facto recognition that the war in Croatia is, for all purposes, over, except for some shelling in border towns as a spillover of the fighting in Bosnia. Clearly the reintegration of these UN-protected border areas into Croatia will remain a crucial point for nationalist agitation in Croatia, and no real development of democratic politics and a democratic political culture is possible in Croatia without a return of these areas. Equally clearly, no peaceful reintegration of these areas back into Croatia is remotely possible without negotiations with the representatives of the local majority Serbian population. Those negotiations in turn will produce no results until the Croat authorities stop mistreating and bullying the dwindling Serbian population under their authority. The actual treatment of Serbs in Croatia is far more significant than all the excellent guarantees in the constitution of the Republic of Croatia. These guarantees, like those in many countries, have little relationship to the day-to-day practice of the police, bureaucracy, and employers. In any case, the fighting has been transferred to Bosnia-Herzegovina and threatens to spread farther south to the Muslim-populated Sanjak area in Serbia and the Albanian-populated Kosovo where the aggressive Serbian regime of Slobodan Milošević began the whole process of destroying Yugoslavia.

The calls for effective UN intervention in Bosnia were in vain because the UN would not intervene without a broad agreement by all major combatants. Such an agreement was unachievable when armed, local, nationalist satraps were outbidding each other in intransigence. It was even less achievable in a situation where informal armed militias could defy any orders to stop fighting and return to a dull civilian existence. Lebanonization had become a realistic possible future for at least broad parts of former Yugoslavia. All that could be agreed on was that sporadic humanitarian aid be sent to the dying cities of Bosnia.

The legal forces in formal control of Yugoslavia itself had proven incapable of either winning the conflicts or making peace. The same can be said of the forces of the individual, newly independent republics. Out of that stalemate a new approach to international peacekeeping will have to be developed. That approach — as has been shown in the case of the UN peace force deployed in the

Serbian-majority Kraina region of Croatia — will have to be less rigidly restricted by respect for local sovereignty, especially when it comes to local political leaders, elected or not, who subject their peoples to endless war and misery. That may be a significant step forward for a world organization previously paralyzed by great power rivalries and an excessive respect for formal sovereignty. The peoples of the new post-Yugoslav states now have the dubious privilege of being the pioneers of one more noble experiment.

Chapter 2

WHAT HAPPENS WHEN ETHNOS BECOMES DEMOS

Yugoslavia: A Relatively Successful Federal State

One of the few solid policies of Tito's Communist regime, or "second" Yugoslavia, had clearly been the relatively successful solution of the festering national questions for which the Balkans had been notorious since the nineteenth century. "First" Yugoslavia struggled mightily and without much success from 1918 to 1941 with the problems of multinationalism until it was destroyed by the German and Italian invasion of April 1941. The disaffection and alienation of almost all the non-Serbian national groups facilitated the swift conquest of first Yugoslavia. A different version of the same disaffection fifty years later has destroyed the second Yugoslav state.

However, internal nationalist disaffection in Yugoslavia also had considerable help from the outside, both times. The bitter irony is that Germany and Austria were prime movers of the formal destruction of both Yugoslavias. One would have hoped that some minimal historical memory of, and shame about, the German responsibility for the genocidal horrors that took place in its satellite "Independent State of Croatia" in 1941–45, as well as the wide destruction and carnage caused by Hitler's aggression against Yugoslavia, would have made the now democratic German states extra cautious about meddling in Yugoslav matters. Unfortunately, Yugoslavia illustrated that the political establishments of neither Germany nor Austria were conscious of the need, imposed by good taste if nothing else, for them to keep a low profile in the East European countries that had been victims of German aggression twice within the living memory of many. Absent such sensitivities, the Germans have ended up as major external factors in the destruction of two Yugoslavias. The first was brutally destroyed by the invasion of the unified German and Austrian Third Reich and its Italian, Hungarian, and Bulgarian fascist allies in April 1941.

The swift demise of second Yugoslavia was assured by Germany and Austria's relentless and unprecedented insistence — against the advice of most of the European Community and the United States — on the unconditional and speedy recognition of the secessionist states of Slovenia and Croatia. The campaign for the recognition of Slovenia and Croatia had been accompanied by a full-blown campaign against the Serbs as a nation, not merely the Serbian political leadership. The campaign culminated in the recognition of Croatia and Slovenia before the end of 1991. The language and imagery used in describing Serbian culture and history in much of the German press can only be described as racist.

In conjunction with that racism, the German press offered no recognition that the Serbian minority in Croatia had any grounds to fear discrimination and reprisals based on widely held notions about their collective guilt for the crimes committed by Serbian militias and other armed forces. The mass media in the two German states have been the first to call for a punitive boycott against the rump Yugoslav state and for its removal from all international forums. Surely there were less obviously partial ways to show displeasure against the brutal war being waged first in Croatia and later even more brutally in Bosnia by the Yugoslav army and its Serbian allies.

When Bangladesh seceded from a united Pakistan, there was no international move to withdraw recognition from Pakistan, despite its brutal war against secession. Unseating Pakistan did not logically follow recognition of Bangladesh. When the Soviet Union dissolved, the largest republic, Russia, was granted the old Soviet seat in the Security Council, despite objections from Ukraine. Surely the passions mobilized against Yugoslavia in its death agony are utterly disproportionate to its historical role. After all, for decades it had been the most open and tolerant of the Communist states.

Why then this eagerness to dissolve all traces of Yugoslavia? Nowhere else in the world was the absolute right to self-determination through a unilateral declaration so ardently defended. Was there really nothing that had to be negotiated before separation? Certainly there was a need to discuss matters such as the fate of the army; responsibility for federal retirees; minority rights for peoples who had suddenly against their expressed will been turned into minorities in the country their ancestors had lived in for centuries; and national and international debts and assets. Why were Germany and Austria, despite the heavy burden of their past history in that area, so very determined to play the key role in determining the policy of the European Community toward Yugoslavia and the states that were to emerge from its wreckage? It is almost as if there was a fatal historical antipathy between Germans and Slavs of the type described in such wonderful detail in *Black Lamb and Grey Falcon*, a masterpiece written by Rebecca West at the outset of the Second World War.

The destruction of second Yugoslavia had been by no means inevitable. Through repeated trial and error and decades of unchallenged rule, the Yugoslav Communists had developed a complex federation that was more successful than other existing models at managing the problems of multiethnicity. This was the consensus of most foreign experts, academic and nonacademic, hostile and friendly to the regime in Belgrade.

To be sure, there had been some loud rumbling of nationalist discontent during the short-lived "Croatian Spring" of 1969–71, when demands for greater autonomy were heard from Croatia. The popular young reformers in the leadership of the Croatian LCY led by Savka Dapčević and Mika Tripalo had demanded that Croatia be allowed to keep a greater share of the hard-currency earnings from tourism and that it be granted more administrative autonomy from the federal center. These relatively mild stirrings within the party were combined with a good deal of overheated and exaggerated nationalist oratory and the usual flood of romanticized history books. The Croatian Spring had been effectively repressed by a skillful and ruthless combination of a crackdown by Marshal Tito and his still powerful center and the new highly decentralized constitution of 1974 that effectively met most of the economic and institutional grievances. Nevertheless, even the reformed constitution could never satisfy genuine anti-Communist nationalists and separatists, but then these were still relatively marginal at the time.

For decades the only debate the LCY was permitted to engage in was that over different ways of representing local interests. To express programmatic political differences about the appropriate road for Yugoslavia *as a whole* would have been to act as a faction within the LCY as a whole. The prohibition of tendencies or factions within the LCY had guaranteed the development of a localist and nationalist discourse in both Communist and post-Communist Yugoslav politics. Yugoslav federalism encouraged the local leagues to defend their own regional interests as a way of broadening their political support, and that guaranteed the development of a league-sanctioned localism. That means that they were encouraged to play with a "controlled" or sanctioned nationalism. However, that required both a finesse and a skill which were not always present; therefore, it was not uncommon during this decades-long period of playing with "controlled" nationalism that local league organizations, leaders, journalists, or writers would violate the ill-defined role of just what was permissible. They would then face sanctions and could be added to the honor roll of martyrs for the national cause.

As historical experience shows, nationalism, particularly in east-central Europe and the Balkans, has been very difficult, if not impossible, to fine-tune, or turn off, when it became inconvenient. Without the voluntary group identities, which can be assumed in a contested multiparty environment, the only group identity that was recognized was the nation, expressing itself through the republic in which it was dominant. This was supposed to be supplemented by group identity in organizations in associated labor — that is, the self-managing enterprises. In a much more attenuated and abstract manner, persons were to have identity as members of the working class. But *classes* in real life most often develop effective identities in counterpositions and conflicts, not in alliances, with other classes. The Communists' claim was that they had eliminated class conflicts and that the ruling managers and politocrats were not a class. Thus working-class consciousness, which might have acted as an ethnically cross-cutting and unifying identity, had been submerged for political reasons in the vaguer category of "working people," which in effect included everyone employed. This was obviously a "soft" and overgeneralized identity that could not generate any deep-seated loyalties. National identity, on the contrary, could generate mass loyalty, particularly with the growing secularization of political faith in socialism and Marxism. By eliminating genuine alternatives in political life and even in discourse, the Communist party's power monopoly may have left traditional national and religious identifications as the most relevant and, for an increasingly depoliticized people, the most passionately held identifications.

This was how the reformist Communist leadership in Croatia got into trouble in 1972.[1] After cracking down on a Marxist left opposition centered on the journal *Praxis,* they encouraged the development of a nationalist euphoria in Croatia that they attempted to use from 1968 to 1972 to leverage concessions from the federation. For a while it worked, but by 1971 they had begun to lose control of their nationalist "followers." Right-wing and traditionalist nationalists, with the support of some of the Catholic clergy, began to enter the officially sanctioned national organizations, like the Croatian cultural society "Matica," and to threaten LCY control. The nationalist tail began to wag the Communist dog.

These nationalists were called to heel by Tito at the time and removed from political life. The trouble was that later there would be no Tito to intervene when a local leadership crossed the boundaries of permissible behavior. In the late 1980s, in the absence of a Tito or an institutional equivalent as a legitimate arbiter, it became much more difficult to deal with a popular populist nationalism. There was no person or institution to set permissible limits on particularized — that is, nationalist — demands on the political community as a whole. When it came to contesting alternate programs, defense of localist and national interests had become the sanctioned artificial substitute for democratic pluralism. In other words, it had become a substitute for democracy. The problem that faced those who wished to shape a multiparty political system was the fear, which turned out to be justified, that such parties would become, as the Communists leagues in individual republics had already become, the local nationalist parties of the different Yugoslav nations.

Despite the claims to the contrary by the Croatian nationalist publicists, Tito's crackdown in 1972 was by no means limited to the Croats who were flirting with nationalism and liberalism. Tito, always in search of a repressive "symmetry" in the treatment of the potentially contentious leaderships of various Yugoslav republics, also cracked down and removed the very popular liberal reformist Communist leaders of Serbia, Slovenia, and Macedonia. That effectively removed the brightest and the best of the young postrevolutionary generation of Yugoslav leaders, a group that had a history of working together and were, at least at the time, almost immune to nationalist intolerance toward each other. There had never been a Serbian leadership more tolerant of Croatian demands, and less prone to nationalist demagoguery, than the liberal leaders who Tito forced out in 1972. The lost generation of liberal reformers of 1972 in the major republics were the logical group to provide an orderly succession to Tito and begin a transition toward democracy. They probably represented the last leadership that could have assured an orderly and democratic transition to democracy.

To be sure, Tito's crackdown, unlike the notorious Stalinist purges, left the victims alive and well. Few went to jail. Most, or at least most of the purged Communists, were given reasonable jobs or retired; all kept their luxurious apartments. The moral and political damage to the Yugoslav political system was enormous, however. An entire generation of liberal Communist reformers was eliminated from political life for two whole decades. To make things worse, this generation had shown that it could cooperate to an extent that was not duplicated by their successors. In addition to purging the "liberal" Communist reformers, Tito's crackdown fatally and permanently alienated a whole generation of non-Communist moderate nationalists and democrats.

A Titoist Constant: One-Party Rule

Looking back after twenty years, it is clear that the crackdown in 1972 was the beginning of the slow, but ultimately and catastrophically total, delegitimation of Titoist Communism. It had proved incapable of seriously undertaking the urgently needed political democratization and economic reforms in the late 1960s. At that time the conditions were optimal. The world economy was in reasonably good shape, and Yugoslavia had ready access to credits and aid. It had, in Croatia, Serbia, Slovenia, and Macedonia, a genuinely popular younger leadership committed both to economic reforms and political democratization *and* to a Yugoslav federation. Tito, however, took a fatal step back from the reforms in the name of a Marxist-Leninist orthodoxy that was in any case sui generis and quite dubious in consistency.

After all, Titoism itself was a major heresy within world Communism, if not *the* major heresy. It had already produced such heretical deviation in economic policy as workers' self-management, decentralization, and a limited market socialism. It permitted almost completely free travel to its citizens from the early 1960s on and as a consequence had a million people working in Western Europe, sending back huge amounts of hard currency. Yugoslavia was a leading force in the nonaligned movement and was far less repressive than other states ruled by the Communist party. Despite all these heresies one important article of faith did remain — the belief in the power monopoly of a party that officially considered itself to be a classic Marxist-Leninist vanguard party. To be sure, a mass-ruling Communist party with more than 1.5 million members hardly resembled Lenin's professional revolutionary "dead men on leave," but that was the contradiction between party ideology and the reality for all ruling Communist parties. More specifically, by the mid-1980s in Yugoslav more and more party intellectuals and theorists defined themselves as Marxists, rather than as Marxist-*Leninists*. Some deviated even further from Leninist orthodoxy and described themselves as democratic socialists. Nevertheless, at least officially, until multiparty elections changed that in 1990, Yugoslavia was ruled by a party that claimed to be the vanguard of the working class.

In Yugoslavia that Communist vanguard had been renamed the League of Communists as far back as the late 1950s. Its power was somewhat reduced and self-limited, and many areas of intellectual and cultural life were permitted considerable autonomy. That autonomy was very wide compared to the other Communist regimes in Eastern Europe and the Soviet Union, but still limited enough to provide for a continual tension and small-scale guerrilla war between the ideological defenders of the regime and the artists and the more independently minded intelligentsia.

One thing, however, did remain irreducible and unnegotiable, both in practice and theory, until the end and the collapse of the league as a Yugoslav-wide organization in 1988. That was the league's unwillingness to compete in anything resembling free elections or even, for that matter, to compete ideologically against any organized group that would politically or ideologically counterpoise itself to the Communists. It would, further, not tolerate competition from a group that accepted most of the postulates of Yugoslav politics. It did not really matter whether the group was nationalist, liberal-democratic, or even (albeit critically) Marxist. The last type of group was most threatening. The 1971 crackdown against nationalism and liberalism was conducted in the name of the unity of the LCY and its continued monopoly of effective power, not in the name of "Serbian domination." If anything, the Serbian leadership and republic tended to get the thicker end of the stick because they were a potential rallying point of liberal reformism in the federal capital itself, which could threaten Tito's declining authoritarian rule. And yet — and yet, if only Tito had retired in the early 1970s, or even better in the mid-1960s, after grooming a reasonable and flexible group to succeed him. Had he done that he would have undoubtedly gone into history as a great and positive nation-building figure, notwithstanding his one-party authoritarianism. He could have been a Yugoslav Kemal Atatürk. Instead there is now a vaguely tragic aura around Tito and his entire era.

Instead of being remembered as the founder of a new, democratic, and multiethnic Yugoslav state, Tito goes into history as a perverse coda on the dead Hapsburg era. He was really the last Hapsburg, ruling a doomed multinational state. By hanging on a decade or two too long, by insisting on maintaining a sentimental ideological link with the Soviet-run Communist world, by his friendships with every Third World dictator who even gestured toward the left, he sealed Yugoslavia's doom. Because of his Soviet and Third World ties he had a genuine antipathy to pluralist parliamentary democracy. He never permitted the development of close ties with the democratic-socialist parties and labor movement of Western Europe. The price would have been respecting human rights and moving toward pluralist democracy. For Tito that would have represented an unimaginable retreat from absolute power. This also explains why he repeatedly turned down offers to get into the European Free Trade Association (EFTA), which would have permitted Yugoslavia to get into the European Community at the same time that Spain, Portugal, and Greece did. Had Yugoslavia done so it could have mobilized European aid in the transition from authoritarianism to democracy — as such aid was used in formerly authoritarian states in southern Europe. With all of its present economic problems, post-Franco Spain has made an orderly and irrevocable transition from a one-party dictatorship to a reasonable, modern democracy. Spain's army is in the barracks while Yugoslavia's army has become completely free of civilian and institutional control and has been waging a brutal war against Croatia. Yugoslavia's fate could have resembled that of post-Franco Spain. That this did not happen is a great pity. Tito sacrificed a European vocation for Yugoslavia to his Soviet and Third World ideological fantasies. He probably thought these fantasies had something to do with the dreams of his leftist youth. But then even that leftist youth was distorted as he became, relatively early, a full-time functionary of his party and then the Communist International. One should never forget that Tito advanced to the leadership of the Yugoslav Communist party in 1938, during the worst period of Stalinist purges in Moscow. Tito's motives were probably the best, and yet we all know what the road to hell is paved with.

No challenge to the political monopoly of the Yugoslav Communists was ever tolerated for long. The consequence was that no responsible and mature opposition was ever permitted to evolve, a fact for which present-day politics of the former Yugoslav states are all too clear a witness. What the Yugoslav Communists did permit, as a poor substitute for democratization, was ever-more decentralization of power and authority. To be sure, that was a decentralization through devolution of power to reliable local cadres of the LCY. Nevertheless, genuine authority and power were devolved to the republics and even lower down to the counties. This evolved into a system in which there were many privileged participants in wielding power; it also meant that the republics rather than the federation eventually became the real loci of power and thus the indispensable power base for the newer generations of politicians.

The Communists Opening the Door to the Nationalists

As the system continued to decay — that is, as the original ideological cement holding the party cadres together continued to crumble — the leaders of the republics increasingly began to represent the interests of their power base, their own republics, against the center. This was a sure road to local popularity. As time went on leaders of the LCY in the republics, particularly after Tito's death in 1980, ever more directly and openly represented the desires and interests of their own republics. A symbiosis of Communist and localist nationalist politics thus evolved. Which of the two components was to remain dominant in the new hybrid was uncertain for only a short while; it quickly became clear that Communist ideology, except when it came to maintaining the party power monopoly, was abstract, while local interests were very concrete indeed. Also, stressing local interests provided a basis for broadening the popular political appeal of the LCY; a stress on Communist ideology only narrowed such appeal.

It was not a long step from that informal symbiosis between local Communist politicians and local interests to an open appeal by local Communist leaders to nationalism. Such an appeal was based on the claim that they, the Communists, most effectively represented national interests and demands, particularly as against competing national demands and against the federal center. The popular and demagogic version of those politics was effectively first invented in 1986 by the leader of the Serbian League, Slobodan Milošević. He first unveiled this new strategy when he mobilized traditional Serbian nationalism combined with loyalty to the party and regime in order to repress the demands of the Albanian majority in the Province of Kosovo for more autonomy. Milošević's response was to mobilize a massive Serbian nationalist hysteria against the Albanians and any others within the federation who might consider Albanian demands to be even partly legitimate. There were quite a number of such people, particularly in Slovenia and Croatia, who either did defend the Albanians' rights to be protected by the Yugoslav constitution and laws or were afraid that they could be the next to be repressed. This set Serbia's leadership in an immediate collision course first with Slovenia and then with Croatia and the Muslim Slavs. Reborn Serbian national assertiveness was Milošević's instrument to win the struggle for power within the Serbian LCY; to topple, in 1988, the governments of the autonomous provinces of Kosovo and Vojvodina; and soon after to oust the leadership of the Republic of Montenegro. In each case he replaced the old leadership with his obedient allies.

The two autonomous provinces were effectively annexed to Serbia, with the silent and very short-sighted complicity of some of the leaders of other republics. This radically changed the delicate balance of power within the federation. Serbia now had four out of the eight votes in the collective presidency that had replaced Tito after his death. That was intolerable in practice since it also gave Serbia an effective veto over all federal decisions. The highest body of the federation, which was supposed to arbitrate differences between the republics, was thus reduced to an instrument of the Serbian leadership and was essentially delegitimized.

These developments were especially dangerous because they coincided with and accelerated the development of multiparty elections in the Yugoslav republics. In reaction to this power grab by the Serbian leadership and the ineffectiveness of the federal leadership of the LCY in restraining Milošević, public opinion in the remaining republics swung increasingly toward the newly formed, openly nationalist, and anti-Communist parties that claimed that they could restrain the expanding Serbian appetite for power. Some claimed that this was possible by no other route than secession. Thus a causal link began to unfold. The choice of decentralization rather than democratization in the early 1970s was at the root of the process. Albanian self-assertion in the Province of Kosovo led to Milošević's awakening of the Serbian nationalist populist genie in the mid-1980s. The fear-ridden reaction of the leaders of the other republics to Serbian bullying tactics had encouraged the reactive growth of varying nationalisms in Slovenia, Croatia, and even among the Bosnian Muslims and in Macedonia. This in turn provoked predictable fears of the minorities about the increasing nationalism of the major national groups in their own republics. There were no instruments at the federal center that could have effectively mediated between the republics. The fat was well and truly in the fire.

Manipulated National Antagonisms

The process sketched above led to open national confrontations and a bitter civil war in Yugoslavia. Probably until the very end of this process, the major political players, certainly those in the LCYs in individual republics, had no intention of actually destroying Yugoslavia. They just wanted more power and were willing to use nationalist real or imagined grievances to achieve that power. The stakes were continually raised until it became impossible to back down. To malignancy, which in its pure form is as rare as pure goodness, one must always add incompetence and miscalculation as major factors in creating political catastrophes. Rather than being caused by a popular upsurge of national hate from below, the civil war was the result of policy decisions from the top combined with an all-too-effective use of the mass media, especially television. I claim this in the teeth of the journalistic insistence by many observers that there is something almost biologically imprinted that, for example, would make Serbs hate Croats and vice versa. Historical evidence shows that except for communal massacres of Serbs by Croatian fascist Ustaše and massacres of Muslims and Croats by Serbian Chetniks during the Second World War, Serbs and Croats have lived together more or less tolerably for four centuries. The majority of Croats were horrified by the massacres, and large numbers participated in the revolutionary war of liberation against the Ustaše and their Italian and Nazi sponsors. In point of undisputable fact, proportionately more Croats from Dalmatia participated in the partisan resistance than did Serbs from any regions but those in which the Ustaše massacres had made resistance the only realistic alternative to death.

There were numerous irritants in Serb and Croat relations throughout history, many of them caused by the relentless sectarian rivalry of the Orthodox and Catholic churches. On the whole the Catholic church was the more intolerant, if for no other reason than that it was favored by the Austrian and Venetian authorities and persisted in trying to use the authority of the state to convert the stubborn Orthodox Serbs, all the way up to the nineteenth century. Nevertheless, for some three centuries, the Serb frontiersmen and the Croats cooperated in guarding the frontiers of the Austrian Empire, Venetian dominions in Dalmatia, and Europe itself against the menace of the Turks. The Serbs were settled in the military frontier of Croatia early in the sixteenth century, well before the Pilgrims landed in Boston. The Croats and Serbs never did live separately in the borderlands where the war raged through much of 1992 until the UN protective forces entered the area.

The absence of a gut hate among the broad layers of population explains the insistence on rigid control of the mass media by the post-Communist regimes in Croatia and Serbia. That control is more rigid today, after "pluralist" elections, than it had been in the last years of one-party Communist rule. Widespread refusal to serve in the armed forces in this combination of civil war and war of aggression against Croatia and Bosnia is testimony to its unpopularity. In Belgrade 85 percent of the reservists were refusing call-ups in the fall of 1991. Large numbers of young Serbs and Croats are staying abroad to avoid serving in an unpopular war. Bosnian Muslims have shown a notorious lack of enthusiasm for fighting despite extreme provocation through massacre and rape by the Serbs and their reputation for great individual bravery. Opposition parties in Serbia are openly defending the right of individuals to refuse to serve in a civil war. The hate had to be systematically *created* and maintained if necessary by horrible atrocities and massacres against Croats, Serbs, and Muslims. These were often deliberately carried out by outsiders and designed to compromise innocent villagers of the other national group. Yugoslavia was not destroyed by vast pressures of discontent from below. It was killed by policies initiated by the political leadership of the various republics. Some did this deliberately, wanting to destroy any possibility of a democratic and decentralized Yugoslavia.

Others — and here I include the leaders of the Serbian and Croatian LCYs, most of the Serbian "democratic" opposition, and the leadership of the Yugoslav National Army — did this through incompetence, cowardice, and an unwillingness to change political habits developed during the long years of the party's power monopoly. Ultimately, of course, Tito must also share in the responsibility for the death of Yugoslavia. He ruled much too long. He did not prepare for any effective succession. As mentioned above, Franco and consequently Spain did much better. The frightening thing is that the leaders of the post-Communist states of Eastern Europe and the new Independent Commonwealth that has replaced the Soviet Union do not offer a reassuring image that they are better, more competent, and more courageous in facing populist demagoguery than their counterparts in Yugoslav states. Quite to the contrary, they are less experienced and skilled than their Yugoslav counterparts were when the irreversible down-slide began.

Therefore it is Yugoslavia, rather than Spain, that unfortunately offers the most relevant lessons for the future of the post-Communist states today. Their future prospects in turn affect the prospects of stability and peace in the entire wider region, and that is why Yugoslavia's current agony is of wide relevance today. To the despair of its peoples, it is, as it has been for many decades, a laboratory where a great number of questions about democracy, modern nationalism, and the troubled transition from authoritarianism will be answered.

The Decentralization of the Yugoslav Economy

Decentralization was widely applied to the organization of the economy. The form it took was in the extension of the system of self-management, or workers' councils, throughout the economy and later to *all* institutions that employed more than a small number of people. While at best the system was a form of self-government, particularly on the microlevel of the enterprises, it was used most often as a substitute for societywide organization of power in the interest of the workers and employees. Yugoslav unions were not that much better than the unions in the more liberal one-party states of Eastern Europe. They represented the interests of the *nomenklatura* and the regime rather than the workers. Attempts to create a nationwide Council of Producers were aborted in the 1970s. Nevertheless, the system of self-management did give genuine authority to responsible bodies elected by workers and *could have been* a massive school in democracy and the responsible wielding of power by broad layers of the working population. Unfortunately, the local LCYs predictably could not keep their hands off. They constantly meddled, above all in personnel decisions.

The Yugoslav system of self-management and workers' control has had bad press both locally and internationally for decades. Much of that is quite unfair and is the consequence of constant interference into the work collectives by the local party *nomenklatura*. What can be fairly said is that there was always a sharp conflict between the idea of self-management, with its stress on direct democracy and the rights of all employees to be involved in decision making, and the rule of a single party. Sharply different political cultures were implied by the rules of the game proposed for the economy and those proposed for the political system. One was democratic, the other authoritarian. It is clear that whatever the future fate of the private sector in the Yugoslav republics, a substantial part of the economy, in all of them, will remain under some kind of social ownership. This is if for no other reason than that the capital to buy up much of that economy is in short supply, and it would be criminal to privatize hard-earned assets at greatly reduced prices reserved for "inside" buyers, as is being done in Poland, Czech lands, and Hungary.

In any of the new, democratic, multiparty states emerging from the former Yugoslav federation a revived, simplified, and revised form of self-management could well be one of the elements of governance of the large socially owned sector. It is necessary first, however, to define clearly what social ownership is; that clarity should then lead to a variety of forms of ownership, from direct government ownership to mixtures of local authorities and cooperatives. A genuine mixed economy would result from the blend of the varying forms of social property with privately owned firms and public firms that sold a part of their shares on the open market. It would be a terrible mistake to wholly reject past economic experiments. The experiences of Yugoslav self-management are far from being entirely negative, and I, for one, consider it clearly superior to bureaucratic, top-down, managerial authority, which is being proposed by many economic reformers. This bureaucratic model is regrettably found in the new laws on the powers of managers passed in several of the major republics.

That particular model is being offered as a "cure" throughout the post-Communist societies. It remains a mystery why giving more authority to many of the same managers who have historically preformed poorly under the old system represents a solution for the problems of the East European or Yugoslav economies.

Why should anybody believe that more authority for managers will increase the willingness of workers to make sacrifices in order to help improve their productivity and economies? To the contrary, the cure is more democracy, more involvement and participation by workers in the day-to-day as well as long-range decisions affecting their lives. That means, in addition to political democracy, industrial democracy — trade unions *and* works councils. Otherwise the grim decisions that may have to be made to save the economies of Eastern Europe and the former Soviet Union will have to be imposed from the top down. Since that will surely provoke resistance, there will then, in turn, be attempts to set up authoritarian governments in order to carry out unpopular economic measures. That certainly does not bode well for any transition to democracy for the post-Communist states. The stark choice may boil down to top-down, Friedmanian free-market reforms *or* democracy. Insisting on economic shock therapy, through a leap into a market economy and the dismembering of the already inadequate social benefits, while very popular among foreign advisers and the international financial community, may well kill the patient. At least it will make democratic options unlikely. It is hard to believe that any genuinely democratic government could apply such a painful cure and remain popular. Therefore, the real-life choice would seem to be: either economic shock therapy involving an enormous drop in living standards *or* popular democratic regimes. The choice is even more stark in multiethnic states where it is almost certain that neither the short-term wages nor the eventual benefits of economic shock therapy would be distributed with anything resembling equity. Nationalism would certainly envenom the economic debates because every national group in a multiethnic state would claim that it was being treated unfairly. That is nationalist political stock in trade.

A Key Problem:
The Organization of Multinational States

The failure to deal equitably and effectively with multiethnicity and develop a successful federal model had contributed mightily to the deterioration of "first" Yugoslavia between the two world wars. The failure to deal effectively with multinationality also contributed to the moral and political defeat of non-Communist parties right after the Second World War. Communist, hard-fisted repression would have without a doubt eliminated them as real contenders for political power in any case. Nevertheless, the "bourgeois" parties' failure to accept the multinationality of Yugoslavia inevitably identified them with the parochial nationalism of their own particular nations and thus made them incapable of presenting themselves as realistic contenders for Yugoslav-wide legitimate power. This failure still haunts the post-Communist political parties of the left, right, and center. Clearly the logic of the way the economy is organized as well as the multitude of links between the various ethnic groups argue that, at some future date, some kind of loose association of Yugoslav sovereign states will be needed. However, that which is needed is not always that which is politically possible.

In any case, the Communists have lost *their* historic claim to represent an acceptable supranational, nonparochial alternative for the peoples of Yugoslavia, one that could be validated in free pluralist elections. The tragedy is that following the political and moral collapse of the LCY, no other Yugoslav-wide political entity or alliance has developed as an effective force for democratization and unification. The long and exhausting battle of the Serbian LCY, led by Slobodan Milošević, against free and competitive elections assured that free elections would first take place in the republics of Slovenia and Croatia.

The Elections: Ambiguous Messages and Missed Chances

The elections took take place at different times, beginning in the two western republics, Slovenia and Croatia, where nationalist and separatist sentiment was most widespread. This arrangement was in no small part the result of bullying tactics of Milošević and the Serbian reluctance to move toward free elections. The results of elections held in that particular way, just like the results in the former Soviet Union, *maximized* the differences and local particularisms. Federal elections would have forced transnational coalitions over political and economic programs to emerge. They would probably have imposed "normal" politics resembling those of Western Europe — with a broad left; a parliamentary, economically liberal right; and nationalist and local parties on the margins. Instead the separate elections in the individual republics guaranteed the victory of the nationalist parties. In Bosnia, for example, the 1991 election resembled a census of the three dominant national groups, and the programmatic parties were completely marginalized. This proved to be the road to complete disaster.

Whether there had ever been a chance to develop a unifying, Yugoslav-wide political force will remain in the realm of speculation. It was never allowed to be tested in elections — no Yugoslav-wide federal elections were ever permitted to be held. That was assured by a suicidal alliance between the LCY organizations in the component republics of Yugoslavia and the forces and sentiments of populist nationalism. The alliance was suicidal for the continued political existence of reform Communists in the republic organizations because they could never be genuinely convincing as advocates of populist and traditionalist nationalism. There would always be more convincing, more authentic, and more full-blooded Serbian, Croatian, Slovenian, and Macedonian nationalists. These were parties and individuals who had devoted their whole existences to their own particular (always "misunderstood and martyred") nation. The alliance was therefore asymmetrical. Nationalists would not become reform Communists or even social democrats, but Communist voters would and could become intoxicated with a nationalism that offered an alternate collective identity. Because this identity was *collective,* it was congenial to voters socialized under a collectivist, authoritarian Communism. A stark example of the effects of such an alliance can be seen in Croatia where the reform-Communist Party of Democratic Change (SDP) dropped in eighteen months from 30 percent of the vote to 3 percent in the polls on the eve of Croatia's independence.

Be that as it may, the leaders of the varied Yugoslav republics moved toward free elections in 1989 with varying degrees of enthusiasm or reluctance, but on one thing they were as one: the reform-Communist Slovene leader Milan Kučan, the authoritarian Serbian Milošević, and the indecisive Croatian Ivica Račan all agreed that under no circumstances were federal, Yugoslav-wide elections to be held. More specifically, they assured that the then widely popular federal prime minister Ante Marković was to be blocked from any chance to test his mandate electorally, and thus test his proposal for a new, democratic, looser Yugoslav confederation.

A democratic Yugoslavia never had a chance to be tested electorally as a proposition. The brutal civil war, fought in Croatia by the federal army and Serbian local home guards and volunteers, has most probably killed the remaining chances that some kind of loose association of Yugoslav states could emerge out of the ruins of "second" Yugoslavia in the foreseeable future. The problem now is how to assure a stable peace that does not reward military aggression. Without this the prospects for democracy in the main successor states — Croatia, Serbia, and Bosnia — are very dim. My own feeling is that the national populist regimes of Tudjman in Croatia and Milošević in Serbia cannot make a stable peace and do not want to move toward a genuine democracy. In Serbia the crass and relentless manipulation of raw national chauvinism by the Milošević regime has resulted in the catapulting of the marginal, semifascist party of the Chetnik leader Vojislav Šešelj into the position of the second party. That party gained some 25 percent of the vote in the second free (though manipulated) elections in December 1992. In the same elections, Arkan, the leader of the most notorious killer squad in the Croatian and Bosnian wars, also managed to get elected to the parliament with a handful of followers. Just as Milošević's and Tudjman's national populists (the fact that one used a right and the other a left demagoguery is utterly irrelevant when it comes to internal policies, where the two are identical) replaced the pale and manipulated pseudonationalism of the local LCYs, there is a real danger, particularly in Serbia, that neofascist ultras may become the real alternative to Milošević. Sorcerers' apprentices who play with elemental forces like nationalism can easily lose control. Others then have to pay for these reckless adventures.

The Yugoslav Tragedy: A Product of Humankind, Not Fate

"Second" Yugoslavia did not die a natural death — it was murdered. Much like in Agatha Christie's novel *Death on the Nile,* the murderers and would-be murderers are numerous. Listing them and their roles is useful even today since Yugoslavia did not face a unique problem in multinationalism. Intended and unintended consequences of the murder of multinational complex states should be of wider interest because multinational states are the rule in much of the world.

From the mid-1950s through to the mid-1980s Yugoslavia had appeared to be the most fortunate country in Eastern Europe. Its Communist rulers were national-oriented and thus a barrier to Soviet domination over their country rather than primarily an instrument of Moscow rule. They did not rule through a mandate from Moscow and thus could not be changed by the will of Moscow. Their generic Yugoslav patriotism was unquestioned and therefore a major asset. As leaders of the nonaligned movement, the Yugoslav Communist leaders had a perhaps undeservedly high prestige and profile internationally. Their specific model of Communism was clearly more flexible and open than the orthodox Soviet-inspired version.

If one thinks of Moscow as the Communist "Rome," Belgrade was then the seat of an "Anglican" church with its own leader in the person of Marshal Tito. This (albeit somewhat stretched) metaphor, which uses the image of Tito as a latter-day Henry VIII, can be extended to the persecution of Communist "Calvinists" — that is, those Marxist intellectuals who denounced the party for not being pure and true to its ideals. A good example of a Communist "Calvinist" was the early Milovan Ðjilas.

Decades before the other "socialist" states, Yugoslavia became open to world trade and established elements of a socialist *market* economy that was decentralized and comparatively dynamic. Those qualities, in addition to the very extensive aid and credits that Yugoslavia received from the West, particularly the United States, provided it with by far the highest living standard in Eastern Europe. The reason this was not always obvious to Western economists and statisticians, particularly those on the left, was that they all too often accepted the official statistics of the East European and Soviet governments. These statistics were often inaccurate, and when it came to translating the living standards in terms of the official exchange rates, sheer fantasies resulted. Thus according to UN statistics Romania had a higher GNP than Yugoslavia! This was a fantasy contradicted by desperate hordes of Romanians trying to flee to Yugoslavia throughout the 1970s and 1980s.

To be sure, in the decentralized federation into which Yugoslavia had evolved by the mid-1960s, the relatively high living standards — which had increased steadily for two and one-half decades — could not be distributed with any degree of evenness. This was particularly painful given the traditional Communist proindustrial bias that skewed economic growth in favor of industry and against agriculture. Thus the agricultural and raw-material producers of the southern region were discriminated against by the decades-long policy of industrial development and growth. This policy made imported technical goods very expensive, thus permitting domestic manufacturers in turn to charge high prices for cars, refrigerators, tractors, and televisions. On the other hand, farmers, miners, and forestry workers suffered a comparative disadvantage, which if anything was exacerbated when incomes of workers were linked to the market performance of their enterprise. The goods that the southern region produced were priced low. This systemic bias was put into effect through rapid urbanization and industrialization. The result was that the more developed regions benefited more from the development of the Yugoslav economy, and the gap continually increased over the decades. The citizens of the richer republics in the north became ever more firmly convinced that their relative prosperity was due to the fact that they worked harder, were more virtuous, were more European, and in general were superior to those in the backward south. Any federal government would be obliged to attempt to even out some of these economic disparities through transfers of funds from the richer to the poorer areas and through the creation of development projects for the underindustrialized and underdeveloped regions. This made the poorer republics in the south more "procentralist" and the richer more "confederalist." Slovenia, Croatia, and Vojvodina showed the same lack of enthusiasm for income transfers to Macedonia, Montenegro, Kosovo, and Bosnia that the "leagues" of Lombardy and the rich north in Italy do for helping Sicily, Calabria, and the south. This natural egoism of the richer regions is made immeasurably worse if it is further argued that the poor are different by reasons of nationality, whether that is defined ethnically or religiously. Then localist egoism becomes something "nobler"; it is turned into patriotism.

For decent and fair collective decisions to be made in a state, there has to be a general agreement as to its boundaries, as to who exactly constitutes the *demos* that is entitled to make controversial allocative decisions in that polity. If the demos is defined only in terms of the ethnos, then when one ethnic group is outvoted in an election it is viewed as more than a political defeat — it is seen as exploitation and robbery of one's nation (ethnos) by other exploiting nations. That dynamic in multinational democracies makes distributive questions matters of national dispute that are often posed in intransigent ways. When national groups are geographically fairly compact, and real or alleged cultural, religious, and historical differences and grievances exist, a veritable witch's brew of issues is created over all redistributive questions. A popular saying in Croatia by the late 1980s was, "We may be brothers, but we do not share the same wallet." By the 1990s the problematic "We *may* be brothers..." was no longer said even jokingly.

There is no question that today *any* — even the very loosest — association of Yugoslav states has become unacceptable to the richer northern republics of Slovenia and Croatia. The continued massive, monolithic hate campaigns in the mass media have done everything possible to demonize "the other side." The brutal crudity of the army and the Serbian state leadership has contributed mightily to making life together unimaginable. One does not have to invent atrocities. They have occurred on both sides in this miserable war without rules. It may be an illusion that the various states will be better off without the unified Yugoslav market, but it is a powerful and popular illusion. The very idea of being taxed in order to assist the "crude, brutal, and non-European" southerners has become intolerable for those in the north. By 1991 the rest of the Yugoslavs had become foreigners to a large number of Croats and Slovenes, much like East Europeans are foreigners today to the members of the European Community. Yesterday they were fellow Europeans fleeing Communist tyranny; today they are a nuisance merely fleeing the economic and political devastation created by that same tyranny.

The Culture of the Present Civil War in Yugoslavia

The Yugoslav civil war is many things at the same time: a civil war in Croatia between the elected government of Croatia and the rebel Serbian minority; an increasingly brutal war of what remains of the Yugoslav federal army against Croatia; and a thinly disguised war of the Serbian nationalist government against the Croatian nationalist separatists. Last, but not least, this has been a postmodern, disintegrative war of particularisms against both the reality and imagery of an orderly if repressive modern society.

It has been a chaotic war against the idea of a secular society by militant Catholic and Orthodox churches identifying with their respective martyred nations (shades of Poland and Ireland!). It has been a war of new-old competing religions following the death of the secular religion of Titoist Communism, which had kept the nationalist demons caged at the price of some repression for forty years. What has replaced Titoism bodes ill for democracy. It may be a grim precursor of what we can expect in the ruins of Eastern Europe and the new Independent Commonwealth.

On the Serbian side this has been a war fought in the name of a systematically maintained nationalist myth based on the Battle of Kosovo lost against the Turkish invaders in 1389 and the centuries of struggles against Muslim Turks to regain a lost independence. The

Croatian nationalist myth is based in part on tales of medieval kings from the tenth century; it is based mostly, however, on protofascist myths of national racial and cultural superiority anchored in the nationalists' ambivalence toward the Ustaše fascist Croat independent state that existed under Nazi patronage from 1941 to 1945.

Neither Serb nor Croat nationalism has much to do with the democratic liberal nationalism of Mazzini's Italy. Both are anchored in myth, tradition, and religious exclusivism. They are the nationalisms of poets, novelists, historical mythmakers, overimaginative ethnographers, and irresponsible populist demagogues. These nationalisms, like those of the other post-Communist countries in the region, are mytho-poetic and antirational. Therefore they are both antidemocratic and antimodern.

In the wake of this rise of nationalist mythology, mad conspiracy theories flourish, and paranoia is widespread. Bookstores in Belgrade and Zagreb are full of books and pamphlets on the mysterious and nefarious dealings of Freemasons and Jews; on the dealings of the agents of the Communist International and the Vatican; on fundamentalist Muslim international conspiracies and German revivalism; and on the work of the CIA and KGB. Most of these are directed against a specific vulnerable and misunderstood nation. To be sure, the mix of villains being revealed in Belgrade is different from that in Zagreb. What both cities have in common is a paranoid political culture and a retreat from rationalism, both of which are being commercially exploited, along with New Age and oriental religions, which are also unsurprisingly enjoying growing popularity. That postrationalism is not unlike the postleft youth culture in Western Europe. Let us call it postmodern. It is the result of years of exposure to mass culture unmodified by either common values or systematically acquired knowledge. In fact, postmodernism is a revolt against both. It also replaced boring "cool" values — like tolerance and democracy — with "hot" values like ethnic identity and possessive individualism.

Fashion, Style, and Postmodern Politics

A bastardized version of the new postmodern youth culture has been visible on the battlefields of Yugoslavia. There are a half dozen armies fighting on both sides. The most effective and least culturally interesting are the regular armed forces — the federal army, the Croatian National Guard, the Croat police, and the Serbian reservists. After that one enters a nightmare world where life copies art and where the question is: What movie has been the model for the particular armed group? There are the Serbian Chetniks, with greasy long beards and hair, traditional peasant caps (combined with the latest model of sneakers), and daggers. They dress like the villains of old Communist-era partisan films. Then there are volunteers, in the hundreds, organized by Belgrade gangsters (junkyard owners and black marketers). These are refugees from movies about Marseilles gangsters and the resistance; they dress in Ramboesque costumes and are clean shaven but for their mustaches. American movies on Vietnam and on special forces have had a heavy influence on Yugoslav military fashions, as have Ninja and Rambo movies.

U.S.-style camouflage has been much favored by irregular forces on both sides. Foreign journalists are warned not to wear funky, semimilitary Safari jackets near the front lines since they will be surely confiscated by jealous leaders of militias. Journalists are also warned that under no circumstances should they drive a new, attractive car, above all not one with four-wheel drive, in the combat zone. It will almost surely be confiscated to serve the Serbian or Croatian cause.

Many journalists have been mistreated and some killed because they did not understand the extreme individualism of some of the armed types they had to deal with. Press passes, documents, and permits from the regular governments or armed forces are of little value. Looting and atrocities by irregular armed groups against civilians abound.

The general atmosphere reminds one of movies about the world after a nuclear holocaust. *The Road Warrior* comes to mind and has clearly been a model. Some Croat guard reservists wear Cherokee roaches with the rest of the head shaved, to which is added a black headband (from Rambo). They favor Kalashnikov submachine guns, which individual soldiers often have to purchase on a black market run by their commanders. One of the past Croat ministers of defense was nicknamed "Mister 10 Percent" because that was his cut on arms bought by Croat patriots, smuggled in for the defense of Croatia. Even crime and corruption assume surreal dimensions in this civil war. That is not surprising since crime and corruption also accompany the privatization of the economy. The usual suspects will be blamed. Jewish graveyards have been desecrated in Split and Zagreb; the Zagreb synagogue has been dynamited. Anti-Communist sentiment has been increasing.

The only good news is that, as detailed above, the young avoid military service massively. While nationalism has infected broad layers of the populations so they hate the "other," this nationalism has not been accompanied by the spirit of patriotic self-sacrifice and willingness to die for one's country. That has been a part of the disintegration of general values and of the notion that communities have the right to make demands of their members. What that also means is that the artificial community of nationalist hate of "others" has limits in its ability to hold the young. It can do so only as long as it remains interesting and does not involve sacrifices. That would suggest that the new European plague of neofascist and anti-immigrant racist skinheads should be met with harsher legal sanctions.

What I am suggesting is that there is a cultural link between the German skinheads, French motorcyclist racists, and Yugoslav irregulars. In point of fact I have talked to French and German mercenaries fighting on the Croat side in what was called a legion, a blackshirt legion, with all appropriate historical associations. They were working-class skinhead types fighting for money against what they thought was still Communism and above all because they had and have nothing at all to do with their lives. In armed militias, wearing the uniforms of their generation gives them a sense of belonging and purpose. Liberal and democratic societies are poor at providing that for the "surplus" young who are increasingly the debris of a postindustrial civilization. They are unneeded. After the civil war in Yugoslavia these young people will become unneeded again. That is why it will be the devil's own trick to get them to give up their arms and return to an empty, purposeless, and impoverished life. With guns they matter, are important, and cannot be ignored.

Chapter 3

TROUBLED TRANSITIONS: POST-COMMUNIST SOCIETIES IN CRISIS

Abstractions, Passions, Victims

Today in Eastern Europe and in the states that have emerged from the former Soviet Union there are few, if any, political ideas and programs that are capable of drawing passionate and committed support. The great secular religion of socialism is either dead or very badly wounded in this region. The most mortal wounds came from the association of the liberating ideas of socialism with the grim, authoritarian reality of Communism, which was in power for decades throughout the region. The very language of socialism and equality has been grossly vulgarized by the ruling Communist *nomenklatura*. It is very likely that when a broad social-democratic movement develops in the region it will consciously use language and symbols different from those of traditional socialism. To be sure, to pursue the religious metaphor, dead gods have been known to rise again, but for the moment this god (i.e., socialism) lies buried, if not in peace. Other programs and ideas are afloat in the region, but they too arouse little passion. Liberal democracy is a popular but pale and very abstract idea for which people may vote but will not fight. If it fails to deliver considerably better than it has in recent years, people may even stop voting for it.

The free market may still be unchallenged — particularly among some intellectuals, politicians, and economic experts — as the imagined cure for all that ails these societies, but it certainly does not inspire any devotion or passion. Worse yet, it is only the *idea* of the market in its pure form — unsullied by any contact with an otherwise grubby reality — that attracts these intellectuals and experts in Eastern Europe and the former Soviet Union. The *reality* of the market and its very concrete opportunities for personal enrichment, at least for a few, attract many of the former members of the *nomenklatura*. Such opportunities also attract all the varied shady dealers who had been on the margins of the state-run economies and the get-rich-quick artists who seem to be growing like mushrooms in fertilized soil after a warm rain.

There is almost no relation between the abstract, elegant, and currently fashionable idea of the market that the East European and Soviet intellectuals have fallen in love with and the reality of the market. To see the future consequences of the reality of the market for Eastern Europe and the former Soviet Union, one should look to Latin America rather than currently successful capitalist systems. And yet for the love of the idea of the market almost as much suffering may be visited on the population of Eastern Europe as had been for the equally abstract idea of centralized planning. There seems to be no limit to how much suffering can be imposed on the living bodies of existing societies in the name of abstract ideas. That seems to be the original sin of intellectuals. They have thus set themselves up to be blamed for the grim consequences of their present infatuation with yet one more abstraction.[1]

Another serious problem that bedevils the reformers and intellectuals in Eastern Europe is their tendency to apply abstract universal norms rigidly to proposals of how to run specific economies and societies. Thus we are given absurd counterpositions: planning or a free market; rigid egalitarianism or the dolce vita of the West; complete dismembering of the federal central agencies of the state or rigid centralism; and so on.[2] A properly organized mixed economy should be a combination of planning, self-management, regionally owned public enterprises, cooperatives, and a small-scale private sector. The choice of particular forms of public or private ownership and administration should be based not on abstract general principles but on the nature of the activity involved.

Another even more serious problem in Eastern Europe is that of how to bring about effective public, popular, and legal control over the power exerted by those controlling the publicly owned sector. Control of this power is a far more urgent problem than controlling the powers harbored within capitalist restoration.

Yet another problem facing Eastern Europe is that of defining the societal purpose of its economics. Classical capitalism worked with the assumption that the massive pursuit of individuals' selfish economic goals would produce social good and an advanced technology and economy, which in turn would improve the lives of all. That assumption about the moral underpinning of capitalism is made mockery of in East European economies where millions are made not by manufacturing or inventing new processes but by speculating, gambling on real estate, and buying and selling former publicly owned property. The road to democratization runs through perilous straits in Eastern Europe and the former Soviet Union. It has a great many enemies. Although few are open enemies of democracy, there are many who are covert. They include a part of what remains of the Communist parties; the bureaucrats in the state and other institutions; and demagogic populists, nationalists, and technocrats. And yet the goal of a decent *rechsstadt,* or a state that respects its own laws and constitution; of a pluralist, democratic society; and of a decent, tolerant, democratic, and socially sensitive political culture — that goal remains as urgent and powerful as ever. East Europeans and citizens of the states of the former Soviet Union include millions, perhaps even majorities, who passionately desire what they often find hard to define or visualize — a stable and functioning democratic society.

It is essential, then, that ideas regarding democracy and the economy be moved out of the realm of abstraction and into the realm of the concrete and passionate. If democracy fails, the field will be left to nationalism and its cohorts — some of the churches of the region, for instance. When the field is left to the clerical and nationalist forces, the victims will not be abstractions but real men and women. Indeed, as the legal, social, and economic gains of decades of Communist-imposed modernity come under an ever-sharper attack from these clerical and nationalist forces, a group that will be singled out as targets will be women outside of the traditional roles as mothers and housewives. Women's right both to abortion and to continued employment in the economy are under ever-widening attack throughout

Eastern Europe. Women will also suffer immeasurably more from the cutbacks of social programs because they have the major responsibility for caring for the family, the ill, and the helpless. This is part of a double load that women carry throughout the region — they have paying jobs *and* the traditional unpaid job of taking care of the children and the household.

The pressure of this double load has made the retreat to the household sound attractive to some overburdened women, particularly when it is combined with the utopian promise of men being paid a so-called family wage. That is a cruel joke in Eastern Europe today, where the trend is to lower the real wages *and* the social entitlements.

Women, of course, are not the only victims when in post-Communist societies the passions of nationalism overwhelm less rousing notions like democracy. Other groups and forces, like community and class solidarity, are also jeopardized.

Nationalism Jeopardizing Community and Class Solidarity

Substantial shifts in the ethnic composition of the population have been created through migration of the workforce during the decades of widespread urbanization and industrialization of the region. This means that the poor and badly paid are often members of different ethnic groups, or are from different regions, and therefore there is often little solidarity among them. This is the case both in Western and Eastern Europe.

Many Slovenes in former Yugoslavia's prosperous north treat the southern "Bosnian" workers who do the work Slovenes no longer want to do with a scorn very similar to that with which the Swiss and Austrians treat their "guest workers." The bitter title of a book on the Bosnian workers in Slovenia by a Croatian sociologist, Sylvia Meznarić, says it well: *What Do Bosnians Do on Saturdays?* That is, what do they do when they are not working at their grim, unskilled jobs? What do they do during their free time in a society where they are treated as unclean and uncultured outsiders? The answer in the case of the mostly male and single workers who are not invited to socialize and meet the local people is that they drink and fight, thus reinforcing the negative stereotypes about Bosnians in Slovenia.

Nationalist exclusivism and xenophobic mobilization against the "others" have become widespread both in prosperous countries of the European Community and in the slightly better-off parts of Eastern Europe and the former Soviet Union. Racism and nationalism weaken the ties of community and solidarity essential to providing a broad political base for a welfare state and income transfers. These pernicious exclusivist ideas make it very difficult to build strong solidaristic trade unions that are essential in this period of economic upheaval.

Racism and nationalism can be easily mobilized against refugees, immigrants, and workers from less fortunate areas who, particularly in times of economic austerity, appear to be competing for already scarce resources and even insist on some minimal rights and consideration. Even fellow nationals — as newly settled Germans from Eastern Europe and the former Soviet Union are discovering when they seek to share in Germany's prosperity — wear out love and consideration, and thus their welcome, very quickly.

The same bitter discovery has been make by Serbian refugees from Croatia in the cities of Serbia and Vojvodina. It was one thing to loudly defend one's fellow nationals "over there" where they were presumably threatened; it is quite another thing to share resources with them at home. Nationalism — unlike socialism, Communism, and the great universalist religions — tends to be ungenerous in its version of the politics of solidarity.

Nationalism and Populism: No Substitutes for Democracy

What is to bind complex multiethnic states and communities of the near future into polities that could be legitimate parameters within which to make political decisions? One thing could possibly be a common concept of social justice and citizenship. These rather general notions could work effectively because the very idea of a political community will have to become much wider, as it becomes clear that ethnically homogeneous states are a thing of the past. If the polity is not to be bound together by the organic ties of kith and kin and by a common traditional and confessional culture, then what is to do such binding? This is a terribly urgent question because more and more states are in reality multiethnic and multicultural, the only difference being that some states accept this reality and others do not. Another basis for accepting the state as a legitimate arena in which to make majority decisions could be the agreement that the rules of the game were fair and just; that newcomers had access to the game on relatively fair terms; that is to say, that the system was democratic and open to potentially new players. Clearly this not an issue specific only to the new states arising out of the ruins of Yugoslavia and the Soviet Union. To the contrary, it is a general issue that will continue to bedevil modern industrial societies as they become more multiethnic with or without also becoming more and more multicultural. What is to tie the immigrant populations with the long-settled inhabitants in the countries of the European Community and in the United States?

A host of questions and related problems arise around these issues. For instance, "foreign" immigrant workers, who form an increasing percentage of the workforce of many advanced industrial societies, are going to be expected to help support an increasing percentage of old-age pensioners by participating in an implicit transgenerational contract. The foreigners will be disproportionately young, and the natives will have a larger share of retired workers needing support through transfer payments in the form of generous pensions. Will the new workers continue voluntary support of such policies if they are not a real part of the polity? Will they support payment transfers if they are expected to leave when they reach old age and are no longer useful workers? And if they do have to leave eventually, then will not the welfare state be financed in good part by those who do not receive full benefits from it? Will this not weaken the moral basis for a welfare state?

Still other questions arise: Can democracy exist at all in the polity if unrestrained greed and plutocracy reign in the economy? And even if the state and economy theoretically could coexist as two separate spheres, can the great barons of the economy be prevented from trying to influence the polity? If they cannot, what then becomes of fair and just political competition among citizens over choices for the state and society? Even posing the question in this manner requires that one acknowledge that this *very theoretical* division between the economy and the state is precisely what is supposed to be the unique advantage of capitalism; one is also forced to acknowledge, however, that maintaining that division requires the kind of restraints on the economic behavior of individual wielders of great wealth that they find obnoxious.

That is an issue that is being resolved unsatisfactorily by the revived national populists in former Communist states and by Islamic fundamentalists in the Middle East and North Africa. Both are implicitly or even explicitly antidemocratic although willing to use democratic mechanisms, such as free elections, to come to power. Both have answers that are capable today of mobilizing passionate commitment and massive support.[3] The answers of both involve in part a blurring of the lines between state and economy. That is why post-Communist populist governments in Eastern Europe are not hastening to sell off the nationalized industries to foreign investors but are keeping them nationalized. The Muslim fundamentalists simply reject the very notion of a separation of religion and state, or the state and society, let alone religion and the economy.

National populists assert the primacy of the nation (or rather the Nation); they hold that the state must express the *ethnos* rather than the *demos*. It is as if all of the East European nationalists had adopted the narrow Zionist definition of the relationship of the people (i.e., the political nation) to the state. In point of fact, contemporary Croatian, Slovak, Polish, and Serbian nationalists, much like the Zionists, even insist on "the right of return" — not for the exiled *citizens* of their states, to be sure, but for the members of chosen respective dominant nations. In defining the legitimate borders of the nation, all kinds of mutually contradictory arguments are used. Zionists, for instance, refer to God's will as expressed in scripture as a means of defining borders, but such a device is used only in reference to Israel. It is no guide to what could be just boundaries between Serbs and Croats, or Ukrainians and Russians, or Kurds and everyone else. The principle of demarcation most commonly accepted among liberals and democrats is usually some version of the Wilsonian argument based on self-determination. Unfortunately in many disputed areas that is hard to establish and even harder to achieve. For example, is it self-determination of the *present* population or of the original population? How far back in the past does one go to determine what is the "original" population? If only the demographic status quo is used, is this not rewarding past forcible transfers of population? Do the Germans who were forcibly removed from the Sudetenland in Czechoslovakia, or Silesia in Poland, have a just claim to return? If not, why not? There seems to be little basis for rejecting such a claim unless theories of race guilt are to be used to make all ethnic Germans guilty of the crimes of the Hitler regime. To be sure, that type of argument about collective guilt of a national group must be familiar to audiences in the United States. After all, they all live on land that had been seized at some past time from the native peoples. What are the mutual rights and obligations involved? How long do these obligations last after the original crime? A century? Two centuries? Half a millennium? How many whites in the United States owe compensation to African Americans for slavery? Only a tiny minority owned slaves, but maybe that is a question about what the society as a whole owes the distant descendants of slaves. Or is it compensation for racial discrimination? Does this include very recent immigrants? The questions and implications seem endless. In any case, these arguments about *collective* tribal rights and responsibilities do run directly contrary to the universalist ideas about *individual* responsibility for one's own behavior and crimes and not those of the family or tribe. Unfortunately the notion of the relative justice of the use of criteria of collective guilt is widespread, and it is particularly widespread among the newly nationalist publics in Eastern Europe.

There is no doubt that the majority of Serbs and Croats regard it proper to punish members of the other ethnic group for the perceived crimes of the government or armed groups of that group. This was explicitly stated in the summer of 1991 in leaflets distributed in Dalmatia telling Serbs who owned summer homes there that they were not welcome and demanding that they publicly denounce the policies of their government. The implicit presumption was that if they did not have the courage to denounce their authoritarian nationalist government, their lack of bravery would be punished by the confiscation of their homes by local Croat patriots. By 1993 most of these homes had been looted or dynamited. Their owners are now banned from visiting Croatia. Similarly, Serbian nationalists demand not only that Croats repeatedly denounce the Second World War massacres of the Ustaše, but also that they acknowledge that the Croat people as a whole owe compensations to the descendants of the Serbian victims. One is moved to ask: Does this include even those Croats — and there were many, particularly in Dalmatia — who fought arms in hand against the fascist Ustaše from the first day of the partisan war?

Conflicting border claims are the norm in much of the world. When convenient, nationalists insist not on those boundaries that reflect the political choices of the present inhabitants, but rather on historical boundaries, meaning those boundaries from that part of the historical past that would support a claim to a disputed territory. Of course in other cases where the historical argument is weak or nonexistent but the ethnic composition of the population is favorable, the plebiscitary (the will of the people) argument is used. Where neither historical nor ethnographic arguments exist, the argument of strategic necessity is used. And when all arguments fail, naked military force or forcible defense of a desired status quo is used. Ultimately, of course, that tends to be the most effective argument of all. That is what makes it popular with those who perceive themselves as the stronger party.

Ironies abound: some East European nationalists see Israel's present relationship to the West Bank as an explicit model of how to treat areas inhabited by other national groups. This even extends to those nationalists whose predilections to right-wing populism and organic nationalism emphasizing "blood and soil" might under some circumstances have been expected to turn to anti-Semitism. The parallels between the right-wing Zionist attitudes toward the Arab majority on the West Bank and the expressed Serbian attitude toward Kosovo (unfortunately for the Serbs, Kosovo happens to be inhabited by an Albanian majority as large as the Arab majority on the West Bank) are striking. These parallels are even explicitly recognized by the Serbian nationalists. But then, Serbian right-wing nationalists also regard Israel and Serbia to be allied in that they both are victims of a worldwide Islamic fundamentalist conspiracy.

The cases of the Israeli right-wingers and the Serbian nationalists have nothing to do with democracy. Some Georgian nationalists go even further: they would give Georgian citizenship only to those who can prove that their ancestors lived in Georgia in 1804! A similar line is taken by the Fiji Islanders and inhabitants of New Caledonia — that is, that the vote must be restricted to the "original" inhabitants, no matter how long the other citizens of the country have lived there. It is an old if not necessarily honorable position that many regions have a "state people," and all others reside in those regions on sufferance and with lesser rights.[4]

Democrats: The Need to Face Nationalism Seriously

Nationalists, in both their traditional and populist variants, pose a major challenge, even obstacle, to the transition to democracy in a great many parts of the world. Because they certainly do mobilize passionate support, any effective democratic program must take into account national sentiments and desires for identity and *combine* them with individual citizen rights for all. That is difficult, but ignoring national feelings is an act of delusion.

Surely an adequate alternative to nationalism for democrats cannot just be the cold bureaucratic-rational community of minimal economic common self-interests projected by the Eurocracy in the European Community and the liberals in the United States. Nor can it be the social Darwinian jungle of the free marketeers who support the most minimal state, except when it comes to repression, and defend the proposition that individual pursuit of greed is the supreme road to achieving a decent society. Nor can a democratic community be built within a state conceptualized primarily as a perpetual bargaining ground, or at best a marketplace, for mutually hostile ethnic, gender-oriented, and single-issue social movements bound by no idea of the common good. Not only is an idea of the common good itself absent in these movements, but a part of the bargaining is also about past wrongs that must be paid off by those who did not commit or benefit from them. (We can leave out the cases where what is sought is not even retribution but vengeance.) Such a polity may be accepted as a potential paymaster for one's *true* community (defined, for instance, along ethnic, gender, life-style, or generational lines). In such an arrangement one bargains for the most one can get, unbound by any sense of mutual interdependence, and it is hardly a legitimate democratic arena for politics.

A basis for a modern democratic political community and state is not provided by the organic, "passionate" politics of *pays réel,*[5] or by the abstract, alienated politics of *pays légal,* or even by the mutually antagonistic and fragmented politics of interest groups and social movements. Such a state and democratic civil society are possible only if there is an overarching idea of the common good, of a purpose for politics. That is theoretically provided by democratic-socialist politics at their best; it is also provided by social Christianity, or even more precisely social Catholicism.

Absolute Right to Self-Determination:
A Dangerous Call

An invincible innocence and ignorance pervade Western prescriptions about nationalism and separatism for the former Soviet Union and Eastern Europe. What is proposed is that which no Western democratic state would dream of practicing. "Pure" market economies are not practiced in the managed capitalism of Western welfare states, and no Western state accepts that provinces — even though they may have had a distinct history and ethnic makeup — have an *automatic democratic right* to separate unilaterally. That absolutist version of the right to self-determination is only for the Soviets and East Europeans. As stated above, such a theory of self-determination, to the point of the right of secession, was not insisted on even in the cases of Third World countries, as the cases of Biafra, Kashmir, Katanga, Eritrea, Timor, and Kurdistan, among others, illustrate. In none of these cases was it proposed to stop aid or mobilize world public opinion against the dominant country unless it immediately accepted the independence of a suppressed and incorporated nation.

No sanctions were ever proposed against France for its stand on Corsican, Breton, and New Caledonian separatism; against Spain for its resistance to a separation of Catalonia or the Basque region; or against Great Britain for its denial of Scots or Irish rights to vote on immediate separation. These proposals for national independence or autonomy were seen as problematic issues that needed, at best, to be debated and *negotiated.*

The situation of the Baltic states was quite different not only from some of these other cases, but also from the situation of other former Soviet republics. To be sure, *all* nationalist movements claim that their own case is unique. Nevertheless, most of the countries of the world have never accepted the Baltic states' incorporation into the Soviet Union, through the Hitler-Stalin pact, as legitimate. That is a view now shared by the Russian democrats. The Baltic countries and Moldavia, therefore, are in a different situation from the other former Soviet republics, at least from the point of view of international law.

However, even in these cases, independence should be something to be negotiated. One very important matter to include within such negotiation is the guarantee of civic, national, and human rights for the non-Latvian, non-Estonian, and non-Lithuanian minorities in the proposed newly independent states. Unfortunately, historical experiences, as well as the present declarations of many of the nationalists, are not reassuring here. Some nationalists in Latvia and Estonia would strip the close to 40 percent "minority" population, including those born there, of voting and civic rights. It does not help matters when nationalists insist that there is nothing whatsoever to negotiate, that all they have to do is unilaterally vote their own independence. This view has considerable support in the West.

Why is it that Western liberals view proposals for radical, egalitarian economic changes as complex and recommend caution, while they view problems of democratization as simple? What are the grounds for assuming that most nationalists and separatists in the former Soviet Union want democracy? Historical experience, the present situation, and statements from far too many nationalist spokesmen argue against such Pollyannaish assumptions.

The Political and Moral Vacuum in Eastern Europe

The sudden toppling of ruling Communist parties resulted in an institutional vacuum. In some republics in Yugoslavia the reform wing of the party itself had initiated the political and economic reforms. The best example is Slovenia, where a continued orderly transition to a pluralist polity is likely. In most of the countries, except Poland, the opposition was small, loosely organized, and relatively isolated. It takes time to build genuine alternative parties and institutions.

The whole point of Communist repression had been to prevent the ties of minimal social solidarity and mutual confidence from developing, for those ties foster democratic opposition. The Communist leaders had in part been successful in crippling the opposition. It remained small and ghettoized until mass popular demonstrations catapulted it — prepared or not — into the political limelight and responsibility.

The democratic revolutions in Czechoslovakia and East Germany followed the scenario of Rosa Luxemburg, not that of Lenin. That is, they involved mass spontaneous eruption from below, rather than careful tactics and strategy planned by a self-selected revolutionary general staff, a cadre leading disciplined troops. While that is heartwarming to radical democrats and democratic socialists, it does leave open the question of where an experienced leadership with broad legitimacy is to be found. Organizational experience and skill are needed within any polity, and once the dust settles and it becomes clear that formally eliminating the Communist party's monopoly of power leaves most problems unsolved, particularly economic ones, that skill and experience will reassert themselves. That is why the Communist parties, under whatever name they take, cannot be written off as future contenders for power in Eastern Europe.

They will probably end up transformed in terms of formal ideology and programs. As in the cases of Hungary and Poland, they may enter into temporary coalitions with national populists, but they will remain an important force on the political scene. This is primarily the case with the Communist reformers; the hard-liners have a much more ambiguous future. It is a future that might well bring them into a direct alliance with the more demagogic nationalists of the organic right.

While the democratic opposition has succeeded admirably in toppling the evidently illegitimate authority of the Communist regimes in Eastern Europe, building new, alternate, legitimate, and democratic authority will be a very difficult task. It will be made ever more difficult by the presence of marginal groups of defeated Communist hard-liners, on the one hand, and right-wing nationalist adventurers, on the other; these are antagonists who share a goal — preventing the stabilization of a democratic order through provocations, riots, and violence if necessary. The scenario for destabilizing democratic regimes was learned by not only the CIA and KGB, after all; there can be other less established players. These forces will be on the fringes of the new, fragile, and democratic former Communist states.

The reform Communists will remain a considerable force in the new East European countries if for no other reason than their presence within the massive bureaucracies that the new governments will inherit. Like the postfascist and post-Nazi structures that were present in Italy and Germany after the Second World War, the new democratic coalition governments will not be able to start with a *tabula rasa*. The bulk of the civil service and other bureaucracies had to be party members, or at least party sympathizers, for four long decades. Again, to pursue the analogy of postfascist regimes, many, if not most, of the experts and administrators who served the old regimes

were mere opportunists and careerists rather than ideological Stalin-
ists. Some of these persons' commitment to democracy will not be
excessively firm, but in fairness it should be added that many of the
Communist reformers have evolved in their politics to a point where
they are genuine defenders of pluralistic democracy and have become
social democrats.

Both the horrendous backlog of necessary reforms and the institutional vacuum have been created by the ruling Communist parties
who bear a historical responsibility for them. That is why those parties will pay a heavy political penalty in any democratic, electoral,
competitive system in the immediate future and will be forced into
coalitions if they are to retain formal power. In some cases, like in
Poland, it may well be in their interest not to take the major political
responsibility for the pain that the economic reforms will cause.

That does not help the non-Communist movements and parties.
These were movements that had learned to oppose and criticize; often
they were concentrated on a single issue; usually they were limited in
membership to intellectuals. Now they have the more complicated
task of learning how to offer alternative national policies for which
they will have to take political responsibility. They will have to learn
how to compromise with stubborn reality, make coalitions with difficult partners, and administer complicated societies that are in deep
trouble. In short, they will have to learn democracy, that same democracy for which they fought for so many years. They will find that
a hard task, perhaps even an impossible task without generous help
from Western Europe and the United States for many years to come.
After all, Western Europe needed the Marshall Plan to develop stable economies and political structures after a much shorter period of
fascist rule.

The beginning of all political and economic reforms was the destruction of the power monopoly of the local Communist parties.
No lasting economic reforms, no liberalization of the political systems had any long-range prospects without that first step. That is
not to say that no reforms were possible without eliminating the legal and very real monopoly of power of the Communist parties in
those societies. What I am asserting is that no *lasting, basic* economic
and political reforms were possible so long as that monopoly was
maintained.

The simple reason for this was that the necessary reforms could be made only within a democratic context, and yet the Communist monopoly could be maintained only by constant limitations of democracy and the right of people to organize their own parties, unions, movements, and institutions. Without minimal social autonomy from the state, genuine economic reforms could not be made because all such proposals were subordinated to day-to-day political intervention. Given all that, the Communist parties will still keep some power and influence in most of these societies for some time, formally or informally. They begin with the advantage of resources and organization. The important question is: How much weight does that carry in the face of widespread contempt and even hatred by the mass of the population in most of the East European countries?

Then what happens if — as is inevitable in some cases — the new democratic governments stumble and plunge the countries into major economic uncertainty and chaos. What happens if the economic reforms do not work, cause immense pain and large-scale unemployment, and create no visible improvement in the living standards of the majority of the population? Worse, what if the reforms cause all these problems *and* create a small, very visible class of newly rich? This is not at all far-fetched given the attitude of Western banks and creditors, on the one hand, and illusions about the magic working of the market, on the other.

What happens when the bad old days of Communist regimes start being remembered as the good old days of relative stability and security? Democracy is a hard-won thing, and fledgling democracies will desperately need massive and generous help. But above all they will need widespread popular support and the willingness of many people to fight and make sacrifices for a democratic social and political order. They will not fight for greater economic inequality and the right of a few to get rich.

New Post-Communist States: A Description

Describing these new social and political hybrids is a very difficult task because they do not fall neatly into categories like "socialist" and "capitalist." For example, for all the talk about privatizing the public sector of the economy and moving into a market-driven economic system, the reality of such a transformation is very complicated. For one thing, certain essential infrastructures of the society will be impossible to privatize. For another thing, much of the public sector is not going to be all that attractive to potential buyers.

Attractive pieces of the economy, and they are few, might be privatized; cheap labor might attract some foreign investment; but neither of those will solve the problem of the bulk of the economy in most of these societies. Much of the public sector, particularly heavy industry, will remain as an example of "lemon socialism," with desperate needs of funding for modernization and reorganization.

These will probably be transitional societies for a considerable time in the future, with a mixture of institutional and economic forms and with a *variety* of forms of ownership — public, state, co-operative, private, and a mix of all of the above. I agree with Alec Nove's argument that such a mix is desirable and sensible.[6] Whether this makes such a society "socialist" or "capitalist" is a definitional problem. My own rough answer is that such labeling will depend on the *specific* balance of organized political and class forces as well as on the specific mixture of forms of ownership in the society. All this will also be complicated by the degree of state intervention through direct and indirect mechanisms. Capitalist economies, one must remember, differ greatly when it comes to such intervention. Clearly the new societies will also develop trade unions that will be genuine and democratic socialist parties, under whatever name.

Whatever else is the case, the struggle for any kind of reformist socialism will be a great deal easier in Eastern Europe once these societies democratize. That which can be given from above can also be taken back. That which is won in struggle from below establishes new power relations. Further, the fate of democratic and egalitarian reforms ultimately rests on the ability of the democratic forces, parties, movements, and trade unions to organize effectively.

For democratization to succeed the democratic forces in Eastern Europe must be able to organize and offer viable political and economic alternatives. That means talking about alternative policies and not endlessly about the past errors and crimes of the Communist regimes. The first is exceedingly difficult to do; the second comes naturally, unfortunately. The mix will differ from country to country, as will the radicalness of the break with the past and the speed with which the various countries begin to construct new democratic societies and political cultures. Given the powerful forces of nationalism and right-wing populism, this entire process will be stormy, difficult, and conflict-ridden. In some cases there will be coalitions of former Communists with right-wing nationalist and populist forces. Some of these countries, but by no means all, will evolve into democratic societies that are no longer politocracies. It will be a hard and bitterly contested road, one that can be made smoother with generous help from the richer societies of the European Community and the United States. But "societies" do not help; genuine help comes from real political and social forces. For the democrats from Eastern Europe and the former Soviet Union that help will have to come from the European trade unions and social democrats. As conservative a figure as George Shultz, President Reagan's Secretary of State, understood this when he linked democracy to the existence of free and strong trade unions.[7]

Democracy does not have a chance in the region without strong and independent unions. Without strong unions, Eastern Europe and the states of the former Soviet Union will represent a threat to the living standards of the workers of the European Community, for they will be a pool of cheap and ununionized labor. If they are such a threat, they will be faced with hostility and xenophobia on the part of the Western Europeans. It will greatly delay their entry into the European Community. With strong trade unions — and help is desperately needed to organize these — Eastern European democrats will have natural allies in the European Community. These allies will not be merely men and women of abstract goodwill. The real allies will be the largest voting block in the European parliament — the democratic socialists, the social democrats, and their allied trade unions.

The World Market: A Hard Place for Fledgling Democracies

The rules of the world market have a universalist character, and they measure the former Communist regimes in Eastern Europe and the former Soviet Union by yardsticks very different from those to which they were accustomed. There are no effective safety nets. There will be no "soft" budget constraints. The new regimes will have to try to produce *and sell* goods of decent design and quality at reasonable cost if they are to have access to competitive markets. To begin to achieve this with the present antiquated industrial plant and organization of the economy at anything like economic prices requires increasing productivity while holding wages down. Cutbacks in social entitlement will likely be demanded.

Such Draconian economic measures will only and at best add to the continued stagnation and the continued checkmate between class forces. The democratic reforms will not really affect this stalemate since most reforms that are proposed by the liberal reformers, even by many of the former democratic leftists, would, at least initially, increase work discipline, increase unemployment, and cut back on the already low living standards of the workers. All this adds to a consolidation of class consciousness on the part of the workers; on the part of the middle class and intellectual strata, it merely adds to their self-consciousness of their separateness. The dilemma has been very clearly stated by Valery Vyzhutovich, a Moscow legislator and backer of the democratic reformers: "Having taken over the functions of power on a large scale, the democrats did not cope with management. To cope with it, one has to either refuse utopian attempts to manage everything, and give society a chance to regulate itself where possible, or cease to be democrats."[8]

One way in which a democratic society can "regulate itself where possible" is through the intervention of powerful trade unions representing their members and forcing compromises known in the West as social market economies or the welfare state. Whatever else takes place in Eastern Europe in the future after the turbulent upheavals in 1989, one thing is clearly in the cards. The region will see the development of *genuine* mass trade unions — good ones that will represent their members and try to build a democratic political order and bad ones that leaders will use for their own enrichment. Some will arise out of the wreckage of the official unions as they are transformed into that which they had never been — organizations defending both the specific interests of their members and the interests of the working class as a whole.

In some cases, as in Poland and parts of Yugoslavia and Hungary, sections of the old official Communist trade union leadership will attempt to turn their organizations into genuine unions. Other types of unions will develop as well. These will be new and independent and will sometimes even take the form of narrow craft unions. Still other unions will develop among the scientific workers and teachers, as in the case of the independent unions in Hungary. All of these and other forms will develop in response to the opening up of these societies and to the clear threat to the living standards of the workers. Many, unfortunately, will be run by irresponsible adventurers.

Most of the reforms proposed thus far have the workers bearing the brunt of getting the economies out of the mess into which the Communist politocracy had gotten them. These proposals are not accompanied by any effective mechanisms for an equality of sacrifice. To the contrary, most proposals include greater rewards for those who can operate within the market, and some provide even better rewards for middle-class professionals. Workers are being told that it is they who are technologically redundant and overprotected.

Middle-class reformers think that any excessive wage egalitarianism is oppressive per se. For many, *any* tendency toward egalitarianism is excessive. This is visible in the uncritical acceptance of the ideological defense of the market as the master instrument of economic reform. I am not questioning here the desirability of introducing some market principles in the economy as one of the needed measures to leverage the *nomenklatura* out of economic control. Nor is there much question that the market is an efficient allocator of consumer goods and indicator of consumer preferences. It can, however, act in those ways just as well in an egalitarian society. The market does not necessarily require great social inequalities in order to perform its distributive and allocative functions.

What I am questioning is the present love affair that many East European reformers have with the "market" as a synonym for the economic dogmas of Milton Friedman and the social policies of Margaret Thatcher. After all, that is not the only market model that exists. Clearly the advanced welfare states of Western Europe, like Sweden, Holland, and West Germany, are also market economies. However, most of the market enthusiasts in Eastern Europe have fallen for the ideology of the raw Darwinian market, not the social market of the social democrats. This is ironic because most of the intellectuals who prattle about the "pure" market would starve to death in any real market economy. The Communist parties are properly held responsible for the horrible economic and cultural mess of these societies. One of the cultural and social messes has been the creation of vast masses of unemployable, well-educated generalists with a traditional contempt for manual or "merely practical" work.

These members of the new middle classes are generally enthusiastic supporters of market reforms. Given their own unsuitability for the rough and ready realities of competitive market economies, this is a little like turkeys demanding that every day be Christmas.

Some of the Communist regimes have also given birth to a very specialized, antisocial, and semicrooked class of entrepreneurs whose skills have been honed at cutting legal corners and finding ways through bureaucratic mazes. They are used to quick profits and corruption and are not about to invest, even if they had the means, in the kind of dynamic and innovative private sector that the economic reformers hope to encourage. One should also pause and consider just how proposals to privatize sections of the economy will work out in real life. Some genuine horror stories are emerging. Just who will be able to buy what parts of the nationalized sectors of the economy for what price and under what circumstances?

Given the tendency in the East European societies to insiderism and manipulation of informal networks, one can guarantee that enormous amounts of corruption and favoritism will occur during the scramble to privatize and "marketize" these societies. There are already signs of this in Hungary, Czechoslovakia, Croatia, and Poland. More are sure to come to light as privatization at all costs continues. This will be even more the case when this privatization involves foreign capital buying into nationalized enterprises. This will occur because there will be more money at stake than ever before, and East European politocratic elites have a notoriously low resistance to financial temptation. Furthermore, wielders of foreign capital have even been known to engage in bribery in other countries, Milton Friedman and the Chicago school notwithstanding.

Corruption will be even more present, however, when the would-be buyers come from the old political elites and the local petty capitalists. Corruption has been their forte, after all. It is almost the only thing they were ever good at. The new East European petty capitalists will clearly exacerbate class antagonisms through their very visible consumption of luxuries, avoidance of taxes and regulations, and attempts to corrupt the local government and political parties. That is probably unavoidable, but what is essential under those circumstances is that trade unions and genuine social-democratic parties develop to assure that the marketization of these societies does not develop in ways that are antisocial and that will threaten democracy.

Democracy will be vulnerable if it is accompanied by massive corruption, increased class differences, and unemployment. At the very least this will increase the tendency for the growth of populism, which has a nasty tradition in the region.

My prognosis is that the societies, politics, and economies in much of the former Soviet Union and Eastern Europe are going to go through a process of *Mexicanization*. The term refers to a mix of private and state-owned sectors accompanied by a hybrid political system that involves elements of free elections, often modified by corruption and deals among elite groups. The political elite will include the local barons and operators on the national scene, the new rich, the technocrats, corrupt and genuine trade unionists, and a plethora of leaders of popular organizations, some more real than others. Freedom to travel and freedom of the press and speech will exist, but will be limited in such a way that they do not interfere with the real wielding of power. To continue the metaphor of Mexico: this will occur within a highly charged and ambivalent relationship to the dominant regional colossus, in this case to the west rather than to the north. All this might still represent a step forward in the complicated real world and a better terrain for further struggles for genuine democracy.

However, the present situation as regards democracy and economic reforms is at best ambiguous. It inspires little political enthusiasm, nothing remotely beginning to compare with the struggle against Communist authoritarianism. With the old enemy defeated there is little, outside nationalism and religion, in the way of positive beliefs about how society should be organized and even less about how individuals should live their lives. Identity is not the same as a program that inspires broad support. The cost of this increasingly widespread ideological vacuum has been widespread cynicism and apathy about *organized* politics and often even about *organized* oppositional politics, above all among the young. There is increased apathy about voting throughout the regime. It will increase if nothing changes — after all, democracy was supposed to improve the lives of the large majority. To date it has not.

Social movements are more congenial and appear "purer." There is a genuine youth subculture that has transcended class barriers. This culture is mostly apolitical, hedonistic, and materialist; it is very consumerist and tends to copy the latest from the West. Among the working-class and lumpen young, there is an alienated punk and skinhead subculture that is open to xenophobic and nationalist mobilization. These could be the shock troops of a new nationalist fascism if there is an economic breakdown and democratic legitimacy is eroded. Social movements are by no means limited to the progressive end of the spectrum.

Many aspects of the youth culture are antiauthoritarian, egalitarian, and seem open to other-directed goals and activities, provided that this is not stated in the used-up old jargon of socialism. This in part explains the attractiveness of alternative peace and ecology groups throughout the area. Under the Communist regimes, democracy had been the primary goal of most of the opposition. That democracy had never been particularly clearly defined, but it was clear that it was a good thing in itself. The problem now, in post-Communist societies, is to give more flesh, more content, to the previously abstract idea of democracy. In the past, democracy had been largely defined in counterposition to the real practices of the authoritarian Communist regimes. The goal of the democrats today has to be the creation of the following: a legal order in which the judiciary system is independent of the state; a richly varied civil society that is autonomous from the state and the dominant political parties; genuine, mass, democratic trade unions; and a multiparty parliamentary democracy. In other words, their goal must be to move beyond the terrain of the social movements and populist nationalist quasi-parties to *institutionalize* a democratic state and organizations.

These are necessary but insufficient prerequisites for a possible later struggle for genuine egalitarian democracy that would include workers' control in the workplaces; popular, grass-roots, participatory authority in the various institutions; and the abolition of gender oppression. These democratic-socialist demands are not *counterposed* to the institutionalization of a democratic polity; to the contrary, fighting for these goals requires stable democratic institutions and the development of a democratic political culture.

A lively and tolerant parliamentary democracy with powerful unions, parties, and social movements is the optimal terrain on which to work for democratic socialism. This argues against pushing political and national differences to the extremes, at least until democratic institutions develop some firmness and stability. However, what makes good sense in the long run — or even the medium run — is all too rarely the same policy that appears to make sense in the immediate present. Tolerance of differences is essential in order to build stable democratic regimes. It is the precondition for a democratic civic culture. That means no revenge, no matter how justified: no witch-hunts of former Communist hard-liners, no attempts to illegalize Communist parties, and above all no hunt for scapegoats for what will be economic and social grim times for most of post-Communist Eastern Europe. Those scapegoats will be, all too often, either those who are ethnically different — the minorities and Jews — or intellectuals, political liberals, and leftists.

The temptation to use nationalist, ethnocentric, and populist pseudoegalitarian demagoguery will be very great, and it will continue to pay off in the short run. Sometimes that demagoguery will be used by what remains of the old Communist *nomenklatura,* institutions, and cadres. This will be more likely when there has as yet been not enough time to develop genuine broadly based programmatic political parties and movements to fill the political void created by the collapse of the Communist parties as credible political organizations.

It is madly utopian to expect that years of grim repression under Communist regimes would have left behind a mass political culture that is in its essence democratic and tolerant. The values of the democratic and human rights activists have been relatively ghettoized to the better educated publics in much of the region. It is important not to assume that the huge turn against the Communist regimes was and is programmatically inspired by the politics and values of oppositional activists. That opposition was and is far broader and includes a visceral and massive anti-Communism that has precious little in common with democratic values.

As noted above, the post-Communist politics of Eastern Europe will in many ways resemble politics in contemporary Latin America, with all its present ambiguities provided by its mix of corporatism, corruption, a dynamic private sector, and a multitude of political parties, most of which have no effective access to power or broad support. One must not push the analogy too far, but it is richly suggestive. In the post-Communist societies the role of international financial institutions and banks will be very important as well as a source of great internal hostility and controversy. These are a part of the historical penalty being paid by these societies for the lost years under Communist regimes.

Political, economic, and moral pressure from the West European democrats, democratic socialists, and trade unionists can significantly improve the prospects of genuine democracy in Eastern Europe. Political leaders in Eastern Europe and the former Soviet Union have to be informed that it is not enough for them to insist that they are certified anti-Communists. It must be made clear that the quantity and type of aid, let alone the relationship to the European Community, will depend on the degree to which the East European states abide by democratic norms and respect human rights; and it also must be made clear that this explicitly includes independent trade unions and social movements. For that pressure to have any real effect the international financial institutions must cease to demand policies that will impose a brutal austerity that will be hard for any democratic or popular regime to survive. Regimes seek to survive, and if they find it essential for their survival, they will cease to be either democratic or popular. The first attribute that such regimes will shed, with some relief in many cases, is post-Communist democracy, which is admittedly already limited. They will try to hang on to some shreds of popularity by shifting the blame for the visibly dismal economic and political prospects to others; that is a formula for xenophobia and ethnic chauvinism.

Those two traits are among the grim products of a badly flawed transition from Communism to the presently popular models of democracy, models that are linked to a neo-Darwinian privatized market economy, to an assault on job security, and to an assault on the crude welfare state that had been available under the old regime. If the West and the international financial institutions continue to insist on this linkage, then the consequence will be a free fall of living standards for the masses. That, in turn, will be fatal for the prospects of any democracy in post-Communist societies, above all in states that are ethnically mixed or that have large minorities. That is one of the lessons of the death of Yugoslavia.

Chapter 4

NATIONALISM AS THE NEMESIS OF DEMOCRATIC ALTERNATIVES

Many of the troubling national disputes that had racked pre-revolutionary Yugoslavia were by and large successfully settled by the postwar political and constitutional arrangements. This was particularly the case with the so-called constituent nations of second Yugoslavia — the Slovenes, Croats, Serbs, and Macedonians, to which were soon added Montenegrins, who were recognized as a nation almost immediately after the war. By the 1970s the Slavic Muslims living mostly in Bosnia and the Sanjak region of Serbia were also recognized as a constituent Yugoslav nation. The two major minorities, Hungarians and Albanians, received a special regime with autonomy in the areas where they were most numerous, Vojvodina and Kosovo. The treatment of the Hungarian minority of some four hundred thousand was held up as exemplary and was used by the Hungarian government to argue for better treatment of Hungarian minorities in Czechoslovakia and Romania. The Albanian minority, however, had a number of legitimate complaints, one of which was that unlike the "constituent nations" they had never voluntarily become a part of either Yugoslavia or its predecessor state, Serbia. They were, in other words, a part of Yugoslavia by conquest.[1] Up to at least the mid-1960s they were subjected to a grim and repressive police regime answering directly to Alexander Ranković, the Serbian de facto head of the political police and other security forces. His purge in the mid-1960s led to reforms in Kosovo and a more liberal treatment of the Albanians, their culture, and cadres.

The overall policy granting wide national self-determination to the constituent nations and the two major minorities within a loose federal state had been one of the more obvious successes of the post-revolutionary regime. To be sure, violent national chauvinists, particularly those of the traditional right and among the anti-Communist exiles, were bound to be unhappy with anything short of their maximum programs. The whole point of a multiethnic federation, however, was that *no* single national group would obtain its "maximum" program because that could only be done at the expense of others. Thus while the Communist national settlement after the Second World War was reasonable on this question, unlike in the matter of *democratic* rights, it made *all* nationalists unhappy. Most of those nationalists of course were absolutely opposed to any kind of Yugoslavia whatsoever, even the loosest federation.[2] In contrast, the large majority of the people of all national groups found the new Yugoslav state, at least on this question, quite tolerable, and a rather widespread "Yugoslavism" was found throughout the country until the mid-1980s.

The Macedonian National Program

Macedonia, for example, had not been the scene of separatist or anti-Yugoslav agitation since the Second World War, when the Republic of Macedonia was created. That was clearly a popular move that did much to legitimate the postrevolutionary Communist regime in Macedonia. The Macedonian Slavs thus managed to get a state of their own for the first time since the reign of Emperor Samuilo in the eleventh century. To be sure, there had been all kinds of ambiguities attached to a modern Macedonian nationalism and the very idea of a Macedonian nation. Things were particularly and bloodily complicated by the fact that the nationalists of *all* neighboring nations, Greece, Bulgaria, Serbia, and even Albania, have vehemently denied the existence of a separate Macedonian nation.

The Greek nationalists have generally claimed that it was all a question of false consciousness, that Macedonians are "Slavophone Greeks" — that is, Greeks who just happen to speak a Slavic language and stubbornly deny their Greekness. Greek political polemicists further confuse the matter by insisting that the eternal quality of the geographic name "Macedonia" is determined by defining the *national identity* of the peoples who live there now. Clearly, however, the present inhabitants have nothing to do with the "Macedonians" of Alexander the Great (who were not Greeks in any meaningful sense of the word). Waves of subsequent invading peoples have passed through and settled in the area known as Macedonia. The odd thing is that since the rise of modern nationalism in the nineteenth century, no one, except Marxist revolutionaries, has proposed that the local people exercise self-determination. Instead rival claims have partitioned what was clearly a heterogeneous population in which most of the peasants were Slavic-speaking Christians of the Orthodox faith and in which the small number of urban Christian elites identified as Greek, Bulgarian, Serbian, or Macedonian.

The Serbs continue to base their rather unconvincing claims on the territory on the relatively brief rule over that area by the medieval Serbian Empire at its greatest extent, and Serbian nationalists call the area "southern Serbia." Bulgarians in turn base their claims to Macedonia on the fact that the area was clearly a major part of the medieval Bulgarian Empire, and the language is much closer to Bulgarian than to any other language. More to the point, a major faction of the Macedonian nationalist revolutionary organization, the Internal Macedonian Revolutionary Organization (IMRO), had been pro-Bulgarian since the end of the nineteenth century. The other faction was for an independent Macedonia as a part of a Balkan federation of nations. Even more to the point, most of Macedonia was partitioned — without any regard for the preferences of the local inhabitants — between Serbia and Greece when they emerged as victors of the Second Balkan War (1913), and the Bulgarians emerged as the losers. Although there are many arguments and counterarguments about the inhabitants' nationality, it should be reasonably clear that the only politically relevant national identity is subjective — the people are what think they are.

On the basis of most of the evidence I am familiar with, it would appear that the vast majority of Slav speakers, who are a clear majority of the population in the Republic of Macedonia, feel today that they are *Macedonian* by nationality. As to the historical issues, only one additional point needs to be made: massive settlements of Greeks from Turkey in the 1920s and a systematic policy of assimilation and repression of the national identity of Macedonian Slavs in northern Greece have reduced the Slavic Macedonians in Greece to the present small minority. It is shameful that Greece does not treat this minority decently, like, let us say, the Italians treat the German speakers in the Tyrol-Adige area. There is no conceivable way that Greece can be said to be threatened by the existence of a small, independent Macedonian state. The new Bulgarian post-Communist government has paved the way to normal relations between Bulgaria and Macedonia — two states that are closely related ethnically — by being the first to recognize the independence of Macedonia in 1992. A model could well be the relationship between Germany and Austria.

The present major national problems of Macedonia itself are with its growing Albanian minority, which now numbers around 25 percent of the population and which has been antagonized by Macedonian nationalist politicians. Given the large number and rapid growth of the Albanian population in Macedonia, the attacks against their basic rights by Macedonian nationalist parties augurs ill for the future stable national relations within that republic. However, the situation of the Albanians in Macedonia is incomparably better than that of their fellow nationals in Kosovo and, at least economically, even in Albania proper. During 1992 and 1993 the major Albanian parties in Macedonia participated in a left-center coalition government, something unfortunately unimaginable in Serbia.

With their absurd territorial claims on parts of Macedonia, aggressive Serbian nationalists may succeed in making active enemies of the Macedonian political parties. That could lead to conciliation between the Albanians and the Macedonian majority. In any case, Macedonia had clearly benefited from its association with Yugoslavia. Its future as an independent state outside of Yugoslavia, in contrast, is fairly problematic given the unfriendly past relations with Greece and Bulgaria.[3] Macedonia is vulnerable to an economic blockade from Greece, and the Greek government has been unremittingly hostile.

The 1974 Settlement of Croatia's Economic Grievances

When Tito, with the support of the Yugoslav National Army and the LCY hard-liners, cracked down in 1972 on what he considered to be

the excesses of the "Croatian Spring," Savka Dapčević and Mika Tripalo — two popular, reformist leaders of the Croatian LCY — were
purged from the LCY but not jailed. The real problem was that the
two had lost control of the movement to genuine (that is to say,
anti-Communist) nationalists. The anti-Communists were jailed in
large numbers, and they form the core of the new nationalist *nomenklatura* of independent Croatia. Many went into exile where they
were welcomed by the existing anti-Yugoslav right-wing émigré communities, some of which were dominated by the Ustaše, who had
been allies of the Nazis in the Second World War.

Both Savka Dapčević and Mika Tripalo have reemerged in 1989
and the elections of 1990 and 1992 as leaders of the moderate
democratic nationalists. Tripalo tends to stress democracy; Dapčević
stresses nationalism. The non- and anti-Communist veterans of the
1969–71 "Spring" play a major role in post-Communist Croatian
politics, covering the whole nationalist political spectrum from liberals and populist democrats through to genuine fascists with their
own paramilitary, uniformed, blackshirt thugs.

The economic and political settlement enshrined in the constitution of 1974 had almost completely solved the original economic and
political grievances against supposed excessive centralism, control on
the part of Belgrade, and domination of Serbia within the federation. As a consequence it was the Serbian *nationalists* who tended to
be the vocal aggrieved parties when it came to the constitution and
the functioning of the economy and the political system of the post-
1974 federation. Their complaints soon found an echo in the Serbian
Academy of Sciences and (albeit very discreetly during Tito's lifetime)
among some of the political leaders of Serbia. Most foreign experts
have also argued that Yugoslavia was far too *decentralized* by the
1974 constitution, making difficult economic and political decisions
all but impossible to make, at least legally.

The 1974 Constitution and Paralysis after Tito's Death

The new constitution was fine for good times when no urgent decisions needed to be made, when no external or internal danger
threatened. That boded ill for the post-Tito era when that hard-
headed and tough arbiter would be gone, and when increasingly

difficult decisions about the economy would have to be made. The problem was not only that the federation was constitutionally extraordinarily loose; the further problem was that what made it function at all were the extralegal, informal agreements of the top LCY leaders, not the formal political system. These all-important informal ties and arrangements began to break down even before the formal system did. The formal decision making by the federal center was almost completely blocked through insistence on consensus and the sovereignty of the republics. This is a cautionary warning to other multinational states: an excessive emphasis on the autonomy of the national subcomponents of such a state may paralyze it. Further, if through paralysis it proves incapable of governing effectively, it will lose legitimacy just as decisively as if it is too repressive.

The Yugoslav constitution of 1974 practically gave each republic and each province a veto over any legislation that might affect it negatively. The result was an almost complete paralysis of the federal system when economic and political crises arose during the 1980s. This doomed to failure all the successive governments of Yugoslavia that followed Tito's death. Their failure in turn created increasing contempt for and irritation with the federal system, while the continued monopoly of power by the LCY prevented any moves to generate broadly acceptable alternatives. The brief exception was the government of Ante Marković, which for a brilliant moment seemed to be about to make a breakthrough with economic reforms and the stabilization of currency, producing a "hard" convertible dinar in the fall of 1990.

This economic breakthrough by the federal government collapsed in the face of a combined assault by the leaders of Serbia, Croatia, and Slovenia, who were united in their determination to topple any successful federal government through insuring inadequate and insufficient support by the European Community and world financial institutions. Marković's success might have led to all kinds of dangerous things: free multiparty federal elections, the creation of a non- or even antinationalist arena for legitimate politics, entry into the anteroom of Europe, and a consequent defusing of nationalist and separatist mobilization. Therefore, if nationalist leaders were to survive at all, Marković had to fail. And fail he did by the summer of 1991. By that time Europe's stinginess and the continued disintegration of Yugoslavia had given birth to a brutal civil war and a

pathological decay of the federal institutions, particularly the Yugoslav National Army, which was by now obviously independent of the
last vestiges of civilian control.

Top-Down Organization
of the Serbo-Croat Disputes

Despite the paralysis of the federation, the Serbo-Croat dispute up
to roughly 1987 was, for the most part, reduced to endless boring
and repetitive polemics between amateur, and sometimes more rarely
professional, linguists and historians and, of course, the pamphleteers
and journalists. The disputes did not become politically important
until the political establishments entered the fray. The Serbs clearly
started the process of disintegration of a federal Yugoslavia. In the
early 1980s they began pushing for changes in the 1974 constitution to give them control over the autonomous provinces of Kosovo
and Vojvodina. Meeting resistance from the more liberal western republics of Slovenia and Croatia, the Serbs organized a huge media
campaign that reached a frenzy when opposition in the other republics began to harden toward constitutional changes and the Serbian
heavy-handed repression of Albanians in Kosovo.

In 1988 the Serbian nationalist intellectuals and politicians in
Croatia started to organize the Serbian minority to pressure the
Croat party and government to support the policies in Kosovo. With
considerable aid from Belgrade this was done through mass rallies and utilization of the symbols of extreme Serbian nationalism.
Thus, aggressive Serbian nationalist mobilization in Croatia began
long before the election of Tudjman's Croatian nationalist government. This also means that Serbian nationalists began their attacks
on Croat moves toward a looser federation or confederation *before*
they could have considered their rights in Croatia threatened in any
way. That pressure backfired very badly indeed; for one thing, it
guaranteed Tudjman's victory. What had been a dispute over Serbian
repression in Kosovo increasingly turned into a showdown between
Serbia and *both* Slovenia and Croatia about the future, if any, of a
joint state. The western republics would not be bullied into support
of Serbia in Kosovo and began insisting on a much looser federation, or confederation, and free elections. By 1988 the result of

the dispute was already the breakup of the federal LCY; this led to free elections in 1990, the first being held in Slovenia and Croatia; those elections swept the LCY out of office everywhere except Serbia and Montenegro. The LCY in these two states metamorphosed into new nationalist-Communist hybrids, new types of parties that will not be rare in Eastern Europe and in the states of the former Soviet Union.

By 1989 the nationalist disputes between Serbs and Croats had begun to metastasize at a breakneck speed that was even further accelerated by wild, jingoist campaigns in the controlled mass media. This process was exacerbated when the hard nationalists won the elections in Croatia in 1990 and proceeded to purge and take over the media, especially television, radio, and the daily press. The post-Communists' control of the media in Serbia and Croatia was harsher and more direct than the control asserted by the Communists in their declining, or decaying, years. The Serbian media were in any case firmly controlled by the Milošević regime even before the elections.

As Milošević's government transformed itself from a faithful, even dogmatic, Titoist regime into an anti-Communist nationalist regime, it maintained all the old mechanisms of control, including the political police and the bought-and-paid-for press. Overnight, and very comfortably, the members of the regime were transformed from Communist authoritarians to anti-Communist nationalist authoritarians. The authoritarianism remained constant, if now somewhat subtler. Zagreb and Belgrade entered in a disgraceful and mendacious jingoist competition in which truth and any possibility of joint coexistence were only the most obvious victims.

Even more pernicious has been the seemingly endless polemics about the relative degrees of guilt for communal massacres during the Second World War. The latter is a nasty dispute involving some leading Serbian and Croatian historians. However, little is written today in Serbia about the massacres of the Muslims by the Chetniks; and today in Croatia in the popular journals even less is written about real Ustaše massacres of Croat antifascists, Serbs, Jews, and Gypsies. Films and books on unpleasant topics like the German role in the Second World War or the role of native fascists have been discreetly withdrawn from circulation in Croatia as now being unpatriotic and inappropriate.

Interethnic Struggles within the Republics

The Serbs in Croatia had been disproportionately numerous in the LCY. Given the position of the LCY in the political system this gave them overrepresentation in the governmental bodies.[4] They had as a consequence been blamed as being responsible for all the mistakes, crimes, and errors of the Communists over their more than four decades of rule. This made them the target of considerable hostility when the LCY's history and the history of the partisan war of 1941–45 started being rewritten by the Croatian nationalist pamphleteers. These were often the former hacks of the old regime, now writing with even less respect for truth than when engaged in the original Communist and partisan mythmaking.

The leadership of Bosnia-Herzegovina, inured to elaborate intranational minuets in the distribution of power in their own ethnically mixed-up republic, had not permitted the expression of any nationalism whatsoever up to the first multiparty elections in 1990.[5] Despite the very ethnically mixed nature of the republic, the 1990 elections in Bosnia produced a huge majority for the nationalist parties of, respectively, the Muslims, Serbs, and Croats. As some observers noted, the election resembled a census. The reform Communists and the other nonnationalists did poorly and became the parliamentary opposition, obtaining around 28 percent of the vote. This was an early warning of doom for the prospects for a peaceful post-Communist evolution of Bosnia. The programs of the hard-liners among the Serbian and Croatian nationalist parties, and they were to prove dominant, were inimical to the continuation of any kind of unified, independent Bosnia. Both the Serbian and Croatian nationalists preferred, with varying degrees of frankness, a partitioning of Bosnia-Herzegovina and the unification of the respective parts with the "home" nations of Croatia and Serbia. This could only be done at the expense of the most numerous ethnic group, the Muslim Slavs.

This was a disaster for the prospects of continued ethnic peace. The Serbian party in Bosnia was totally subservient to Belgrade and committed to breaking up Bosnia and grabbing as much as possible for a Greater Serbia. The Bosnian Croats voted for the Bosnian branch of the ruling nationalist party in Croatia. Only the Muslims and the leftist antinationalists were really committed to trying to keep Bosnia together and outside of the Serbo-Croat conflicts that were rapidly developing into a general intranational war. The disintegration of Bosnia has been accelerated by the recognition of Croatia by the European Community. That all but guaranteed that the Serbs and the army would extend the war to Bosnia unless a general peace settlement between Croatia, its own Serbs, the remnants of the Yugoslav army, and Serbia could be brokered.

The Yugoslav political system, which had been monopolized formally by the LCY although it was consociational in all but formal description, had made impossible the development of a responsible and legitimate opposition that would be forced to develop and offer alternative national, Yugoslav-wide programs.[6] Through a combination of repression and co-optation, opposition outside of the LCY had been limited to intellectual circles that could not offer alternative programs. They therefore dealt with questions of fairly abstract theory or, worse yet, with the eternal national question in its endless historical, linguistic, literary, or political guises.

The current cycle of national disputes that led directly to the destruction of Yugoslavia began in the mid-1980s in two unpredictable places and in one that was all too predictable. The predictable place and the problem from the very beginning was Kosovo. The unexpected places were Slovenia and Serbia (that is, so-called Serbia-proper, without the two autonomous provinces). Neither had a history of nationalism and separatism. To better understand the destruction of Yugoslavia one must, then, explore the specific cases of and relationships among the nationalisms in Slovenia, Serbia, and Kosovo.

Slovenia: Democratization and Intolerance

Before Yugoslavia plunged into its final crisis, Slovenia was by far the most prosperous and advanced republic in the federation. Before 1988 it had less than 2 percent unemployment, in contrast to the Yugoslav average of over 14 percent, and 10 percent of its workforce was composed of immigrant workers from the less prosperous southern republics. The immigrant workers were mostly poorly educated, often single, males. They were also often Muslim and spoke Serbo-Croatian, the language of the huge majority of Yugoslavs. They were the "guest workers" of Slovenia. However, as Yugoslav citizens they also had considerable rights so long as Slovenia remained in Yugo-slavia. Their visible presence had awakened a popular, grass-roots Slovenian resentment because the Slovenes, being a small nation numbering under two million, felt that their future national existence could be in question if too many "outsiders" resided in the area. Their reaction had therefore been less than fraternal or sisterly to-ward the guest workers. The Slovenes wanted and want no part of a national melting pot in their republic.

The Slovenes' popular resentment of Yugoslavia had also been fu-eled by the feeling that they had long paid an unfair share of the federal budget and that those funds were mismanaged by the lo-cal political leaders of the less-developed republics. The resentments were still further exacerbated when the political leaders of the south-ern republics backed the Serbian proposals in 1987–88 to alter the structure of the federation to centralize economic decision making — that is, to make it easier for the federation, and those who controlled it, to get access to Slovenian economic resources. Relations were worsened even further when the Serbian press, acting with the ob-vious approval of Slobodan Milošević, began a hysterical campaign attacking the Slovenes' tolerance of social movements, political op-position, and a somewhat countercultural youth organization of the LCY.

Mladina, the lively journal of the Slovenian LCY youth organi-zation, was on the cutting edge of struggle and debates about civil society and civil liberties in the country as a whole throughout the early 1980s. Like the rest of the Slovenian political establishment, Communist and non-Communist, *Mladina* backed the human rights and the right to organize of the Albanians in Kosovo, earning the bitter hostility of the Serbian press and nationalists. In the sum-mer of 1988 the journal was the target of an army trial regarding the handling of secret army documents that it did *not* publish. The documents dealt with contingency plans for a military intervention in Slovenia in the case of an "emergency," much like the real-life botched army attempt to intimidate Slovenia in the spring of 1991.

The Slovenian political establishment and general public were increasingly antagonized by Serbian repression in Kosovo and by Milošević's blocking of the democratization of the political system in the federation as a whole. This culminated in 1988 when the Slove-nian delegates walked out of what turned out to be the last unified congress of the LCY. Shortly afterward the Slovene reform Communists organized the first multiparty election in postwar Yugoslavia, to the horror of all hard-liners. When the reform Communists lost the elections in the spring of 1990, they turned over the government to the victorious anti-Communist coalition and went into opposition. Their chances of regaining power through democratic elections are very good; by 1993 they became a partner in a left-center coalition government.

Continued exhausting confrontations between Slovenia and Serbia within a crumbling federal structure have worn out any remaining affection for the Yugoslav federation. Although the Slovenes offered a loose confederation of independent republics as an alternative as late as the spring of 1991, the federal army's unsuccessful intervention and attempt to reimpose federal authority have snapped the remaining emotional ties to any form of Yugoslavia, at least for the time being. That is a pity because Slovenia contributed mightily, out of all proportion to its size, to the possibilities for a programmatic evolution of Yugoslavia toward a confederation of equal nations.

Slovenia had benefited greatly from its link with Yugoslavia, within which it had developed as a modern nation. The bias against raw-material producers and the high import duties on manufacturing had subsidized the Slovenian economy for four decades. However, that subsidy was invisible, while the Slovenes' contribution to the federal funds for the underdeveloped regions was politically very visible. As a result, substantial parts of the Slovene public have regarded their republic as an exploited victim of the Yugoslav economy and political system.[7] Since the early 1980s the Slovenes' living standards have been falling, as in the other republics, and they had naturally blamed the national economy. Their subsidies to the underdeveloped regions meant that they had paid a large share of the federal subsidies for Kosovo over the years, thus financing a policy universally objected to in Slovenia.

The future of the Slovenian economy is going to be far different from its past. Independent Slovenia's new military establishment will probably cost more than the Slovene share of the Yugoslav defense budget had been. A new foreign office and diplomatic establishment will not come cheap. In exchange Slovenia will lose its source of low-priced raw materials and even worse the protected market for its manufactured goods. The Slovene living standard will almost certainly continue to fall sharply, and once out of Yugoslavia, there will be almost no social consensus on how to distribute the burden of economic sacrifices. The large new unions are not inclined to accept a Mexicanization of Slovenia. Their own dream model is closer to contemporary Austria.

Serbia: A Dangerous Populist Nationalism

The Roots of Serbian Nationalism

Serbia had been the traditional center of the more democratic and liberal-minded intelligentsia and political elites. It was, however, the only republic whose nationalism could be — and was — fatal for the federation as such. Serbs had been the largest national group in the federation and the dominant group in the army officer's cadre. Traditionally, from the revolution to the mid-1980s, Serbia was one of the areas least prone to national separatism because Serbian nationalism had traditionally tended to be Jacobinic. That is, it was both democratic *and* centralist, and that made Serbs populistically intolerant of any *group* rights for minorities in a multiethnic state. France had been their main mentor in democracy, and it is useful to remember that France is one of the most centralized states in Europe.

The Serbs have always played a large role in the army and the police and could therefore only with difficulty have considered themselves oppressed in either post- or prerevolutionary Yugoslavia. On the other hand, current revisionist novels and journalistic and historical writing have tended since the early 1980s to stress the role of Serbs as the victims of the Yugoslav idea and unification. The stress is on the huge sacrifices that Serbia had paid in the First World War for the new Yugoslav state, and on the role Serbs played both as victims and soldiers in the civil war and revolution. This does have some historical basis although the Dalmatian Croats, for example, played a proportionately larger role in the revolution than the Serbs in Serbia did. It is the Serbs from Croatia, Bosnia, and Montenegro who provided the bulk of partisan fighters and most of the civilian victims, not the Serbs from Serbia. However, those are merely uninteresting, dull facts; the political problem lies in what conclusions are drawn from the mix of myths and facts found in the living popular culture. A pathological image of national suffering has emerged from the marginal and subterranean sections of the nationalist intelligentsia and petty bourgeoisie, and has become a part of the general language of contemporary Serbian politics and culture, above all in the mass media.

In any case, the Serbian nationalists feel their contributions have not been honored and respected. After all, Marxists, and Marxist-Leninists especially, have regarded the First World War as an imperialist war. Glorification of the Serbian army that fought in that war therefore became one of the rallying points of nationalism from the time of the Communist takeover.

Further, the historical treatment of Serbia's role in the unification of Yugoslavia in 1918 has caused additional complexities of Serbian nationalism. There are essentially two ways of treating that unification: it can be viewed as a voluntary coming together of South Slav peoples from a disintegrated Austria-Hungary in one state with Serbia and Montenegro; or it can be seen as the result of the Serbian army's liberation of their oppressed brothers and sisters. The second version of the unification myth dominated the prewar royal Yugoslav state and caused endless mischief. Such historical myths are pure political poison, particularly when used by irresponsible chauvinist journalists.

Serbian Nationalist Myths: The Role of Kosovo

Untangling myths from historical reality is very difficult and often tries the patience of nonspecialized readers. I will try to simplify without distorting. There are three central nationalist myths in Serbia: that of the heroic role of the Serbian army in the First World War; that of the martyrdom of Serbs in the Second World War, especially in Croatia; and that of Kosovo, which undergirds the other two myths. The first two myths have been treated elsewhere above. Thus I will focus now on the Kosovo myth.

The Kosovo myth begins with the medieval Battle of Kosovo, in which the invading Ottoman Turks defeated a mixed army of Serbian feudal nobility aided by Albanian and Bosnian contingents. The battle itself is documented historical fact; almost everything that is popularly believed about it is a myth.

Prince (Knjaz) Lazar, who was defeated at the Battle of Kosovo, was not the king of Serbia, although he ruled over most of the Serbian lands. Rather, the title of the king of Serbia was contested by at least two figures: King Tvrtko of Bosnia, who was crowned with the traditional titles of the Serbian kingship, and King Marko, who was a Turkish vassal and died in service of the Turks. Unfortunately for historical truth, legends and epic songs were enormously important in a land where the oral tradition was strong. These legends and epic songs make King Marko the hero of many a heroic story while King Tvrtko is hardly mentioned, although he ruled over most of Bosnia, Dalmatia, and a good part of western Serbia. The probable reason is that it was the Serbian Orthodox church that shaped the myths among the masses, and Bosnia was always a suspect place teeming with both Catholics and Cathar (Bogumils) heretics. King Marko was at least safely Serbian Orthodox.

The national liberation movements of the Balkan peoples, including the Serbs, were directed against the Turks for centuries. Kosovo symbolized the Turkish victory and conquest of the Serbs and other Balkan Slavs. Because the Turks were the government officials as well as the landlords and tax collectors, the nationalist revolts were both nationalist and crudely democratic and egalitarian. When the armies of the Christian Balkan states of Bulgaria, Greece, Montenegro, and Serbia defeated the Turks and other Muslims in the First Balkan War (in 1912), it marked the end of years of foreign domination and rule in the Balkans. It was one of the first victories of movements of national liberation against a foreign oppressor and had many similarities with the anticolonialist struggles of the mid–twentieth century. In the Balkan wars of liberation, however, it was the Muslims who were oppressors and Christians who were victims. The wars were directed against the Turkish Empire, the paramount Muslim power, and thus reinforced the identification of nation and religion.[8] The victory of the Christian states in First Balkan War therefore had great symbolic significance. It was simultaneously liberation for the Christian population in Kosovo, Macedonia, and Thrace and the conquest and subjugation of the Muslim Turkish and Albanian population.[9]

The focus of Serbian nationalism on Kosovo with all of its historical and mytho-poetic association has led to a revival of Serbian Orthodox religion in public life. The Serbian Orthodox church has been all but synonymous with Serbian nationalism, and both in turn are bound to the mythology of the Kosovo cycle of epic poems. The church created a number of myths, with a particular focus on the supposed martyrdom of the Serbian nation as such. The Kosovo of the legends has almost no resemblance to dull historical reality, just as the role of the Serbian Orthodox church in the church-inspired legends has almost no similarity to its role as a centuries-long collaborator with both the Ottoman and Austrian empires.

The Kosovo cycle of heroic ballads has played a crucial role in the birth of modern Serbian nationalism and in the rebirth of the Serbian nation itself in the nineteenth century. Serbian nationalism has always included the Montenegrins, who are at the same time the most traditional of Serbs and have a history of separate identity as the first of the Balkan peoples to gain their national independence. When dealing with Albanian national aspirations, Serbs and Montenegrins have acted as one national group, although regarding other issues within the federation they have often gone their separate ways.

Kosovo is where the greatest monuments of Serbian medieval culture are located. It is the battleground where the medieval Serbian kingdom was destroyed by the invading Muslim Turks, who ruled over the defeated Serbs for five hundred years. Just how traumatic Turkish rule was is historically problematic. During its first two centuries it probably represented a substantial improvement in the lives of the peasantry. The last two centuries represented a decline and rapacious exploitation, and that has shaped the national and mythical memories. It is described as traumatic darkness by the Christian novelists and historians who helped shape the modern national consciousness of the Serbs and Montenegrins. The same is the case with Greek, Macedonian, and Bulgarian national memories; the long centuries of Ottoman rule as well as the shared Christian Orthodox tradition provide for a certain common heritage and influence contemporary political culture.

Serbian Nationalist Grievances against Yugoslavia

Serbian nationalist complaints against postrevolutionary Yugoslavia were long-standing. One was that Serbs were divided between four republics and two provinces. Serbian nationalists regarded this division as a loss, while anti-Serbian nationalists have always considered this to be an unfair advantage because it maximized the chance of a

Serb to serve in the top offices of the federation. A Serb could theoretically serve as a representative of Serbia, Vojvodina, Bosnia, Kosovo,
or even Croatia or Montenegro. There were reasonable historical,
if not ethnic, grounds for such division. No republic is nationally
homogeneous; for that matter, Croats, for example, were divided
between three or four federal units.

The lack of a unified Serbian state led to minor nationalist complaints, mostly on the part of writers and academics, up to the early
1980s, when a group of leading intellectuals drew up a draft programmatic memorandum for the Serbian Academy of Sciences. While
the memorandum, which proposed a national program of unification
for the Serbs, was suppressed at the time, it had a great influence and
is considered by many to represent the *real* program of the Serbian
government of Slobodan Milošević.

The major disputes in Serbia until the present leadership took
over in 1987 had been between the political and economic "liberals"
in the LCY leadership and the democrats inside and outside the LCY,
on one hand, and the LCY hard-liners, on the other. Hard-liners
had been marginalized throughout most of the 1960s and 1970s,
so that the debates in the press and among the intellectual elites
were between the economic and political liberals and the egalitarian
democrats.

Over the past decade the developments in Kosovo have led to a
fundamental realignment of politics in Serbia and the growth of a
dangerous, defensive, populist, and officially sanctioned nationalism.
This nationalism was initially focused on the defense of Serbs from
the pressure of the local Albanian majority in Kosovo. That pressure
included assaults — more often threats of assault — against an increasingly small and aged minority. A breakdown of law and order
has been an almost permanent feature of the life of that province.
That breakdown affects the Albanians in Kosovo as well, of course.
There has been a massive migration of Albanians, as well as Serbs,
from Kosovo.

The increasingly common use of the term *genocide* to describe
the situation of the Serbs and Montenegrins in Kosovo is a monstrous and chauvinist exaggeration. The danger point on Kosovo was
reached when the responsible political leadership of the Serbian LCY
and government and leading intellectuals and academics took over
that grotesquely abused term from a hysterical yellow press and thus

legitimated it in the mid-1980s. Genocide obviously has to be fought without mercy, if necessary with arms in hand.

The Serbian intransigence about Kosovo was easily extended to the defense of Serbs supposedly also threatened with "genocide" in Croatia and Bosnia. The ideological mechanism was the same. Much of the intellectual underpinning and respectability for the xenophobic nationalist developments among the Serbian intellectuals and academics continued to come from the Serbian Academy of Sciences. Alas, this includes some of the Belgrade group of *Praxis* who had played a heroic role for decades in fighting for a democratic and humanist socialism.[10] The hard nationalist line unsurprisingly also draws the support of those who seek to revise the history of the revolutionary war of liberation so that it better harmonizes with nationalist and increasingly pro-Chetnik views.

All this has made for a frightening degree of national homogenization in Serbia. This homogenization, which extends from the traditional nationalist right to much of the more dogmatic traditional left, has been pushed actively by the government leadership in Serbia and with sheer euphoria by the local press. There is no effective opposition to the national circling of the wagons in Serbia. If there were it would have great difficulty in getting access to the mass media. Even the very tame democratic opposition is relatively marginalized in the media.

Modern Kosovo: Repression and Tragedy

A Dangerous Ethnic Mix

Kosovo is tragic, is central to Serbian national myths, and is also the place where modern Albanian nationalism was born in the late nineteenth century. It is also an area that, whatever its history, today has an absolutely clear and growing Albanian majority. Even if there were no extralegal pressure against them, and there have been such pressures, the majority of Serbs and Montenegrins would not continue living with a huge Albanian majority, whom most of them consider culturally more backward. Instead they continue to flee. This is similar to the well-known phenomenon of "tipping" or "white flight" that occurs in the United States and Western Europe when minorities that historically have been considered inferior move in and start becoming majorities. At a certain point vast migration of the former dominant group takes place. In the case of the Serbs and Montenegrins, there is a place to migrate where economic and social conditions are better, and where their language is spoken. Also, because they tend to be better educated, many Serbs and Montenegrins have left Kosovo to go to more developed areas. The result is that Kosovo is becoming inexorably more purely Albanian through both migration and demography.

Albanians in Kosovo have by far the highest birthrate in Europe. Because the Albanians are both heavily rural and Muslim, they have resisted education about birth control and the emancipation of women. The social pressure of the traditional patriarchal society encourages young marriage and deters women from entering the nondomestic workforce. As in all traditional agrarian societies, large families are an asset and insurance. Attempts to enforce Yugoslav laws and modern norms are seen as an assault on traditional Albanian culture and have been passively resisted for decades.

The pre–First World War Serbian Marxists believed that the Albanian majority had a right to self-determination and that Kosovo had been unjustly conquered in 1912, when the Albanian majority was much smaller. The Serbian socialist leadership of that period had the rare courage to fight that nationalism that is most difficult to fight — the nationalism of one's own nation. The views of Serbian socialists, however, were not taken seriously by either the Serbian or the Yugoslav intrawar governments. They treated Kosovo as a long-lost part of Serbia, and the Albanians as interlopers. Serbian and Montenegrin colonists were settled in Kosovo between the wars, often on land confiscated from Albanians. To be sure, Albanian brutal abuses of the local Slav population, including seizure of land throughout the last years of Turkish rule, were also well documented and remembered.

Albanians, who never have been consulted about their own desires, quite naturally regarded both Serbian and, later, Yugoslav rule as alien conquest. As a consequence, during the Second World War the Albanians collaborated broadly first with the Italian and then with the German occupiers who left the local government in their hands and promised the establishment of a Greater Albania. Albanian nationalists resisted the partisans and the new Yugoslav National Army for several years after the war. The area had to be reintegrated into Yugoslavia by force. With the exception of the few

Albanian Communist and partisan cadres, Kosovo was pretty much run by the local, mostly Serbian and Montenegrin, political police up to the time of the removal of the Serbian head of the political police, Alexander Ranković, in 1966. Everybody was subject to police repression, but Albanians were particularly vulnerable.

In the years after the removal of Ranković, the Albanian demands for greater autonomy, symbolized by the demand that Kosovo be given the status of a republic, were raised. The demand for republic status was first publicly raised in the mass student demonstration in 1968, and then in the demonstration of 1981. These demonstrations were denounced as counterrevolutionary by the political leadership of Serbia and of most of Yugoslavia, and participants were jailed en masse.

Since 1981, any raising of the issue of a republic status for Kosovo has been attacked in the Serbian press and by Serbian political leaders as counterrevolutionary. It was not on the face of it an unreasonable demand. In a normal law-abiding state it would not have been counterrevolutionary to propose to change a constitution that has been changed a number of times. The demand was *not* that Kosovo secede from Yugoslavia, but that it change its status within Yugoslavia. Right or wrong, such a demand should have had a place in the normal political debate of a country that was democratizing and evolving toward a more open society. The fact that it did not contributed to the unfolding of the death of Yugoslavia. In any case, radical changes of the 1974 constitution regarding the relations of the two autonomous provinces to Serbia were exactly what the mass "noninstitutional" demonstration and the Serbian political leadership demanded and achieved in 1987 and 1988.

While Kosovo received the lion's share of federal and republic economic aid for decades, it fell ever further behind the rest of Yugoslavia. Poor as it was, and its per capita income was one-sixth of that of Slovenia in 1987, it remained far better off than Albania. However, quite reasonably, the Kosovo Albanians did not compare their living standards with the country they did not live in, but with that of the country in which they did live. There was probably little or no popular sentiment for unity with Albania until the collapse of Yugoslavia. Albanians *could* imagine themselves as equal citizens of a multinational Yugoslavia. They cannot imagine themselves as a minority of a Serbia, particularly one that denies them basic rights.

Kosovo and Yugoslavia were fated to remain together; Kosovo and Serbia cannot.

Young Albanians have been refusing, on principle, to learn Serbo-Croatian, the language spoken by twenty out of twenty-four million persons in former Yugoslavia. The result is that they have been and are locked into a self-made ghetto as far as decent employment outside of Kosovo is concerned. That is one of the reasons so many Albanians work as unskilled manual workers or run small pastry shops outside of Kosovo. It is also why there is such a high ratio of administrative workers to other workers in Kosovo: work had to be found for at least some of the graduates of the vast Pristina University system. The problem of unemployment in Kosovo is catastrophic. In 1988 only 229 were employed out of every 1,000 of working age, compared with 693 in Slovenia and a national average of 450. And the economy has worsened since. Women have systematically withdrawn from the nondomestic labor market, and half of the population is under sixteen years old. This explains why the pressure on land is so great in Kosovo.

A major dispute between the Albanians and Serbs in Kosovo is over land. All kinds of pressure — including the offer of hard-earned money from members of Albanian land-purchasing families who are working abroad, suggesting prices way over the real value of the land — have helped fuel the emigration of Kosovo Serbs. Existing racist laws prohibiting the sale of land from Serbs to Albanians simply do not deal with this land hunger and with the problems of an aging and increasingly female population on the Serbian farms.

Women's Rights in Kosovo: A Critical Issue

Unless Albanian women in Kosovo are pulled into the workforce through the creation of decent jobs, the Albanians' birthrate will continue to explode and an ever-larger pool of educated and bitter unemployed young people will be created. Their resentment is going to be directed against the marginally better-off Serbian minority in their midst (better off because of smaller families, if for no other reason) and more and more against the Serbian state.

The same Communist political elites, police, and courts that in areas like Kosovo and Macedonia had been all too willing to jail demonstrators, student dissidents, and irreverent writers have tolerated child marriage, the removal of female children from the school system, and other illegal patriarchal practices. These violations have deprived and continue to deprive women in the less-developed areas of Yugoslavia — particularly in areas inhabited by Muslims and Albanians, but also in Macedonia, Bosnia-Herzegovina, southern parts of Serbia, and Montenegro — of the rights guaranteed by the constitution. This is one more argument why, particularly in a state with a wide range of cultural diversity, protection of individual rights cannot be left only to the local courts and police. Leaving enforcement of women's and general civic rights and laws to local authorities has been a part of the problem, as repeated complaints from Kosovo, Bosnia, Macedonia, and the less-developed parts of Croatia and Serbia have shown. Female emancipation and modernity go hand in hand. So do democracy and egalitarianism.

Although many of these problems stem from local authorities in more backward areas, the Serbian and Montenegrin police and authorities in Kosovo, or for that matter in their home republics, also harbor backward patriarchal norms. They have been reluctant to move in cases of rape unless the rape in question "was motivated by nationalist motives" — that is, unless it is a rape or accused rape by an Albanian of a Serb or a Montenegrin. Most rapes within the same national group remain unreported or underreported, and claims of rape or abuse are usually met with skepticism or hostility by the police. Rape is always outrageous. There are many more rapes of Serbian women by males of their own nationality and of Albanian women by their own nationals in Kosovo than there are cases of intranational rape. The outrage of so-called normal, nonnationalist rape seems to escape the attention of both the press and other organizations in Serbia. It is a scandal that it has also escaped the attention of official Serbian women's organizations. This is why such little discussion as there is in the various Yugoslav republics about issues of women's rights and feminism has taken place outside these organizations.

Funds sufficient for the effective development of Kosovo are simply not available given the otherwise grim economy, and, in any case, without a drastic cut-back in the birthrate increased funding would do little good. But a cut-back in the birthrate can only occur voluntarily, and that requires economic aid and the generation of jobs. The establishment of punitive measures such as those currently proposed in Macedonia, which would penalize a family that had a third child by cutting back child allowances and social benefits, is exactly the kind of reactionary policy that can only backfire. Such measures are obviously unjust because they penalize the child. One cannot push birth control as a solution to a nationalist dispute without raising all kinds of racist and reactionary political issues.

The left parties that form the governing majority in Macedonia fail to take the lead on this question in good part because they treat the issue of women's rights as a formalistic and unurgent question particularly in the less-developed areas. Of course, those are exactly the areas where women's rights are most vital. In this respect the leftists in Macedonia are not different from their cothinkers in other post-Communist societies. They fail to see that demography, the education and employment of women, and the social reproduction of a nation are not just women's issues but are also general societal issues. Because of this oversight, they leave the solution of these matters to the distant future, after the "more important" problems are solved. The trouble is that apart from being immoral this position is impractical. The "more urgent" issues cannot be solved without addressing women's issues.

Repression in Kosovo and the Breakup of Yugoslavia

Kosovo was the issue that directly led to the split of the LCY into competing parties and to the loosening of the federal arrangement to the point where Yugoslavia could have survived only as a confederation, if at all. There were three reasons for this. First, to keep Kosovo under Serbian control required constant violation of the rights of an ever-angrier and more alienated Albanian majority in that province. The rest of the federation became unwilling to continue to use its resources and prestige in pursuing a policy that was increasingly condemned internationally. Second, the Serbian Communist leadership reacted to this by attempting to take over the LCY, thus leading to a split of the LCY through the walkout of the Slovenian delegation from the fourteenth (and last) congress in 1989. The Slovenian Communists were later joined first by the league of Croatia and then by the leagues of Bosnia and Macedonia. Third, assertive Serbian nationalism initially mobilized over Kosovo began to threaten other federal units and provoked a Croatian national populist counter-part that defeated the profederalist Croatian Communists and elected Tudjman's nationalists.

The mass nationalist-populist demonstrations in Serbia had thus provoked a showdown between the Serbian leadership, which used and supported the demonstrations with their demands for complete Serbian authority over the autonomous provinces and a tough line in general, and the rest of the federation. That in turn led to a rapid weakening of political authority to a point where the army has been pushed, against all of its original instincts, into intervening first into politics directly and then into combat in Croatia. The more democratically minded leaders in the other republics had feared that the Serbian leadership wanted to provoke a complete breakdown of intrarepublic relations and force the army to take a stand, and their fears proved justified. The future existence of even the loosest Yugoslav union based on anything but sheer repression therefore became impossible.

The assumption of the hard-liners was that the army's natural bias was toward more centralization and order and presumably toward a hard line in Kosovo and other Albanian-inhabited areas in Macedonia and southern Serbia. To these biases one has to add the sensitivities of the army — given the national composition of the officers corps — about any threat or even perceived threat against the Serbs in Croatia and Bosnia. The hard-liners had guessed right. Their alliance with the armed forces killed Yugoslavia more effectively than any combination of internal and external enemies.

Kosovo festers and will continue to do so until genuine negotiations with representatives of the Albanian majority take place. Since there is no longer an option of maintaining Yugoslavia, the negotiations can only be about the separation of Kosovo from Serbia. During the last two years of Yugoslavia's existence (1989–91), the Serbian leadership lost countless opportunities — offered in turn by Slovenia, Croatia, and Bosnia-Herzegovina in alliance with Macedonia — to preserve some kind of a loose Yugoslav confederation.

The Serbian leadership bears the lion's share of the responsibility for the destruction of Yugoslavia. That destruction ended in a bitter war of the army, Serbia, and the Serbian minority in Croatia against Croatia. It has also made inevitable the intraethnic civil war in Bosnia-Herzegovina and civil wars or at least major internal dis-

turbances within Serbia and Croatia. There have already been huge
numbers of victims of the war: hundreds of thousands of Croat and
Serb refugees; thousands of dead and tens of thousands of wounded,
mostly from the ethnically mixed areas where Serbs and Croats had
lived together for centuries; thousands of Croatian civilians killed
by the army and Serbian volunteers in the armed aggression against
Croatia; and hundreds of Croat and Serb civilians butchered by un-
disciplined volunteer forces on both sides. The conflict in Bosnia
promised to be even worse from the very beginning. It is there that
by far the worst atrocities have taken place. Not only have there been
vast and well-documented massacres of mostly Muslim civilians by
Serbian militias, but concentration camps and massive forcible population transfers, known as "ethnic cleansing," have also been used
to change the demographic realities of Bosnia. The worst of the horrors has been the systematic use of organized, repeated mass rape by
Serbian militias of non-Serbian, mostly Muslim women as a part of
"ethnic cleansing." To be sure, there have been cases of rape by all
sides, and the UN has documented that Croats and Muslims have
committed massacres and run concentration camps. What was unprecedented was the organization of mass rape as a matter of policy
in a manner that could not have been unknown to the highest military and political authorities of the so-called Serbian Republic of
Bosnia. One obvious victim is the prospect of a tolerable and decent
life together after the war.

Public opinion polls show that the large majority of Croats now
consider the majority of Serbs in Serbia, Croatia, and Bosnia collectively responsible for the war against Croatia and for the atrocities
committed by the few. Likewise, Serbs in Croatia and Muslims hold
the majority of members of opposing groups responsible for the war
and for atrocities of the few. For far too many on all sides the ties
of trust essential for people to continue living side-by-side have been
unraveled. Democracy and a law-abiding society itself are hardly possible if the principle of collective guilt is maintained. Unfortunately
there is little or no chance that those responsible for this huge tragedy
will ever be brought to justice. Neither those who have committed
atrocities and murders nor those who have helped destroy Yugoslavia
with their pursuit of reckless political ambition will ever pay for what
they did. That is a terrible example for other reckless gamblers with
nationalist passions throughout the region. The example of leaders

like Milošević and Tudjman says this: if you win, you can get away with destroying a country, even if the consequences are enormous carnage and an economic wasteland; you may even get international recognition. On the other hand, if you lose, a financially comfortable exile is probably the worst that will happen to you. Reliable information indicates that the Serbian leadership has transferred millions of dollars, apparently mostly to Cyprus, for a comfortable safe haven if the "worst" (that is, peace and a democratic government) should ever occur. A number of Croatian politicians maintain a second passport and businesses in the West for a similar contingency. The worst of the war criminals head bands of looters who long ago guaranteed a prosperous future for these gangsters.

By hanging tough and refusing to negotiate the Serbian leadership effectively killed all possibilities for any kind of Yugoslavia. If a new one is ever reborn it will be because the present political players in Serbia, and probably Croatia and Slovenia, are no longer dominant on the political scene. This tangled story contains interesting lessons for the post-Soviet states in dealing with their own even more explosive national problems.

Imagine a disintegrating nation where several emerging states have nuclear arms. Imagine a multinational commonwealth composed of independent but not always viable states, where the largest nation can easily dominate the rest by force and threat of force. Then imagine increasingly bitter economic and political disputes without any mechanism for resolution. Alas, none of these things needs to be imagined, for they exist. The Yugoslav experience with such problems, even after decades of experience, resulted in a catastrophe. What is there to give any hope that the road of the post-Communist states emerging from the former Soviet Union will be any smoother? The Yugoslav experience argues against any optimism about the future fate of the former Soviet Union.

In reaction to an aggressive Serbian nationalism, four out of six republics declared by the spring of 1991 that they would stay in Yugoslavia only if it becomes a much looser confederation where no republic could be outvoted by any combination of others. The alternative was secession and/or a civil war. By choosing to push the war in Croatia, the armed forces and the Serbian leadership closed the door on the possibility of either a confederation or an association of Yugoslav states. Such relations are only possible among states that are friendly to each other. For the time being the war in Croatia has strained that friendship beyond the point of return. In contrast, many natural economic, cultural, and geographic interests do argue for some kind of association among what are complementary economies bound with all sorts of informal personal networks. Stranger things have happened, and a grim economic present may make a past association look much more attractive. In any case, any new association would have to be based on freely and explicitly agreed upon terms. A surprisingly large number of political and intellectual actors in the newly independent states of former Yugoslavia are open to some kind of minimal new association.

Chapter 5

NO DEMOCRACY WITHOUT BOTH UNIVERSALISM AND MODERNITY

If you fight dragons long enough, you will become a dragon; if you stare into the Abyss, the Abyss will stare back into you.

— Friedrich Nietzsche

Nationalism: Barrier to Contemporary Democracy

Eastern Europe and the former Soviet Union are densely populated today with ghosts of chauvinist, clerical, populist, right-wing, and corporatist parties and movements. These political throwbacks to the troubled era between the two world wars have emerged all too well preserved after decades of Communist rule. They are almost all that has been preserved and all that has survived of a pre-Communist political culture in Eastern Europe and to a lesser extent in the former Soviet Union. An alternative, modern, universalist political culture had its heart leached out by decades of Communist rule through the visible contrast between the egalitarian and democratic rhetoric and the authoritarianism and privileges of the ruling Communist *nomenklatura*.

If democratic pluralism of any meaningful sort is to have a chance in that region and if stable democratic polities are to emerge, then it

127

is essential to try to keep these ghosts quiet and if possible to re-bury them. Otherwise a Hobbesian universe of a constant struggle of all against all, with the basic loyalty being focused on the tribe, will turn the whole area into a murderous battleground of rival, mutually exclusive nationalisms, and democracy will be only one of the more obvious victims. Exclusivist nationalism provides no meaningful basis for constructing stable, popular, democratic regimes that can obtain and keep legitimacy, particularly in modern nationally heterogeneous societies.

It is as if all the predemocratic political movements, folkish sentiments, populist prejudices, and vaguely religious nationalist identities had been preserved in amber during the long years of Communist power in Eastern Europe and the Soviet Union. In those countries, these relics of the political past had been preserved from the political and economic changes in the political culture of the rest of Europe. A kind of Rip Van Winkle staggered back to life in 1989 and has had a desperately difficult time in trying to catch up with the long, lost years.

The revival of nationalism and the politics of ethnic identity is primarily responsible for the return of these political ghosts from an unlovely pre-Communist past. Nationalism is the red meat of the organic, "authentic" Heideggerian national community that is all too easy to mobilize against a mere "cool," legal, and rational democratic universalism. Nationalism, whether old or new, provides a collective identity that is a powerful magnet in this era when old universalisms are collapsing. Those politics are dangerous because, by definition, they exclude a number of subjects of the new nation-states from full citizenship, which is limited to the ethnically dominant national community.

Nationalism is a form of mass communitarian politics. It defines the nation, the ethnic group, as the most relevant community, certainly the most *politically* relevant community. Therefore modern nationalism in the form that it takes in most countries represents a problem for democratic politics in a great number of places besides the post-Communist societies. Politics of identity, unlike "crass" politics of interest, are not normally negotiable. Nationalism and other politics of identity, such as those of fundamentalist or nationally identified religions, are therefore a continual threat to those who would build a multiparty, democratic, parliamentary legal order based on tolerance and pluralism. A difficult task is thereby made almost impossible. Intransigent advocates of nationalism see negotiations, concessions, and compromise as treason and betrayal of irreducible national rights or the doctrines of the religious community. Treason, of course, is not a concept to be debated but something to be fought.

When nations that have been submerged within multinational states and federations are reborn as independent states, it seems they spring up fully armed with grievances, with historical friends, and above all with enemies. If no universal and enforceable norms are developed that can address these historical problems, and above all if no norms are developed about how current disputes are to be settled, the rise of newly independent nations will be a catastrophe through much of the region.

There are enough particularistic past and present, real and imagined, grievances for the whole area to swim in blood for decades. Because about the only things some of the post-Communist states have in overabundance are large armies with a great deal of conventional, and in the case of Russia nuclear, hardware, there is no guarantee that violence will be limited to home ground. To the contrary, *external* aggression may buy time and, at least temporarily, domestic unity and relative peace. Thus, new and greatly strengthened international institutions, including a much stronger UN, are now desperately needed. The institutions have to be international because it is entirely possible, as free elections in many post-Communist states as well as in Algeria have shown, for a majority to democratically elect a xenophobic nationalist or fundamentalist majority. The result of such elections can be not only the repression of those who differ and a massive attack on the rights of women (the state of such rights almost always being an excellent barometer of human rights); such governments are also prone to employ illegitimate measures in both internal and external conflicts and wars. This is not only an obscure regional problem; it can easily overflow its regional boundaries with terrorism, kidnapping, international arms trade, and other allied phenomena.

As I have argued earlier, the rise of nationalism and consequently of national and communal conflicts throughout Eastern Europe and the former Soviet Union will directly affect much wider regions. It will affect the European Community with spreading instability and floods of desperate refugees fleeing for their lives. It will also affect the Middle East and Muslim world because at least some of the conflict will involve national-communal conflicts between Muslim-identified national groups and nations and Christian-identified groups and nations.

An excellent example of a blend of nationalist and religious passions, no matter how doctrinally inconsistent, is the case of Muslim fundamentalism. This is particularly true when such fundamentalism turns to the political arena, as in the cases of Algeria and Iran. Just as in the case of nationalism, which is almost always defined by what it is *against,* Muslim fundamentalism is against "Western" values like secularism, pluralism, and equal rights for women, which, it is argued, are imposed by cultural colonialism and threaten the "genuine" identity of the nation and of Islam. (This, with only a minor shift in labels, is what most of the nationalist rhetoric sounds like.) Islam for the fundamentalists, then, is not merely a religion but a way of life that permeates every pore of society; it is a community of the faithful. Fundamentalism grows when a religion is threatened, and Islam is threatened both by cosmopolitanism and secularism. Thus the communal conflict will inevitably spill over from areas where Christians and Muslims have lived together for centuries to conflicts where there are new Muslim immigrants in Western Europe. This communal conflict, in part using traditional Christian-Muslim rivalries as a framework, will almost surely affect not only wide areas of the former Soviet Union, but also Bulgaria and parts of former Yugoslavia.

Democracy and Egalitarianism

Genuine political democracy requires at least minimal commitment to social justice and egalitarianism. Effective political equality cannot coexist with great differences in wealth. Great wealth — in real societies, outside of civic or economic textbooks — is all too often translated into *political* power, or at least the ability to influence that power. This is all the more the case in post-Communist societies, where financial resources are scarce and where universalistic norms about proper separation of the personal from the public, when it comes to mobilizing influence, are all too rare. In practice, these have been particularistic societies for decades, whatever the normative

claims by those who enforced the official ideology. Particularism —
that is, connections and acquaintances — had provided for a high survival and advancement rate in the years of authoritarian Communist
rule.

In these societies, connections and influence (known as VIP [*Veze
I Poznanstva*]) have represented the most valuable currency in political and economic life for decades. The smart operators — who will
form the core of the new capitalist entrepreneurs in post-Communist
societies, including those of the independent republics of former
Yugoslavia — are still masters at the art of mobilizing connections
and influence for personal ends. Large quantities of money in relatively impoverished societies provide very great leverage. These
operators are therefore dangerous for democracy, much in the same
way that they made the workings of an impartial legal state so
difficult in Latin America.

More to the point, the social solidarity required to make the sacrifices necessary to modernize the East European economies without
authoritarianism cannot be generated with a so-called pure market
economy. Solidarity requires that the social order be considered at
least minimally just and committed to the general good, not just to
the maximization of production and profit. But economists love models, and models in order to appear clear must simplify; they therefore
almost always leave out the social and political dimensions. Economists all too often ignore the social consequences and political costs
of their proposals. Sensible people, on the contrary, must insist that
there is no such thing as a "purely" economic policy that can be
isolated from social and political consequences. In real life, when it
comes to making politico-economic decisions, academic economists
should be kept at a distance. Professors Friedman and Sachs should
certainly be kept at a distance from policy making in Eastern Europe
today. They are dangerous to the prospects of democracy.

Local Religions and Nationalism

Religiously based national intolerance is all too familiar to Yugoslavia with its own mixture of national populism and hard-liners in
Serbia, clerical right-wingers in Croatia and Slovenia, and religiously
identified Muslim Slav nationalists. Popular hostility to the previ-

ously dominant Muslim groups, whether Albanian or South Slav, still fuels a populist Christian Orthodox nationalism. It should go without saying that these "Christian" and "Muslim" nationalists have almost no connection with the teachings or sometimes even the institutions of their religion. Religion here serves merely as a national identifier. Thus one can have a "Christian" or "Muslim" atheist. What is important in the politics of identity is that the labels define both the inside community and — sometimes even more importantly — the outside community or "the other."

Similar, often religiously identified, nationalisms are found throughout most of Eastern Europe and in the former Soviet Union. That hostility to the cultural and religious "other" is also tearing apart former Soviet Transcaucasia. It seems that traditional national disputes are vastly multiplied when the factor of historical Christian-Muslim rivalry is added. But then, for so many centuries religion was the only recognized national identifier throughout the region, and explicitly so under the Ottoman Empire. This is especially the case in places where specific nationally identified churches exist — for example, the Georgian Orthodox church, the Serbian Orthodox church, and so on.

Roman Catholicism lost much of its universalistic (i.e., trans- or supranational) appeal in Eastern Europe when the clergy began identifying with the popular strata and began developing *national* churches in the nineteenth century. The process continues to evolve: when the Catholic church becomes less hierarchical and more popularly based, lower ranks of the clergy begin flirting with populist, corporatist, and sometimes raw right-wing nationalist politics. This identification of the Roman Catholic church's clergy with their own given nation is very much present in Slovakia, Slovenia, Croatia, and Poland and is only slightly less so in Hungary and the Czech lands.

While this national identification dates back to the mid-nineteenth century, this trend has been considerably strengthened under the current Polish pope. He was almost the arch-symbol of a church that resisted the initially nonnationalist Communist rulers and became the repository of national identity, even for many non-religious Poles. In this sense one could say that the Catholic church in Poland has acted much as the Orthodox churches have acted elsewhere, particularly during the long years of Communist repression. By becoming closely nationally identified, these churches also took on the specific traditional, national hostilities toward the historical rivals of their chosen nation. Thus the churches exacerbate rather than mediate ethnic conflicts. Also, after the toppling of the Communist regimes, the churches have come forward to collect the reward for their long struggle against Communism. They demand the return of the old church institutions, schools, hospitals, rest homes, and sometimes land and industrial properties. More ominously they demand the imposition of religious teachings on social and political matters. Divorce, abortion, and contraception are under attack, and there the churches readily find allies among nonreligious nationalists who are profamily and natalist for demographic as well as ideological reasons.

In Transcaucasia one of the first effects of Gorbachev's glasnost was that for the first time in decades age-old hatreds and grievances could be expressed. In Georgia and Armenia this included some Christians' demand that historical grievances, sometimes dating back for centuries, be settled with their Muslim minorities. This was even more acute in places where the Christians' Muslim neighbors had their own independent states with boundary disputes to be still settled. Under the Ottoman and Persian empires the Muslims had lorded it over the Christians, and memories of past grievances are long. For the Armenians, there are relatively "recent" grievances of massacres under the Turkish rule culminating in near genocide in 1915. Even before Armenian independence that historic grievance generated anti-Turkish terrorism by the distant descendants of the victims of the 1915 massacres.

Gypsies as the Ever-Present "Other"

In traditional societies the ethnic or religious "other" is essential for maintaining the boundaries of one's own community. That explains the dialectics of the survival of the Roms (Gypsies), who in Eastern and Central Europe are subject to an almost pathological hatred, to vast discrimination by the society at large, and to physical attacks by skinhead types. And yet the Gypsies in large numbers have survived both the Nazi Holocaust and decades of attempted assimilation (that is, cultural extinction) by the Communist regimes. They survived and found specific caste-defined niches throughout Eastern Europe. They have even adapted to new roles that flow logically out of their traditional ones. Thus Gypsies have been very visible in the transfrontier black market trading, that is, smuggling. They are dominant in used car dealing. And they have learned how to use and abuse the asylum and welfare laws of the rich West European countries.

It would be hard to imagine a more sharply defined "other" than the Gypsies. The Gypsy stereotypes brazenly mock all the aspirations to modernity, order, cleanliness, productivity, and hard work of the masses of East Europeans seeking to become just like their idealized versions of West Europeans or Americans. Gypsies are the very opposite of Central European petty bourgeois respectability. Gypsies horrify the lace-curtain, upwardly mobile types who make a cult of cleanliness, sobriety, and kultur. It is as if they represented, in an extravagant and more colorful way, the rejected folk life that is only a generation behind so many striving Central and East Europeans. This is why it was possible for Germany and Austria to get away with no compensation to the *Gypsy* victims of genocide. This is also why the Gypsies' claims for asylum can be almost universally mocked, although they are clearly subject to discrimination and persecution in most of the East European countries. As times get worse, they will be in ever greater physical jeopardy.

The Need for Effective International Peacemaking Institutions

The tragic death of Yugoslavia has shown that the existing international institutions, traditional diplomacy, and a mechanical respect for national sovereignty are inadequate for the new post-Communist realities in Eastern Europe and the former Soviet Union. They do not really work in most of the world. They cannot stop civil wars and massacres. They were probably always inadequate. In the past, the Cold War and the rigid anti-interventionism of the nonaligned movement made any solution to this inadequacy impossible. Did Bokassa really have the sovereign right to massacre his own people? Did Pol Pot have that right in Cambodia? Can the Sudanese government wage an endless genocidal war against the black non-Muslim population of its south with complete impunity? Do the various Somalian warlords have the sovereign right to destroy their "own" country and people? Does the "Yugoslav" army have a right to wage a war against a secessionist Croatia or Bosnia-Herzegovina, particularly after those states' independence is recognized by most of the world's states and they become members of the UN?

Will an independent, internationally recognized Croatia have the sovereign right to settle accounts with its own Serbian minority as its (probably right-wing nationalist) government and police see fit? At some point, and it would be better sooner than later, the problem of building international peace-making mechanisms with teeth will have to be addressed. There will have to be ways of *imposing* arbitration on warring and squabbling new nation-states. However, for such mechanisms to be truly effective they will have to deal with established larger states as well, at some time in the not-too-distant future. The alternatives are either murderous chaos involving ever-greater regions of the world or an equally unattractive *Pax Americana* or *Pax Europeana* or even a *Pax Germanica*.

I am arguing that the Yugoslav tragedy was not the result of some exotic or particular and unique problem. It was not based on the peculiar Byzantine tradition of the Serbs or the alleged Croatian national affinity toward genocide. The mechanisms that have been invented to deal with the Yugoslav tragedy, no matter how jerry-built (no pun intended) and inadequate, will have, of necessity, a far wider application. That is why a great deal of thought and caution is needed. That is also why it will not do to reduce the tragic death of Yugoslavia to heroes and villains — in genuine tragedies the roles of the real players are more complex and ambivalent.

A legitimate state must be able to combine both high support and high compliance from most of its population; otherwise it will be unable to carry out its decisions. Both internal and external factors may make it impossible for a state to maintain legitimacy in the eyes of the majority of its nominal subjects. If this happens there are crises, revolutions, and disintegration of authority. That was the fate of an initially popular Gorbachev, and the same process led to the demise of Yugoslavia. Low voluntary compliance with laws, directives, and regulations is a major and widespread problem throughout the post-Communist states. However, to obtain compliance through repression is politically unacceptable and probably organizationally unachievable. In any case, to even attempt such repression would jeopardize the other vital dimension of legitimacy — that is, popular support.

Historians and Ethnographers in Service of Nationalism

A major disservice to scholarship as well as to intraethnic peace has been performed by generations of national historians, ethnographers, writers, and poets who labored mightily in trying to prove the special role and virtue of their own ethnic group. I am most familiar with that problem in Yugoslavia. The best-known Serbian ethnographer, Jovan Cvijić, argued that mountain *Dinaric* types (who just happened to be mostly Serbs and Montenegrins) are the people with hardy state-building virtues. In contrast, the mild *Pannonian* types (who happen to be mostly Croat) have a more gentle and servile mentality. Dinko Tomašić, a Croat ethnographer, accepted this division of typologies but argued that the Pannonians were the natural democrats and state-builders, while the Dinarics were suited for war and violence and therefore traditionally turned to police and military careers and to authoritarian rule.

I am very uncomfortable with all this essentialist talk about "mentalities" and find the recent revival of that fashion among intellectuals in the West alarming. Talk about black or Hispanic mentalities seems just as potentially dangerous as were the teachings of the French human geography or ethnographic school on these types of matters. On the other hand, environmentally shaped historical and political cultures and socialization are valid and interesting topics of debate and research.

Historians in former Yugoslav republics have argued about which principalities in the early Middle Ages could be called Serbian or Croatian. To understand the context of these disputes one must know that the last Croatian national kings were contemporaries of the preconquest Saxon kings in England. The great medieval Serbian monarchs existed at the time of the Wars of the Roses in England. As a minor colorful detail, the city commune and state of Dubrovnik was *never* a part of Croatia until the foundation of Yugoslavia. Dubrovnik was also never a part of Serbia. Yet such is the power and poetry of historical mythmaking that obscure medieval monarchs are treated as relevant to contemporary politics and frontier disputes between Serbia and Croatia!

Serbs and Croats are not uniquely history-ridden. Slovaks, Bulgarians, and Ukrainians all try to create a medieval history appropriate for their present national goals. Sometimes this is more or less based on documentable history; at other times it is wholly fabricated. Romanian and Albanian national historians, writers, and poets try to go even further back, to classical or even pre-Roman times, for their nations' times of greatness. Poles and Lithuanians get nostalgic for the time when *their* commonwealth stretched from the Baltic to the Black Sea. Hungarians remind all and sundry that they had a powerful medieval state that dominated Croatia, Slovakia, Romania, and sometimes parts of Bosnia, Serbia, and even western Ukraine.

The trouble is that to most nationalists this ancient history matters. It is the basis for contemporary border claims and for present-day sympathies and antipathies toward neighboring peoples. It is irrelevant how much of this history is accurate. In point of fact, documentation on the Middle Ages in Eastern Europe, the Balkans, and Russia is very scarce. Hence the history that today is politically relevant in Eastern Europe and the former Soviet Union is the product of romanticized pseudohistories and historical novels and poems from the nineteenth century on.

Parallels with this pseudohistoricism as a basis for present claims for settlement of past and present grievances, real as well as imagined, can be readily found in the rise of African Studies and Black Studies in higher education in the United States. Real and pseudohistorians among African Americans are playing a role analogous to that of Slovak, Ukrainian, Croat, and Slovene historians. That is, they are trying to reconstruct, or construct, as an act of mytho-poetic imagination, a repressed national identity. We should note, for example, that "African American" is a recent, artificial construct that conflates the very obvious existence of varied national groups among sub-Saharan Africans who were brought over as slaves; it also ignores the fact that the genealogies of many members of that group contain as much (if not more) "European" ancestry as African ancestry. This mass self-delusion is not limited, of course, to African Americans and East Europeans — it is also prevalent among West European national groups. These groups too are artificial constructs composed of very diverse ancestry and were only consciously turned into "nations" relatively recently. This origin of national groups does not make nationalism any less intense and passionate. Sometimes these identities are based on completely mythical creation stories, like the legends of the Nation of Islam among blacks in America. Creating modern national identity has been for the most part a conscious project. Truth has little or nothing to do with such a project.

Multinational States and Self-Determination

Those who supported self-determination *à outrance* in the case of the secession of the republics of Slovenia and Croatia from Yugoslavia based that support on the formula that a one-time, unilateral declaration of independence suffices to make a national group eligible for international recognition. As I have argued above, if that formula were generalized, very few states in Africa or Asia would survive in their present form. Many states would also face unilateral secessions in Europe and the Americas. To name only a few nations (the names of some local peoples prone to secession are given in parentheses) that would be directly affected: India (at least the Kashmiris), Pakistan (Sindhis and Baluchis), Iran (Kurds and Turkmen), Turkey (Kurds), Iraq (Kurds and Shiites), Ethiopia (at least five national groups), Nigeria (remember Biafra!), South Africa, Sudan, Kenya, Uganda, Mozambique, Zaire, Sri Lanka, Burma, Indonesia, the Philippines, China (Tibetans and the people in Sikang), Guiana, Suriname, Canada, Spain (Basques and Catalonians for starters), the United Kingdom (the Scots, Welsh, and Catholics in Northern Ireland), France (Corsicans and others), and Italy (members of the Lombard Leagues and the Sardinians are only the best known). Czechoslovakia faces dissolution; minorities in Romania and Bulgaria now stir ever more restlessly.

Xenophobia and nationalism have an established but so far modest place in the Western European parliamentary as well as extra-parliamentary scene. Tribalism is popular and ascendant; in a few places it is associated with the left but mostly with the hard right. It becomes dangerous when it is activated outside its marginalized existence by being taken over by the more respectable players on the political scene. That phenomenon is emerging in Europe as the electorates face a combination of European unification and stagnant economies; in that situation more and more politicians are pointing to immigrants as the source of problems.

Respectable politicians in France, Austria, and Germany have begun to show excessive understanding for the ultranationalists. Le Pen in France, the Freedom Party in Austria, the Lombard Leagues in northern Italy, and the Republicans in Germany are emerging from their relative ghettoes. The complex of issues stewing in this witches' brew will easily produce a neofascism, particularly when there is no broad, decent, and democratic left to contest for the masses drawn to nationalism and populism. The alternative to politics of passion and identity cannot be mere defense of a cool, impersonal, liberal, and legalistic status quo. Historically the left and nationalists competed for the same voters and supporters. But the left is today wounded and in a moral crisis. The longings and issues raised by the renewed anti-establishmentarian nationalism can be countered only by a revived and large class-based and gender-sensitive left. It must be gender-sensitive because — if for no better reason, and there are better moral reasons — so many women are in the workforce and so many more are dependent on the social services of a welfare state.

A veritable Pandora's box opens up for the states that have replaced the Soviet Union. In that area no frontier even resembles an ethnic frontier, and hundreds of national groups with more or less articulated aspirations for national independence exist. Those that have not yet been heard from can soon be expected to join in the atonal chorus demanding their very own national states. That situation highlights the issue of boundaries, which is also posed when the international community faces the matter of recognizing new nation-states, particularly those that do not have a prolonged history of independent existence within internationally recognized frontiers. What are fair boundaries? Ethnic boundaries very rarely coincide with state or administrative ones; in any case, all boundaries have been subject to both voluntary and *involuntary* shifts of population. How far back in history should one have to go to right injustices caused by forcible migrations? For example, what about the admittedly unjust massive expulsion of Germans from the Sudetenland, Silesia, Pomerania, East Prussia, Vojvodina, and Slavonia in 1945? This was obviously unjust because the principle of collective guilt and punishment was applied, and individuals were indiscriminately punished for the crimes of their national state, in this case Nazi Germany. Should that injustice be rectified? Do Russian and other non-Baltic nationals have *national* rights in the newly independent Baltic states, where they form up to 45 percent of the population? The majority were born there. Then, of course, there is the absurd

contradiction that those who deny any legitimacy and legality whatsoever to the former Communist regimes and their decisions *insist*
that the frontiers drawn by those regimes are legal and legitimate!
That is particularly notable in the case of the boundaries separating
the states of the former Soviet Union and Yugoslavia.

Then there is a question drenched in blood in Yugoslavia today:
Do minorities in the new nation-states have the same right of self-
determination as the majorities? For example, do the Serbs in the
Serbian-inhabited regions of Croatia have the same right to secede
unilaterally from Croatia that Croatia had to secede from Yugoslavia? For that matter, why do the Croats claim rights for their
people in Bosnia-Herzegovina (who number barely 17 percent) that
they absolutely deny to the not much smaller Serbian minority of
13 percent in Croatia? The Croats claim that "their people" have the
"right" to set up a "national community," the Croatian quasi-state
of Herzeg-Bosna, which is independent in all but name from the rav-
aged sovereign, independent state of Bosnia within which it exists.
The ramifications of this logic are many. Do the Albanians living in
Macedonia have the right to join with those in Kosovo? Do they
have a right to merge with Albania and create a unified state? Can
the Hungarians in Transylvania secede from Romania, where they
have been mistreated for years? What about the Muslims and Turks
in Bulgaria? Do they have a right to independence? If not, why not?
Does Crimea have a right to decide democratically to secede from
Ukraine? It was after all quite arbitrarily attached to Ukraine by a
Communist dictator in 1954, which is relatively recent. These are
only some of the more obvious questions. Dozens of far smaller nations that have been internationally recognized with seats in the UN
have far more dubious prospects than the potential East European
petitioners for independence.

Some prefer historical to ethnic boundaries. That raises an even
worse set of problems. Which historical boundaries? Every national
group has its preference — the historical moment when it was at
its peak. To repeat an example, why should Crimea be a part of
Ukraine? There are certainly no ethnic justifications. In an act of
obscure generosity Khrushchev attached Crimea to Ukraine in 1954
without its population being allowed to utter a mumbling word
about this. Should *that* decision bind the present inhabitants of
Crimea, not to say the Russian republic? The upshot of all this is that

no matter how one attempts to define these boundaries — whether ethnically or historically — in most instances the populations are far too mixed for reasonable approximation of a fit between boundaries and the national distribution of population. There will always be minorities on both sides of the proposed new frontiers.

Therefore, if the new states are defined as *national states* — that is, as the homeland of a politically dominant nation — then they will always have at least two classes of citizens: the majority, the full members of the political nation; and the minority (or minorities), who will be tolerated and given fewer rights. The minorities will never be fully equal members of the political nation *if that political nation is defined ethnically.*

Ethnicity is ascribed, not acquired. You are born with it or you are not. Presumably you can lose it by forgetting or renouncing your language and customs, but you cannot acquire an ethnicity. Citizenship, on the other hand, can be both acquired and ascribed. That is why the only possible kind of decent, modern, democratic state is one that is, at the very least, defined as the state of all of its citizens, irrespective of national origin or religion. The nationalist leaders and advocates of the new national states emerging from the ruins of Communist rule reject this proposition as false universalism. One hears the echo of the old Stalinist accusation of rootless cosmopolitanism against the Soviet Jews. As a result of the widespread insistence on authentic national roots as the foundation of the new post-Communist states, democracy faces a very dangerous future throughout the republics of former Yugoslavia and throughout most of Eastern Europe and the former Soviet Union. Because of that insistence, it was always very dubious that the Independent Commonwealth would survive even a relatively brief time.

Modern Nationalism's Ambiguous Relationship to Democracy

Modern nationalism as we know it has been on the scene from the early nineteenth century. Most historians agree that there was little or nothing of it in the world before the end of the eighteenth century. Before that time people were familiar with loyalty to a monarch, a religion, a region (*pays réel*), a canton, a village, a city, or a stratum or class. However, loyalty to the *nation* — that is, nationalism — dates essentially from the French Revolution. The leaders and armies of that revolution carried the message of nationalism wherever they went. By the time the cycle of revolutionary wars had ended in 1815, they had even infected some of their enemies with nationalism. From that time on — despite the best efforts of the Holy Alliance to crush it — nationalism flourished, more often than not in intimate alliance with another idea popularized by the French Revolution: democracy. When Marx and Engels wrote their manifesto, it was no specter of *Communism* that haunted Europe; rather it was the very real threat of revolutions for national independence and greater liberty. Most writers, then, recognize nationalism as something essentially modern.

Since the early nineteenth century nationalism has gone through many phases in symbiosis with many different movements, democratic, imperial, liberal, socialist, fascist, and Third World. It has obviously served at times to expand the boundaries of the political community and participation and to attack privileges of the anational aristocrats and merchants. It often represented the defensive reaction of disadvantaged and undereducated classes to the metropolitan centers. This was particularly the case in Eastern Europe, in the distant provinces of the multinational empires of Austria-Hungary, Russia, and Turkey, especially when those provinces were inhabited by peoples who did not speak the imperial language of administration.

At some times nationalism had popular but also profoundly conservative roots, examples being the Carlists in Spain, Rexists in Belgium, Breton nationalists, national populists in Hungary, and the Serbian Narodna Odbrana. At still other times it was very contradictory, combining modernization with military conspiracies — examples of this being the Young Turks, Zveno in Bulgaria, and the Greek pro-*enosis* (unity) conspiracies on Cyprus. Still other nationalisms were fused with fascism throughout Central and Eastern Europe, like the Iron Guard in Romania, the Arrow Cross party in Hungary, and the Ustaše in Croatia. Clearly nationalism by itself is almost nonexistent as a force. It is almost always fused with a broader program to which it adds a specific national flavor. Thus nationalism can be formally left-wing or right-wing in theory. In practice, particularly in the last few decades, nationalism — when not directly involved in defending an oppressed nation — has in essence been populist whatever the nature of its formal program.

That is, nationalism places primary emphasis on the people of a given nation, as against an emphasis on classes or programs. It may treat the "people" or the nation (or a fusion of the two) as an oppressed or exploited category, but it is violently hostile to dividing the people or nation by raising divisive class or political issues. The political language used by nationalists almost always stresses *unity* against the outsider or the enemy, real or potential. Nationalism in modern politics establishes a boundary separating "us" from "them" and bases that boundary on inborn, that is to say national, characteristics. You are born, more rarely adopted, into a national group. There is no nonsense about individual choice.

Therefore nationalism threatens both individual liberty and democracy. Liberty is negated because the citizen or subject is *assigned* to a national or ethnic category without having any choice in the matter. Democracy is threatened because individuals are ascribed — through birth — to national parties and groups, and therefore there can be no alternations in power based on democratic elections. Elections are reduced essentially to national censuses, and politics, at best, consists of deals and compromises made between leaders of national communities.

The best present-day working example of a blatantly nondemocratic system based on national parties is probably Malaysia. Despite the mix of three national groups, Malays, Chinese, and Indians, the native Malays are explicitly privileged when it comes to civil service jobs and even in the economy since every major firm must have Malay co-owners. A similar system is evolving in the Fiji Islands. There are far worse alternatives in the world today — for example, systems in which no deals are made, and the multiethnic community breaks down into intraethnic violence or war, as was the case with Sri Lanka, Sudan, or Yugoslavia. There are also far better alternatives in how to deal politically with multiethnicity in the world today — for example, designing the state and its laws so that they are neutral as to the national origin and identity of citizens and making certain that political parties, unions, and movements do likewise and concentrate on ethnically cross-cutting issues.

It would be naive to expect that this is an easy solution. How does a democratic country *prevent* nationalist, xenophobic, and racist political mobilization? Does it do so administratively? It is possible to imagine a multiethnic federation in which the national groups all have geographically fairly compact units and in which it would be a requirement that a party have at least a certain percentage, let us say 4 percent, of the votes in each unit to be represented. This, however, still does not prevent nationalist or even racist agitation, and it does discriminate against legitimate regional interests. For that matter it improperly discriminates against national parties. Such parties, in a democracy, can only be defeated politically, not administratively. However, the problem remains: In a democracy to what extent can one prevent the imposition of undemocratic restrictions and norms by a majority of the voters?

Many nationalist parties, and religious parties for that matter, insist on the right, indeed duty, to impose their majority or even minority norms on the society as a whole. The role of religious parties in Israel; the issues of divorce and abortion in Ireland; the proposals to enforce Catholic norms on such questions in Hungary, Croatia, Slovenia, Poland, and both the Czech Republic and Slovakia — these examples immediately come to mind. In Poland despite clear public support for the right to abortion, the church managed to bully the parliament into passing a law in late 1992 that provides a two-year jail sentence for a doctor carrying out an abortion. And yet I do not know any way of dealing with such issues except through democratic debate and decision making.[1] To be sure, qualified majorities (two-thirds, for example) should be normally required in any democratic state to alter constitutions and basic laws. But it is the case that nationalism, particularly when intimately bound up with religion, poses the question of protection not only for minority rights but, probably even more, for individual citizens who do not identify with any particular tribe.

Thus, for example, the Province of Quebec permits only children of English-speaking parents to opt for an English-language education. All others are obliged, by legislation passed by the French-speaking majority, to go to French-language schools. Now, while this legislation might have had a perfectly worthy and rational aim — to preserve a French-speaking community in the midst of a vast English-speaking realm — it clearly violated the rights of immigrants who come from non-English-speaking countries. Their personal rights and liberties to make important educational choices for their children have been substantively limited.

To be sure this also raises another thorny question: In determining how, in what language, and according to which norms children should be educated, how does one balance the rights of parents against the interests of the community or the state? After all, do children unconditionally belong to the parents? Do Muslim parents have a right to insist that their daughters wear veils in public schools? Do fundamentalist parents have a right to demand that their children not go to biology and sex-education classes? These are some relatively benign examples of a kind of issue that has bedeviled mixed communities for a long time. As societies become, as they undoubtedly will become, more ethnically mixed these kinds of issues will multiply. Clearly, democracy and liberty are in a very tense relationship with national and communal goals when it comes to education and the political socialization of the young. Another perhaps more politically relevant example: Do minorities have a right to insist on teaching history and literature in a way that stresses their national identity and pride? In the United States that is called multiculturalism. What about national states in Eastern Europe and the states of the former Soviet Union? What will these states do when the national history of one group consists in large part of greatly distorted, chauvinistic lies and grievances against another national group? How are histories likely to be presented in a nationalist-dominated Serbia or Croatia? What are the Croats likely to teach in their schools about the role of the Serbs, and vice-versa? Who is to make such politically and nationally charged decisions about the education of future citizens?

This is an especially painful question because school teachers, and especially school teachers of national history, have been a major element in inventing passionate modern nationalisms. It is said that school teachers taught provincials in France that they were Frenchmen and Frenchwomen. To do this they warred relentlessly against the *patois* spoken in many regions, as well as against Basque, Breton, and Occidental (Provençal), which were established languages. School teachers and priests reinvented the Slovaks as a nation, as well as a number of other almost lost peoples who had to be reinvented in the nineteenth century.

The cossack leader of the great revolt against Poland in the seventeenth century, Bohdan Chmelnyckyj (Kmelnisky), is a great hero of Ukrainian nationalist histories; he also led huge, murderous anti-Jewish pogroms. It is not too difficult to guess how such a blood-stained figure will be handled by school teachers in a new nationalist

Ukraine. For that matter, how will revisionist historians treat the various Ukrainian nationalist (and violently anti-Semitic) organizations — like the rival branches of the Organization of Ukrainian Nationalists — that fought side by side with Nazi Germany and against Soviet tyranny during the Second World War?[2] Radical revisionism about right-wing nationalist groups allied with the Nazis during the Second World War will appear throughout much of the region. It will be present in, at least, the Baltic countries, Hungary, Romania, Slovakia, Croatia, Serbia, and Albania. In all of those countries right-wing nationalists were allied with the Nazis. Their retroactive rehabilitation will necessarily involve a revision of the estimate of the role of Nazi Germany *and* in some cases revision or at least relativization of the Holocaust against the Jews. To be sure, *Communist* historiography in the last few decades also minimized the Nazi war of extermination against the Jews.

In any case, in a period of nationalist euphoria, it is extraordinarily dangerous to leave the questions of the national content of education to teachers. On the other hand, when one considers what demagogic games will be played with this type of question, can it be left to the politicians, albeit democratically elected?

The only concrete beginning of a solution to these kinds of questions and dilemmas is an internationally supervised and enforced bill of rights for minorities and for human rights in general, collective and individual, throughout the area. Certification of adherence to such a bill of rights should be the condition for aid and continued recognition of the new national states. This will almost surely be called interference and tutelage by nationalists in these countries. They will charge discrimination, pointing out the many violations of such rights throughout the world and even in the Western capitalist democracies.

"Why begin with us?" will be the general outcry. There are at least three good answers to this question: (1) one has to begin somewhere, and there is a great urgency today to deal with these matters in the post-Communist states; (2) the offended pride of these "nations" is an abstraction; individual people and members of minorities whose rights are jeopardized are very real; and (3) a state is not weakened by having to adhere to democratic and human rights norms. One could add that any state that would be seriously weakened by adherence to democratic human rights does not deserve to survive. To the contrary, by defending and insisting on such rights the international community contributes to giving democracy — which requires decent, law-abiding states controlled by their citizens — at least a fighting chance.

Material aid is desperately needed by the post-Communist countries of Eastern Europe and the former Soviet Union; however, material aid alone will not provide a fighting chance for democratic options to win out. Their people need, despite whatever their political leaders say, energetic help from the European Community and the United States in preserving the minimal rules of the game so that democratic development has a chance. In addition to help from governments, massive engagement by trade unions, women's organizations, peace groups, lawyers' organizations, human rights groups, and monitors is needed. In other words, all the institutions of the civil society in the Western states, and particularly the women's groups and the trade unions, should take it upon themselves to seek out and help their opposite numbers in the new Yugoslav republics, Eastern Europe, and the former Soviet Union.

The Transitory Present and Future Change

A dangerous, widespread, common fallacy holds that the present political situations and the present widely accepted paradigms about how societies and economies should be organized are very long-range trends, if not irreversible. We live, however, in an era of truly cataclysmic changes, the most recent of which have been the upheavals in the former Communist-ruled states and the radical transformation of the world from the brink of a nuclear holocaust to a post–Cold War situation. Yet it is widely assumed that the fragile, temporary, and very shallow political consensuses in advanced industrial societies and the post-Communist countries will last. Why should this be so?

Why, for example, assume that the left is dead rather than dormant? Why assume that a broad and dynamic left cannot revive, perhaps under a different name and using a very different language and imagery? The forces and impulses that had provoked the rise of egalitarian and democratic movements, in practically every country on the globe, are as present on the scene as they were a century ago.

Superior communications and the presence of mass media make people living in misery aware that this is not immutable and God-given. Mass media make most people aware that there are places where ordinary people live better than they do. Television and radio now make knowledge and more often illusions about the rest of the world universally available even to illiterates.

Masses of people in Eastern Europe and the states of the former Soviet Union now believe that it is possible for things to be better. Badly organized and repressive societies are not inevitable; political systems, societies, and economies are social constructs made by people. As Marx had noted long ago, people make history and societies, not out of whole cloth to be sure, but there is a great deal of discretionary leeway. Therefore more is now demanded of political leaders and states than used to be. They are expected to change the economies and societies to make them function better in the interest of most citizens. Passivity in the face of economic misery will no longer be tolerated. Limited democratization has radically raised expectations. The hope for a decent, democratic, political *community of all of its citizens,* a polis that treats all of its citizens equally and fairly, will almost certainly rise again.

New, modern democratic movements will rise out of such demands and desires with programs that will be very much like those of modern social-democratic parties. The heart of such programs is the demand for a democratic and egalitarian advanced welfare state adapted to the material and political conditions of specific countries. The politics of such movements will be modern, democratic, socialist politics appropriate for a post–Cold War era, an era in which slaying the dragons of an aggressive and expanding Communism can no longer be evoked to postpone dealing with an overloaded agenda for meeting human needs. These movements will open the terrain for debate about what a desirable society should be like. They will also provide room for the indispensable elements of utopian imagination and hope.

Chapter 6

NATIONALISM, GLOBALISM, AND DEMOCRACY

When I look at the present dim prospects for democracy and socially just societies developing in the states emerging out of former Yugoslavia and other post-Communist countries, I feel anger, pity, and sorrow, distributed in more or less equal doses.

I feel terribly and helplessly angry at the numerous overambitious, unprincipled, provincial mediocrities who had through various sleazy pseudoelections managed to take over and hang on to the political leadership of the two largest republics, Serbia and Croatia. Their shallow, primitive nationalism combined with political bungling had effectively made it impossible to proceed peacefully with democratization of Yugoslavia. Their work has also led to constant confrontations among the ruling "natiocracies," ending up with a bloody war on Croatian soil in the summer of 1991 followed by a predictably far bloodier carnage in Bosnia-Herzegovina. In the Bosnian war the Serbs and Croats are both rivals and accomplices in a tacitly agreed-upon partition of that hapless state at the expense of the largest ethnic group, the Muslim Slavs.

They were aided in their destructive role by the incompetent political hacks controlling the monster of the whole story, the Yugoslav army. The army, however, did not always act without provocation. In fact, the Slovenian separatists who won the first free election in Slovenia hastened to provoke an armed confrontation with the federal

army by forcibly seizing border and customs posts on the international border separating a still-existent Yugoslavia from Italy and
Austria. This, of course, in no way justified the army's gross over-
reaction in invading Slovenia, but the Slovenian nationalists were
certainly no mere innocent victims in this case. To them any means
justified the end — in this case, establishing an independent, separate
Slovenian state.

The Slovenian nationalists were desperate to secede from Yugoslavia because of the gross violations of the constitution and laws
of Yugoslavia, for at least the three previous years, by the Serbian
nationalist leadership under Slobodan Milošević, a Communist hack
who managed to combine the old Communist party and state appa-
ratus with populist nationalist demagoguery. More to the point, he
had the support of the army. To differing degrees all these people
are responsible for the mass slaughter and physical destruction that
have driven the Yugoslav states, individually and collectively, from
the doorstep of Europe to the fringes of the Third World.[1] They share
the responsibility for having unleashed and mobilized nationalist separatism and hatreds that predictably produced enormous destruction
and war and set back the clock of political democratization and the
economy for decades.

But then, the leaders of the various Yugoslav republics have also
included honorable and competent men; at least the presidents of
Macedonia, Bosnia-Herzegovina, and Slovenia can be reasonably so
described. These honorable and competent men were not able to
prevent the catastrophe. And the frightening thing is that when one
looks at the leaders of the other post-Communist states facing nationalist and populist challenges in Eastern Europe and the Independent
Commonwealth, one sees that honorable, competent (not to say experienced) political leaders are very few. They are the exception. On
the whole, the Yugoslav political establishment had been above the
average in competence for one-party regimes. That is a frightening
thought!

In unleashing their destruction on Yugoslavia — whether for the
stated purpose of maintaining the status quo or for unconditional,
absolute, and immediate sovereignty of their own nations — the political elites of the individual Yugoslav states have sharply reduced
the actual independence of their peoples and have created a situation
in which their nations must in the long range become protectorates

to be jointly overseen by the UN and the European Community. In any case their separate pursuits of narrow nationalist goals have indefinitely postponed any realistic prospect of entering the European Community, with the possible exception of Slovenia. Poland, Czechoslovakia, and Hungary now have an agreement with the EEC that has launched them on a path that is to lead to eventual entry into the organization. Yugoslavia's case for EEC membership before 1990–91 was, if anything, better than that of these other nations. In fairness, it must be added that the Serbian leadership, broadly supported by its population and intellectual establishment, bears the lion's share of the responsibility for the rapid deterioration of Yugoslavia's prospects to survive with the same status that Hungary, Czechoslovakia, and Poland now have.

Was the result of nationalist self-assertion worth the price? Were the national grievances of the various Yugoslav nations, always excepting the Albanians in Kosovo, so burning and obvious that it was necessary to call for desperate and extreme measures to satisfy them immediately? In any case, would not most real and imagined economic and political grievances have been resolved much easier had Yugoslavia managed to get into the European Community? Up to the late 1980s, none of the many informed foreign observers who were writing about Yugoslavia noticed any really burning and unsolvable *national* grievances, again always excepting the Albanians. One could have usefully compared Yugoslavia's situation with that of post-Franco Spain, where long-overdue democratization would also produce stronger national assertiveness and autonomies, as in the case of Catalonia. The crucial difference was that in Spain democratization was not forced to wait for all the national questions and grievances to be solved first. There would have been no chance to democratize Spain if the precondition had been the solution of the Basque national question. Some national questions take more time than others, but they can usually at least be defused and become more manageable by a government that moves toward democratization with energy and does so with the support of Europe.

Be that as it may, the specific stated and visible national grievances of the Croats, Serbs, Slovenes, Muslims, and Macedonians appeared to be relatively minor, quaintly old-fashioned, and marginalized before the late 1980s. Social, economic, democratic, and human rights issues were a different matter altogether; there legitimate and visible grievances did exist.

The fragmentation of a relatively successful state and economy[2] that followed in the late 1980s, under the assault of separatist nationalisms reacting to Serbian attempts to impose a de facto hegemony, exacerbated an already excessive dependence on international and transnational institutions that were remote from the citizens and unaffected by any semblance of democratic decision making.

In "Jihad against McWorld," a seminal article in *Atlantic Monthly*,[3] Benjamin Barber cogently argues that both the world market — with its leveling consumer culture and world-encompassing economic institutions — and exclusivist, antirational, and antimodern nationalism are in their very different ways inimical to democracy. Neither is subject to democratic popular control, to the give-and-take of democratic political processes; both are essentially antipolitical and therefore antidemocratic.

Political helplessness breeds cynicism, and one price of widespread cynicism about the possibility of politics is democracy itself. Ever-lower political participation and growing intolerance[4] throughout the post-Communist states that have emerged out of Yugoslavia, and throughout Eastern Europe and the new states of the former Soviet Union, are evidence of just how badly democracy has been injured.

Politics of Theater and Politics of Identity

Democracy is the direct victim of the failures of the old and new political classes in former Yugoslavia. This is all too typical also of the situation in Eastern Europe and the Independent Commonwealth. The pity is that in the post-Communist elections, destructive and overambitious bunglers — often uncritically supported by a West relieved to see the last of the Communists in power — were able to get more or less popular mandates from their nationalistically self-indulgent electorates as well as from a substantial part of the intelligentsia. These electorates wanted to give way to and celebrate their own repressed, traditional, atavistic, and exclusivist tribal urges. As an old Montenegrin saying goes: "What good is freedom if you can no longer cut the throat of a Muslim?"[5] The worst part of all of this, I believe, is that most of those demonstrators and voters who indulged themselves in a little "harmless" national assertiveness against their Albanian or Serbian minorities actually believed they were engaged only in a theater of politics — a playing out of political passions that was not really meant to be taken seriously, that is, to have anything real to do with the economy, or tourism, or international relations. Many in the West asked: What could be the harm of playing out some scenes in the theater of identity? For an answer one need now look only to Yugoslavia, the former Soviet Union, and scenes elsewhere in Europe.

The know-nothing politics of identity in the case of various Yugoslav and other East European nationalisms had a great deal in common with the riots of rival soccer fan clubs throughout Europe. Both engaged in a politics of spectacle where the game itself, like politics in an increasing number of societies, was carried on by professionals. The public was there to cheer. Sometimes, given the emptiness of their lives, the unemployed and underemployed young who composed the soccer fan clubs desperately wanted to do something more than simply passively cheer; they then actively rioted. Analogous groups in Croatia and Serbia became the core of the nationalist paramilitary bands (sometimes these were even based around soccer fan clubs). They did not take elections and political decision making all that seriously; it was not "real." Elections were primarily a way of letting off a little steam, of sending a harsh message to those in real charge. The assumption was that those in charge would stay in power anyway.

The voters expected that after they let off a little steam the reins would be pulled in by *someone*, as Tito had so often done during his lifetime, or that some institution would act as the indispensable tutor. This was an inheritance from years of authoritarian, Communist top-down rule where politics and protests were shadowboxing and sandlot politics, a little like that of student governments in the United States. Popular politics were all shadow and no real substance. Therefore one could say anything and pass any resolutions or decisions because they would never be carried out. Democracy in the post-Communist states was *expressive politics* and had nothing to do with political responsibility and legitimacy. Weakness and repression breed irresponsibility. Weakness corrupts just as much as absolute power. There was no place for the peoples of former Yugoslavia, or

Eastern Europe, or the former Soviet Union to learn responsible politics, to learn that what they decide and who they elect matters, and sometimes can matter a great deal. The experience for almost half a century was to the contrary — politics had been a sham. Years of authoritarian manipulation breed a bone-deep cynicism. The ramifications of this sorrowful process extend beyond Eastern Europe and the former Soviet Union. Indeed, to the marginal and poor in the United States and Western Europe politics must seem increasingly to be but a spectacle with the majority as passive onlookers or at best a passionate fan club.

In the case of Yugoslavia there is also the sense of terrible waste — the waste of resources; the waste of opportunities; the waste of the huge sacrifices by so many, the great pain and suffering of the innocent and not so innocent; the enormous waste of human lives; the waste of idealism. A good part of that idealism had already been burned out from all but the most naive by the cynical careerists and bureaucrats, and in some cases by brutal policemen and jailers. That was a story repeated over and over again by battalions of former Communist dissidents like Milovan Ðjilas. Still one should not forget that it was idealism and Promethean vanity that initially inspired many to try to build a modern, egalitarian society in backward wartorn societies, and specifically in Yugoslavia. At that time, the "really existing" political alternatives to the Communist-led partisans had been discredited or compromised by passivity or collaboration with the Nazi occupiers. To understand the present alternatives in Yugoslavia it is helpful, then, to reexamine with some precision those alternatives after the Second World War.

The Real Alternatives after the Second World War

At the end of the Second World War, the only alternatives to the Communists that had a chance to win were the juntas controlled by Serbian officers; if victorious, those juntas would have been dominated by the armed nationalist Chetnik movement of General Draza Mihailović. That non-Communist alternative could only have triumphed if there had been a long civil war — like the one that was waged between the Royalists and Communists in Greece between 1945 and 1948 — that produced fertile ground for such a backward and reactionary authoritarian regime. A Yugoslav right-wing regime would have been *worse* than the repressive Greek regime of the Colonels given the intraethnic hatred caused by the communal massacres in the Second World War. Because it would have represented only the Serbian side, a nationalist right-wing regime in Yugoslavia could not have avoided a bloody vicious circle of nationalist revenge and counterrevenge.

The Communists did not represent any single national group — in practice from the very outset they repressed *all* nationalisms, as they did all alternative political currents. The new regime was indeed very repressive at the outset, but with the exception of the Albanians no national group was oppressed as such.

The abstract idealism of the Yugoslav Communists led to acts of great cruelty, and that idealism is no justification for the crimes of Communist repression. Many devoted Communist activists and partisan combatants suffered greatly, and fought bravely, with no idea of personal gain or advancement in mind. Clearly, the great majority of them passionately believed in building a state where the various national groups would be fully equal. This first generation of Communists in power was ultimately betrayed by those for whom the revolutions were a road to personal advancement and power. They were also betrayed by the great contradiction in their own ideology: the incompatibility of the Stalinist version of Leninism that they had learned with genuine popular power and democracy. Titoism from the moment that it became an independent variant of Communism was a history of repeated attempts, ultimately unsuccessful, at internal reform in Communist systems, the point of those reforms being to solve that contradiction between an increasingly attenuated authoritarian Leninism and democratic empowerment through self-management.

The Yugoslav party theorists experimented with various mixes of decentralization and party (i.e., LCY) control for almost four decades. They introduced semisyndicalist models of workers' councils, drastic administrative decentralization down to the levels of county government, and ever-greater autonomy for the republics and provinces. The LCY also experimented with increasing marketization of the economy and excessive decentralization of the large enterprises down to "basic organizations of associated labor." The LCY even experimented, with considerable hesitation and inconsistency, with its own withdrawal from direct control of culture and the arts.

These experiments, which were utopian and frequently egalitarian in inspiration, often sounded very good and often brought about real improvements in power relations on the microlevel in the enterprises. The decades-long experiment in workers' self-management was not merely a sham. It did substantially limit the powers of managers, and it did involve large numbers of workers over prolonged periods of time in managing their own enterprises. There were, however, many problems and weaknesses with those experiments. One of these was that self-management was carried to absurd lengths, fragmenting enterprises into ever-smaller units. But the basic weakness was that, without a single exception, all these experiments, the good and the bad, the successful and unsuccessful, were brought in from the top down by a party that insisted on maintaining its own power monopoly. These measures thus provided no genuine sense of empowerment that victories gained in struggles bring to the mass of the people.

By the time of Tito's death, in 1980, the Communists had effectively given up control of the major Academies of Sciences in Belgrade and Zagreb, which had become strongholds of traditionalist Serbian and Croatian nationalisms. The LCY had lost control over the universities and the intellectuals and by the early 1980s barely maintained its hold over the major media. And yet, it kept a dead man's grip on the political system. In what was in all other ways the most open society in Eastern Europe, the Yugoslav Communists insisted, up to the very last moment, in trying to keep the political monopoly of power.

The most that even the most liberal reformers in the LCY in Croatia and Slovenia were willing to grudgingly concede as late as 1988 was that there could be a "nonparty" system. This would be a system in which LCY membership was no longer necessary for candidacies for the legislatures. Nonparty single-interest groups or other groups of citizens would even be allowed to propose candidates. What the LCY would not accept was the organization of rival political parties that could propose alternative programs. What an absurdity! How absurd it was to propose to move toward democratization without any responsible alternative parties and programs that would offer some choices to the electorate, and for which identifiable groups stood. This death grip on the various levels of political power is in good part responsible for the catastrophic collapse of Yugoslavia, for its sudden unravelling, and for its downward slide with no effective controls or brakes.

Nationalism Substituting for Democratic Mobilization

The LCY's systematic prevention of the normal development of responsible opposition groups, journals, and parties had created an intellectual and moral desert. That manmade desert became a veritable fertile oasis for charlatans, adventurers, and demagogues who came to prominence overnight as the system collapsed. There had been no time to develop alternative views and politics to be tested by debate and mutual criticism. Instead the "new" non- and anti-Communist politicians had to develop overnight. Quite naturally the new politicians did not build their programs out of wholly new materials. Rather, they used whatever political materials were available in the consciousness of the electorate, and what was available was, by and large, pretty terrible, or at the very least inappropriate for democratic politics and pluralist give-and-take in what was a complicated, modern, multinational federation.

Among the passionate alternative political views on how to organize the state and society, the most readily available were supplied by the émigrés, who had preserved a nasty kind of traditional xenophobic nationalism from the years between the two world wars. Centrists and liberals could not arouse passionate commitment; the democratic left was weak, fragmented, and compromised by the similarity of its rhetoric with that of the Communist reformers. Many voters disillusioned by the squabbling and incompetence of the Communist reformers and hard-liners turned to their declared enemies. Hostility to the Communists developed among many future voters.

Much of that hostility to Communists in Yugoslavia in the late 1980s,[6] even among the beneficiaries of their rule, was based on an "echo effect" — that is, many people reacted to the *general* collapse of Communism throughout the bloc. It did not matter that the performance of the Yugoslav Communist system was substantially different from that of the Communism of the East European states or the Soviet Union. It was tarred with the same brush, and

the ambivalence of some Yugoslav Communist ideologues and of
Tito himself toward a continued identification with Communism
as a world system helped align the Yugoslav Communist system in
popular imagination with the rest of them.

Communism was no longer a wave of the future — it was now
seen as a worn-out, inefficient, unmodern, and intellectually unfashionable ideology. Countries one admired for being orderly and
progressive and for having a high living standard — that is, the countries of Western Europe and North America — were emphatically not
Communist. For the young, Communism also suffered from the most
fatal of all sins — it was quite simply *boring*. In any case, for many
reasons (and love of democracy was one of the least important ones
for most), Communism became an enemy to many. It was responsible
for all that ailed the society. Communism was now widely considered
responsible for the economic backwardness, low personal incomes,
poor access to consumer goods, disintegration of traditional values,
disrespect from the young, repressed national grievances and resentments, poor working habits, and everything else that prevented life
in the Yugoslav republics from resembling that of a much-idealized
Western Europe. On the other hand, all the advances of the society that had occurred under Communist rule were now seen as the
product of the hard work of the citizens of one's own exploited and
unappreciated republic and nation. No wonder the Communists were
now the enemy, particularly of the young and less educated. Reason-
ing that the enemy of their enemy must be a friend, they turned to
the alternative, the nationalist right, without knowing or much caring
what the nationalists' program consisted of.

Most Serbian and Croatian political émigrés were both right-
wing and clerical in political orientation. During the more intense
periods of the Cold War, this position had been useful for gaining
acceptance as loyal anti-Communist citizens in their new countries.
Émigré politics usually included a mishmash of clericalism, romantic historiography, and pseudoscientific nationalist ethnography and
were laden with arcane conspiracy theories involving the Freemasons, Jesuits, and espionage agencies. All this had been preserved
in the micropolitics of anti-Communist exile groups and journals
and was now made available to the new anti-Communist, nationalist
politicians. Those nationalist metapolitics were packaged with financial aid that, especially in the case of Croatian right-wing émigrés,

was provided for the most convincingly anti-Communist of the new politicians.

Conspiracy theories and forms of political paranoia had long been popular in former Yugoslavia. They were vastly encouraged by the ceaseless efforts of the political police and the police's favorite journalists to develop a "security consciousness," that is, a general paranoia about all foreigners, potentials spies, and all those who were different and might threaten the political order. Thus there was ample ideological room in all of the Yugoslav republics for a cultural symbiosis between the right-wing émigrés and the police-inspired journalists and publicists. Both loved dark plots with undefined alien forces of great power and malignity shaping the world and the nation. In that they were not very different from the far-right nationalists in Western Europe and the United States.

Protofascist and Communist-inspired paranoias fit together very neatly and helped corrupt and infect an already insecure public that could discern no readily available alternatives to the well-known and comfortable beliefs and social and political systems that were collapsing. These are politics for intellectually and morally lazy people — almost everything is explained by conspiracies against one's own poor, victimized nation; the conspirators are in alliance with the traditional national rivals; and unity is needed to battle the internal and external foes.

Thus for the Serbian nationalists it was self-evident that the Albanians are in cahoots with the world conspiracy of Islamic fundamentalism and eternally lust after pure Serbian womanhood. The Croats are obviously an extension of the permanent plot of the Vatican against Orthodox Christianity, or alternately the German march to dominate Eastern Europe. For the Croat nationalists, the Serbs are representatives of the barbarian non-European hordes of treacherous "Byzantines"[7] who are presumably out to destroy Western civilization and Christian (that is, Catholic) culture; they are also natural Bolsheviks and are even biologically inferior or at least impure. (One of the popular terms of abuse for the Serbs, popularized by soccer gangs, is *Cigani!* — Gypsies!) All this is wonderfully easy to use to increase the circulation of a mass, yellow, chauvinist press and the influence of television and radio. It is a politics of identity reduced to its crudest form, "we" versus "they." It is a politics reduced to sound bites. But then, such politics are not exactly unfamiliar in the United

States or even Western Europe; it is all a matter of scale. Such politics steer clear of the notion that differences may be based on legitimate disagreements and grievances that could be subject to negotiations and compromise — that is, subject to the mechanisms of democratic political processes.

Many Belgrade intellectuals continue either to support a rump Yugoslavia dominated by a larger and more united Serbia or quite simply to support a Greater Serbia. Those goals cannot be achieved by any democratic government, particularly not in the teeth of almost unanimous hostility from the world community. The choice is therefore either Serbian nationalist aims as defined by the regime *or* democracy. National populism in Serbia has turned out to be a part of a more general wave of an unpleasant future dominated by mutually incompatible, xenophobic nationalisms in the post-Communist states facing disintegration and the desperate need to reform.

However, the mass populist and nationalist demonstrations in former Yugoslavia cannot be explained away so simply, for they also represent a distorted attempt at a popular, communitarian, and grassroots expression of the growing disenchantment of very broad layers of the population. The extent to which national political systems are increasingly helpless within a more and more globalized world economy is a complex question. But one thing is clear: more and more decisions intimately affecting peoples' lives are settled on a supranational level. The world economy is not "accessible" to democratic decision making, particularly not that of a small, independent state. The tendency is to increase the number of questions that are settled in arenas out of reach of ordinary citizens or the national states. The new post-Communist states have lost control of their economies and cannot assure law and order, personal security, and safety of property for their citizens. The demonstrations are a protest against these situations and are also a penalty for the blocking of the political system for far too long. The mass demonstrations are also a plebiscitary, a bastard and populist form of democracy taking the place of a genuine democratization of the political system. The new political system has lost a considerable amount of sovereignty and has become to no small extent a protectorate of the world community. The IMF and the World Bank will dictate the parameters of economic revival and reconstruction after the war, and the UN forces will attempt to enforce a peace and law and order that the governments of newly independent Croatia and Serbia could not. Bosnia will long remain a basket case. How can the citizen affect politics in a polity that is increasingly dependent on forces and decisions that are anonymous, many degrees removed, alien, and inaccessible?

A democratic option has been made almost unimaginable now in Bosnia through Serbian brutal "ethnic cleansing" and the Croat complicity in effectively partitioning that state. Such an option remains difficult in Serbia and Croatia because the Serbs and the Croats waged a bitter dirty war for maximalist national aims with horrendous losses of lives and property. No one won. The war was a moral and political disaster for both Serbia and the Yugoslav army. In any truly democratic system, those who were directly responsible both for the policies that led to a war and for waging the war incompetently would not remain in power. The Serbian leadership, though, remains.

On the other hand, the Croats have hardly won a famous victory. Vicious Croat nationalist triumphalism, right after the first free election in 1990, helped make support for the war far greater than it would have been within the Serbian minority in Croatia. Modest concessions by the Croat nationalist government in the spring of 1990 would have marginalized the Serbian minority's support for the war. The result of the war that was fought entirely on Croat soil was not only vast destruction of cities and creation of some six hundred thousand refugees, but Croatia has also lost effective control of some one-quarter of its territory for an indefinite period. Fighting the war encouraged the existing tendencies toward authoritarian presidential rule by degree and censorship of the media in Croatia.

When the war moved from Croatia to Bosnia in the spring of 1992, intercommunal violence and open warfare reached near-genocidal proportions in Bosnia-Herzegovina. Most of the victims were Muslims, but all sides were murdering civilians and running concentration camps mainly designed to create ethnically "pure" cantons in what had been an exemplary multiethnic society. Again the main culprits were the Serb nationalists. They were clearly being seconded by the Croats, who not only were grabbing twice as much territory as their proportion of the population (just like the Serbs), but also were in open agreement with the Serb nationalists that any "unitary" (i.e., noncantonized) Bosnia was unacceptable. That is, both the Serb and Croat nationalist leaders in Bosnia rejected the idea of a state based on the rights of citizens as distinct from the rights of ethnic or national groups. Partition is then the only answer, and an ethnically based partition is impossible without transfers of population. These transfers cannot be voluntary: peasants do not readily leave their ancestral homes; they have to be terrified out of their minds. Therefore, cantonization of Bosnia and the creation of nationally "pure" states necessarily lead in a straight line to massacres, atrocities, looting, gang rape, and concentration camps as instruments of the new demographic policy. While Serbian nationalists have done by far the most of this, there have also been huge transfers of Serbs from Croatia and Bosnia, three to four hundred thousand refugees, and none of these population transfers was gentle.

Have any of the genuine grievances and insecurities of the peoples involved been solved? Are the Croats more independent and prosperous than they were in the Yugoslav federation? One-quarter of their state is under an indefinite international trusteeship and control (underpinned by an ever more watchful and suspicious German sponsor) supervising their human and minority rights performance. International aid cannot begin to make up for the vast destruction by the Yugoslav army and the loss of the Yugoslav-wide markets. Slovenian independence was gained at a lesser price. Clearly Slovenia had benefited greatly from being in the Yugoslav economy. The Serbs are less secure in Kosovo despite, or rather in good part because of, their repression of the Albanians. The Serbs now certainly also have good reason to feel less secure in Croatia and Bosnia-Herzegovina than at any time since 1945. The Serbian politicians' bullying and the Serb's massive self-indulgence and romantic national chest thumping have frightened and antagonized every one of their neighbors, including a good number of their Montenegrin cousins. They are now much poorer and more isolated than ever. Macedonian independence promises a great deal of economic hardship and political suffering; it promises absolutely no improvement either in the very real cultural and political self-government Macedonians have had for decades or in their economic situation. The suffering of the Albanians is the result of relentless Serbian repression and a confrontational leadership that failed to use the political openings that the first free elections offered. The repression of Albanians in Kosovo cannot last; the only thing worse than the situation of Albanians in Kosovo is the situation of Albanians in Albania.

The Rogue Army: An Explanation

Reliable inside information from top officials of the last legal federal government[8] makes it clear that the Yugoslav National Army had become an independent force at least a year before the breakup of Yugoslavia. The final breakup took place by June 1991 when the irreversible step of military intervention in Slovenia occurred. That was the point of no return. The military and above all political failure of that invasion and the widespread rallying of world and European public opinion in support of Slovenia's unilateral declaration of independence encouraged the Croat separatists to follow.

This means that it was essential to demonstrate unmistakably to both the army leadership and the Milošević government that their murderous goals were not achievable except at unacceptable cost. That is why a real blockade was a necessary step — but only a step — to changing the Serbian policies. Complete and enforced protection of Bosnian air space — permitting the Bosnian government to arm itself and providing protection for deliveries of aid, food, and medicine — should have been organized much earlier. Many lives would have been saved, and perhaps the government in Belgrade would have been changed. The more complicated ethnic picture in Croatia, with a large (13 percent) Serbian minority that was both manipulated by Belgrade and thoroughly frightened by the maximalist oratory of the triumphant Croatian nationalists, guaranteed a war in Croatia. This would be war that combined a civil war (on the part of a large segment of the Serbian minority, which seized as much territory as it could) with ever-clearer involvement of the Yugoslav army on the side of the Croatian Serbs against the legal Croatian government. In any event, the army lost this war politically and doomed the Croatian Serbs to a marginality that would sharply reduce their numbers and influence in a Croatia that would gain international recognition. Once Croatia won its independence, Bosnia-Herzegovina's move was but a matter of time. To stay in the remains of a Yugoslav federation after Slovenia and Croatia had departed would have subjected the Muslim and Croat majority of Bosnia to Serbian domination. Bosnia clearly could not stay in a completely Serbian-dominated federation. Equally clearly the Bosnian Serbs, numbering 32 percent of the population of Bosnia, were not going to willingly become a minority in the country in which they had been the most numerous single ethnic group before the massacres in the Second World War had altered the local demography.

The army, which was increasingly composed of Serbs and Montenegrins by this time, was fated to back the Bosnian Serbs as long as it could. The result was the monstrous civil war in Bosnia combined with an aggressive war on Bosnia on the part of the army and Serbia. But that civil war, with its horrendous ethnic cleansing, was quite predictable once the country began to unravel.

Why then did the Yugoslav army, with its extensive intelligence networks, allow itself to be drawn ever further into this doomed adventure? The answer is both nasty and simple. The army leadership was ideologically Communist and, while concerned with preserving Yugoslavia, was even more concerned with preserving Communist political power. They were against the only kind of Yugoslavia that could have been preserved — a decentralized, economically reformed, and pluralistic Yugoslavia, in other words, a Yugoslavia not ruled by Communists. They bitterly opposed any pluralist political reforms and only grudgingly accepted minimal economic reforms.

At least twice before June 1991 the leaders of the army were on the verge of a coup designed to overthrow the reforming Marković government. They were firmly convinced that in this goal they had a powerful ally, the Red Army, which faced similar foes in its own country. They and their political allies saw their last chance in the failed coup against Gorbachev in the summer of 1991. Had the coup succeeded they would have struck with reasonable assurance of at least political and moral backing from allies in what was still the Soviet Union — more to the point a Soviet Union with a ruling, no matter how reformed, Communist party. In effect the Yugoslav army had tied its fate to the antireformist Communism of the military and political conservatives in the Soviet Union. With the defeat of the coup in Moscow both the Yugoslav army and the Milošević government faced total international isolation. In the place of a Yugoslavia that they had sworn to defend they left vast destruction and a number of antagonistic weak states. With the exception of Slovenia and Macedonia these are authoritarian states. Bosnia-Herzegovina today hardly merits the description of a state at all. It certainly cannot protect its citizens' lives or property.

In any case, the fact that ending the war will require vast intervention by the international community sharply limits the legitimacy of the new governments that have arisen out of the wreckage of Yugoslavia. These small, weak, and dependent states will now have their legal systems and human rights performance monitored by rightly suspicious international human rights agencies rather than by their own parliamentary commissions; their economies will be monitored by international financial institutions rather than by their own economic bodies and ministries; their law and order in large areas will be directly controlled by UN forces rather than their own police; and their political systems will be increasingly subject to direct pressure from the European Community. Now one might agree, as I do, that these external pressures, particularly in the field of human rights, are all to the good; however, it is clear that they have sharply reduced the power of citizens to run their own societies and communities. That must certainly increase both alienation from politics and a general feeling of anomie. All this was the result of struggles for *greater national independence* than could presumably be found in the old loose federal Yugoslav state!

The individual new states that emerged from Yugoslavia all now accept a great deal more interference in their own affairs and more bullying from neighboring states than they ever dreamed was possible. While Yugoslavia is today a fairly extreme case, the loss of national autonomy to globalization is a general problem. The tendency to break up complex multiethnic states increases the power of supranational and global forces in which citizens do not have even theoretical possibilities to intervene. Ethnic nationalism, an essentially communitarian impulse to strengthen the immediate national community, results in the creation of political entities that are even more helpless.

Some Reasonable Democratic Goals for Former Yugoslavia

Whoever and whatever forces are collectively and individually responsible for the death of Yugoslavia, that deed is now a historical reality. The old federal Yugoslav state no longer exists, no matter what legal and diplomatic fictions may be invented by Serbian and Montenegrin fragments of former Yugoslavia to claim the name and legal continuity. The demise of a prolonged experiment in building an effective multinational federal state leaves many orphans, not the least being the millions who were offspring of mixed marriages or who simply felt themselves to be "Yugoslav." The experiment is for the time being clearly over.

The question, then, becomes this: What can be imagined as a decent, if not optimal, outcome emerging from this wreckage? In outlining my own answers to that question I use two examples as metaphors — Benelux and the Scandinavian countries. Both are very imperfect, and I am all too well aware of the fact that the peoples of former Yugoslavia are not Scandinavians, or for that matter Dutch or Belgians. The examples are only meant to be suggestive metaphors. What unites both is what is essential for the new states: boundaries between the new national states must be *absolutely* inviolable; however, at the same time, those same boundaries must not be too terribly relevant in the lives of most people and for the functioning of most economic institutions and transportation networks.

The first step toward this would be mutual recognition, basically within their present borders, of all states emerging from Yugoslav as independent sovereign states. Except for the most minor of mutually agreed on frontier adjustments, the existing borders should be maintained. This is for two very important reasons: first, any attempt to redraw the frontiers would lead to military conflict; second (and this is an even more important reason), attempts to redraw the frontiers along "ethnic" lines not only are doomed but reinforce two absolutely deadly myths. The two myths are: first, that it is *possible* to draw borders in such a way as to create ethnically "pure" national entities; and second, that this is *desirable*. Both myths are born out of a desire to create ethnically national states rather than states that are states of all of their citizens. Because mere border changes can never achieve national homogeneity given the demographic realities of former Yugoslavia, a policy of trying to create ethnically compact states must necessarily be accompanied by forcible massive population exchanges. That *is* in fact the conclusion drawn by many Serbian and Croatian nationalists, and they advocate such more or less voluntary population exchanges. Instead of these pernicious dreams of racial and ethnic homogeneity, the new Yugoslav states should be encouraged to pursue the only kind of policy possible in a modern democracy. That is a policy that the states are states of all of their citizens and that there should be a systematic delinking of ethnic and national symbols from those of the state.

That is why it is reactionary and oppressive for Serbian "democratic" politicians to insist on a return of a monarchy and on a special relationship with the state for the Serbian Orthodox church, which is a symbol of unity only for the Serbs themselves; one-third of the population of the state of Serbia is neither Serbian Orthodox nor drawn to symbols of Serbian royalty. That is also why the Croat democrats must accept that a democratic Croatia, rather than being merely the state of the Croats, must be a state of all its citizens. No amount of manipulation of the borders will change the demographic realities. Mass expulsions of minority populations might, but these are quite properly unacceptable to contemporary Europe, a violation of the Helsinki Accords, and would turn the state that tried to carry out such a practice into an international pariah.

So the borders should be left alone, and the populations — of whatever national identity — that fled the war zones must be permitted to return gradually. These refugees must be able to return with guarantees of safety; therefore all paramilitaries must be disarmed, and for a period of time both the police and courts must be subjected to international supervision.

A second step should be to create a Yugoslav-wide free-trade zone; if at all possible, such a zone should be underpinned with a customs union. One reason for such a need is that many of the industries and services in former Yugoslavia are interdependent. Some kind of common currency is too much to hope for now, but at some point it will be needed. Another option would be a readily interchangeable currency, preferably tied to the ECU (European Currency Unit, now worth slightly more than one dollar). The customs union and free-trade zone should be expanded to include neighboring countries that are waiting in the lobby of the European Community. Clearly Hungary and Bulgaria and later Romania and Albania are obvious candidates. The wait to get into the European Community will probably be considerably longer than expected. In order for normal economic relations to develop between parts of former Yugoslavia, some kind of agreed-upon arbitrational and judiciary commissions will be needed to avoid unilateral confiscations in the name of compensation for damages done during the war, or to compensate for private and public property confiscated during the 1991–92 war. It would not be a bad idea to "borrow" European Community judges and codes to avoid constant suspicion of partiality. Such judiciary and arbitrational bodies should also be developed to deal with citizens' complaints about human rights abuses by their own states and with the great many legal matters between citizens of now separate states. An "impartial" judiciary, removed from direct political pressures and nationalist demagoguery, might also be a face-saving way to begin dealing with long-overdue human rights issues in Kosovo as well as with rights of minorities in general. This could also be a preparation for an eventual integration into the EEC.

A third step should be for all new Yugoslav states to sign a nonaggression treaty. Such an agreement might also attempt to deal with three outstanding issues that need to be "defanged." The first problem has to do with members of the old Yugoslav army who have been separated from their homes. A solution would be simply to provide for the right of former soldiers and combatants to return to their homes and apartments or be compensated for them. A second and related problem has to do with making provisions for the pensions of the standing army. The third problem has to do with dividing the hardware of the old Yugoslav army among the states in some equitable way. The long-range goals of any proposal to resolve these issues should be to remove the army as an independent "rogue" element on the political scene, to allow the old commissioned and noncommissioned officers to retire, and to reduce the armed forces of the individual new states to a manageable size, the smaller the better. It would not be a bad idea to revive the idea of the whole area becoming a military-free zone. This would make both civil society and democracy considerably safer than they would be in the presence of national armies composed of necessarily dissatisfied heroes of wars of national independence. It would be safer if they were disarmed. Whatever service would be required should be directed at massive efforts for reconstruction of war-torn areas. Perhaps, instead of military service, something like voluntary "youth brigades" from various independent states can help reconstruct Vukovar, the area around Dubrovnik, and other war-devastated areas. It is a mistake to underestimate the vast potential of idealism among the young. I suspect such a project would have masses of volunteers, if only the nationalists and political hacks can be kept out.

A fourth step would be for all new Yugoslav states to negotiate and jointly agree upon an advanced human rights code with viable enforcement mechanisms. This would or should go a long way to re-assuring the new states that "their" fellow nationals are protected even if they live in a state in which they are a minority. Such a code should also provide for cultural autonomy and the right to keep contact with national cultural institutions in other states. Legitimate worries about the condition of the Croats in Vojvodina and Mon-tenegro, Serbs in Bosnia and Croatia, and Muslims in Serbia and Montenegro would be assuaged. Emphasis on individual as well as collective rights would help to ensure that negotiation of such a code would not become just a bargaining ground for intertribal disputes. I am at the moment much more worried about individual human rights than the more visible "group" ethnic rights. The first are a good deal easier to violate, and after doing so it is easy enough to insist that the issue is only an internal matter for the state in question. Not only eth-nic organizations but also social movements and trade unions should be part of the effort to defend human rights. It would be natural for social movements and trade unions to cooperate across the new state lines; they already do in the rest of the world. We might even see that happy day when the new Yugoslav states compete to determine which one is "best" and most advanced in human rights. This would be a wholly benign competition for a change.

A fifth step, probably far in the future, would be for some new Yugoslav states to share some consular and diplomatic services, both for reasons of economy and because of the scarcity of diplomatic cadres. Other related steps are the following: given the large num-ber of mixed families and friendship networks, it is reasonable to expect that the use of visas and passports between these new states should be abolished, permitting free travel, if not residence, for cit-izens of all states to all states. In the near future some select states might establish a system whereby citizens could work, reside, and collect pensions and health benefits in any one of those states. It also would make sense to work out mutual recognition of diplo-mas, licenses, and insurance. In short, the aim is to have the kind of relations between states and citizens that exist in Benelux and the Scandinavian countries. These strike me as reasonable goals for the former Yugoslav space.

Extensive and systematic contacts between citizens, professional associations, trade unions, and political parties would give content to a loose association of now-independent Yugoslav states. That is where the Scandinavian model comes in. There is every reason to expect that close cooperation between social-democratic parties and unions from all individual states could be institutionalized, and so could a still looser association of liberal-democratic parties, of conservative parties, and so forth. Close mutual support between trade unions in the states of former Yugoslavia is a natural and has already begun among some. Even during the height of the war in Croatia and Bosnia, democrats, social democrats, and trade unionists were meeting and attempting to develop new links based on mutual respect and equality.

A final and very important step is to systematically break the media blockade that has been imposed on the citizens of the separate new states, but particularly Croatia and Serbia. The press, radio, and television must be opened up and freed from direct and indirect censorship and domination by the governing parties. Once this happens, the absurdity of some of the fantasies built up by the regime's press and media — fantasies about widespread Croatian "fascist and Ustaše" sentiments or about massive Serbian support for the aggressive war on Croatia — will be revealed.

Once the present xenophobic, nationalist fever has abated, it will become increasingly clear how much has been lost, how similar are the problems faced by the people of the new separate states, and how essential some cooperation will be if the job of reconstructing a viable economy and society is to begin. However, that cooperation will be effective only if it occurs among equal and independent states.

What are the forces that might fight for such a program? Does it represent more than wishful thinking by rootless intellectuals nostalgic for a cosmopolitan Yugoslavia now replaced by parochial ethnic states? I believe that the ethnic mobilization has very shallow roots. Yugoslavia as a country had a history of seventy odd years, almost fifty of them after the Second World War. A very great deal of cultural and economic integration had taken place. From Bosnia and the borders of the Kraina region have come repeated reports of fraternization, partying, and boozing among soldiers from opposing Croat and Serb sides. I have personally witnessed cases of this. Much of the ethnic stereotyping is only skin deep and not very convincing given the vast similarities of the combatants. The only people who seem convinced that nationalism is a serious business and not a kind of politics of theater, analogous to that of rival soccer gangs, are linguists, romantic novelists, and historians. All of these have a professional stake in exploiting the hard-to-see "differences" between the Serbs, Croats, and Muslim Slavs who speak the same language and whose ancestors have shared the same space for a millennium.

Likewise, the new, widespread, popular anti-Communism is only skin deep. There is a discreet but widespread nostalgia for the "good old Titoist days," days of job security, rising incomes, and law and order in what was the most open Communist-ruled country in Europe. After all, real incomes in Croatia, Serbia, and Bosnia dropped from an average of six to eight hundred German Marks a month to well under one hundred! That is an economic catastrophe for the great mass of individuals and families. Massive dismissals, purely at the discretion of the management, face huge numbers of workers. All vestiges of workers' control and self-management have been abolished. Skimpy pensions have been cut in half. Inadequate social services are being sharply reduced. There are 2.5 million refugees. Every fourth person in Croatia, every fifth person in Serbia, and every third person in Bosnia is now a refugee. Weimar Germany was a paradise of stability compared to the ruins of Yugoslavia, with the exception of Slovenia. More ethnic warfare is on the agenda in Kosovo and the Muslim areas of Serbia.

This means that sharp oppositional politics of the right and the left are being forced on the agenda. It is not at all clear which forces will win out. My best-case scenario is based on the notion that the broad, class-based left has more resources and more resonance in the memories and residual politics of the peoples of Croatia, Bosnia, and Serbia. Small parties that share a common democratic and leftist politics exist in all of the former Yugoslav states, and those parties have maintained loose networks. They control the governments of Macedonia and Slovenia and the opposition in Croatia, Bosnia, and new "Yugoslavia." They have broad support from former non-Communist dissident intellectuals and from Communist democratic reformers. Above all they draw support from the antiwar young and from the increasingly militant and bitter unionized workers. It is not at all certain that these forces can win; much will depend on the solidarity and support they get from the broad social-democratic left in the European community, and even more will depend on their courage in the face of repression and even death squads in some of the new states. However, they do represent a hope, a possibility, and a set of goals worth fighting and taking risks for, and that is as much as anyone has ever really had in Eastern Europe and the former Soviet Union. The alternatives, if they lose, are very grim indeed. Unfortunately, they are no less probable.

Modern nationalism, not only in Yugoslavia and the rest of Eastern Europe, moves by strange and convoluted rules that are sometimes explicitly antirational and antimodern. Many of the hardline nationalists in the 1920s in Europe — in France, Spain, Italy, and Germany — were quite explicitly aware of this dimension of nationalism. They gloried in it and were especially attracted to authoritarian and charismatic nationalist movements immersed in Jungian symbols and the leadership principle. Early Italian fascism was the classic prototype of these movements of national renaissance. Nationalism is a thing of passion and emotion and is therefore postrational and postuniversalist; it is meant to be felt and believed and not coldly analyzed. It is therefore also utterly nondemocratic although populist, and it is emphatically not subject to the compromises and negotiations that are the heart of modern democratic politics. Nationalism when awakened is also inconsistent with building "cool and rational" complex federal or confederal states that are essential if any kind of democratic arrangements are to work in multiethnic states. This is most definitely not merely a problem for the states of former Yugoslavia or the former Soviet Union. Nor is it a problem associated only with economic backwardness and with political "premodernity." The problem of multiethnicity looms not only for Nigeria, Ethiopia, and India, but also for Canada, Spain, and even the United States.

Structuring democracy in multiethnic states in an era of awakened nationalisms will be the major political problem for the early twenty-first century.[9] A second problem will probably be how to maintain meaningful pluralist democracy and effective citizen participation in modern states that become ever-less relevant in making the decisions that profoundly affect the lives of their citizens. A final essential problem will be how to combine democracy, equality, and community with those supranational mechanisms that will be needed to deal with economic and ecological problems and ultimately with the problem of global economic maldistribution — the very issue that in the end will determine if we will live in war or peace.

Chapter 7

A PERSONAL SUMMARY

Autobiographical Note

By the spring of 1991 Yugoslavia was nearing terminal illness. The federal LCY had not been in existence since the withdrawal of the Slovenian and Croatian sections. While the economic program of the federal premier, Ante Marković, had managed to maintain relatively high wages and a stable currency, the crisis was obvious to all. The presidents of the six Yugoslav republics were still holding endless sterile meetings to try to work out an impossible compromise between the Slovenian and Croatian leaders, who were willing to accept at most a loose confederation, and the Serbian leader Milošević, who pushed for a more centralized federation. There was an end-game, apocalyptic atmosphere in the circles of intellectuals I moved among in Belgrade, Zagreb, and Ljubljana. A familiar, worn-out regime was clearly on its last legs, but there was little joy and much fear about the prospects for the future. We did not expect any velvet revolution or magical fixes from the new mantra, "Market and privatization." And yet, none of us could even imagine just how terrible the next two years would be. The more uneasy of my friends were already moving to their "home" republic from both Serbia and Croatia if they were of the "wrong" nationality.

My own case is fairly atypical. I am an only child and was born in Sofia while my father, a prerevolutionary Yugoslav diplomat, served there. Both of my parents were Serbian, and like many Serbs both

descended from immigrants from Montenegro. My paternal grandfather died during the epic winter retreat of the Serbian army through
the Albanian mountains in 1915. The other grandfather, who had
been a Serbian diplomat, was one of the founders of the nationalist conspiratorial group Unity of Death (known popularly as the
Black Hand), which was composed primarily of young officers. The
group was responsible at least for the assassination of King Alexander Obrenović and was accused of having some connection with the
assassination of Archduke Ferdinand. In any case, grandfather Bogdan Radenković was sentenced to death for allegedly plotting against
the prince regent Alexander and the heads of the Serbian government;
he died in prison.

My maternal relatives included a number of cabinet misters, ambassadors, and politicians in Serbia and prewar Yugoslavia, including
the first (still non-Communist) vice president of post–Second World
War Yugoslavia, Jasa Prodanović. Thus I have, if anything, a better
and longer Serbian nationalist pedigree than most so-called Chetnik
leaders in Serbia today. This makes my bitter hostility to all nationalists and above all to my own people's nationalists the more
provocative to Serbian nationalists and completely incomprehensible
to Croat nationalists.

I did not, however, spend most of my youth in Yugoslavia. After
my parents divorced, I stayed with my father outside of Yugoslavia from 1940 to 1964, leaving as a child of eleven and returning
at thirty-five. My father served the royalist Yugoslav government in
London as a publicist and a cabinet minister. As a bitter opponent
of Tito's Communists, he refused to return to Yugoslavia after the
war. During the Second World War, I lived in Greece, South Africa,
and Egypt before settling in the United States in 1946 at the age of
seventeen, after a brief military service.

I have lived in America ever since, and it is there that I have com-
pleted my education, developed my political affinities, and developed
as an intellectual. The irony, given my background, is that I developed as an American democratic socialist active in trade unions and
the civil rights movement. I did not return to Yugoslavia until 1964,
which was when somewhat bemusedly I rediscovered that I had an
extensive and affectionate family and a national identity and roots.
That identity was always problematic, however. I do not think of my-
self as a hyphenated American, a Yugoslav-American, but rather as a

Yugoslav *and* an American. Both those are constructed or intentional identities: that is, I *chose* them. I am also a Serb, an antinationalist Serb to be sure, and a citizen of Croatia — a citizenship that, once again, I *chose*. I am, however, getting ahead of the story.

Once I rediscovered the other half of my identity, the Yugoslav half, I began to spend long stretches of time, once four years in a row, in that country. I did extensive sociological and historical research there. During these decades I developed wide-ranging professional and political links with the social scientists in Belgrade, Zagreb, and Ljubljana, particularly with a circle of democratic dissidents in and out of the LCY. Since I speak the language (both the Serbian and Dalmatian-Croatian variants) without a trace of foreign accent, I have had access in research that was normally barred to foreigners.

Although I thus for many years have had two very different homelands, in terms of politics I have stood for roughly the same democratic-socialist and pluralist ideas in both of them. It is a position that made me an opponent of the political establishments in both countries with rather more access to media in former Yugoslavia, particularly during the last years of Communist rule when vigilance and censorship markedly declined.

Since 1968 I have by choice lived — when not in New York — on the island of Brač near Split. The island is and has always been almost completely homogeneously Croatian, but it was a major partisan stronghold during the war and revolution. Small villages on my island have produced more partisans and paid a heavier price in lives than did villages ten and twenty times larger in Serbia or the heartland of Croatia. It was a "red" island that had clearly benefited enormously from the years of Titoist modernization and from both Yugoslav and international tourism. It was cosmopolitan the way only islands can be, and it was and is the closest thing I have ever had to a home. I have spent more time and lived longer in the village of Supetar on Brač than in any other place.

My only child, a daughter, was born in Supetar. For two and one-half decades that was where I had my "little community" of nonprofessional friends and neighbors — fishermen, veterinaries, farmers, cafe owners, seamen, war veterans, all native to the island. And yet, despite the fact that I was an articulate and well-publicized enemy of the Milošević regime in Serbia, even I began to feel uneasy in the summer of 1991.

Vicious anti-Serb and anti-Yugoslav slogans were increasingly appearing on walls. While the older generation remained tolerant and cosmopolitan, their far more "modern" kids, dressed in the latest youth fashions from the West and listening to the latest hit music from the same West, were now as often as not turning to a kind of pop nationalism, in good part reacting to the Milošević regime's actions and to the behavior of Serbian tourists they saw.

It was weird! Here was a generation that had benefited enormously from Communist rule parroting slogans about how Croatia had suffered all these years within Yugoslavia. Oddly enough these kids were more parochial and apolitical than their elders. The elders were more likely to have been in other republics and to have known people of different national origins. The young ones (I guess this has something to do with the universal youth consumerist culture) might have gone shopping in Trieste or Austria, even worked in Germany, but almost none of them had visited Macedonia, Bosnia, or Belgrade, except during military service. The years of localism and local pseudonationalism encouraged by the LCY elites since the mid-1960s had come home to roost. Although there was a common youth culture and although the young Croat and Serb soldiers were to discover as they fought in the fratricidal war that they shared cultural tastes, there was very little sense of a common Yugoslav identity.

On Brač, then, there was a clearly discernible generational gap. The older generation knew just how much Brač and Supetar had advanced, and they also had had the experience of fighting together with the other Yugoslavs against a foreign enemy. The young ones, both the locals and the young workers from Serbia who were coming to the workers' hostels on Brač to vacation, seemed to have little in common. Since 1985 the Serbian popular press had unleashed relentless propaganda about Croatian war crimes in the Second World War, and that had created hostility where it had not existed before. Serbian tourists' arrogant assertiveness; huge portraits of Milošević displayed on all buses and workers' hostels in Dalmatia and on Brač; aggressive singing of Serbian nationalist songs; chants denouncing "Ustaše" in a region that had been explicitly antifascist and propartisan — all those created an unpleasant and tense atmosphere.

It was clear that something very nasty would happen soon, and we all waited with dread. Our lives would never be the same, and we would all remember the last two decades of Communist rule as a golden era when law and order prevailed, living standards grew steadily, and the society increasingly became open and tolerant. The victory of the nationalists in the first elections in Croatia in 1990 was a shock to those of us on Brač — the island continued to vote for the now-reformed Communists. Our dread was soon justified when the new Croat government attempted to disarm the mostly Serbian police in Knin, in northern Dalmatia, and was met with resistance. Barricades were set up, cutting Dalmatia off from Croatia and ruining the last weeks of the tourist season. I remember how strange the whole thing seemed. Barricades were up, but there was still, at least formally, a Yugoslav federal government!

The war was already on top of us, but it was undeclared. In Belgrade and Zagreb oppositional intellectuals were trying frantically to meet and do something. Others of us were meeting during that desperate summer in, of course, Sarajevo. Only in Sarajevo, of all places, were intellectuals and dissident activists still relatively optimistic in early 1991.

Organizing Democratic Antinationalists

I was deeply involved in the debates in the media throughout the country in 1991. This was in part because (as I mentioned in the Introduction) in 1990 I had joined with some democratic socialists in organizing the first open non-Communist political group in Yugoslavia, the Union for a Democratic Yugoslav Initiative (UJDI). The group was organized in all the major cities, including Zagreb, Belgrade, Sarajevo, Ljubljana, Skopje, Rijeka, and Split. Most of us had known each other through decades of meetings and activities. The UJDI included many of the rebel student generation of 1968, fighters for democratic reforms, some feminists, and peace activists.

We had also gathered most former members of the dissident Marxist-humanist *Praxis* circle, with the notable absence of Mihailo Marković, a major academic from Belgrade and for years a good personal friend. His absence signaled how many close personal friends with whom we had collaborated for years would be lost to Serbian or Croatian nationalism. Marković, a well-known former democratic-socialist dissident, shocked us by becoming the vice president and a very visible and articulate spokesman of Milošević's ruling authori-

tarian Serbian Socialist party, which was the old Serbian LCY with
ever more aggressive nationalist politics, the old political police and
, *nomenklatura,* and none of the virtues of the old organization.

My personal situation was quite complicated. As a dual U.S.-
Yugoslav citizen I would now have to opt for citizenship in one of
the new states emerging out of Yugoslavia. Increasing national polarization put me in a difficult position as a known public opponent of
the Milošević regime and the Serbian nationalists. This made me a
target for both Serbian and Croatian nationalists, the first because of
my politics and the second simply because of my ethnicity. It was a
toss-up where I would be more uncomfortable or more unsafe as the
situation got progressively worse.

I remember my initial shock when in the center of Belgrade in
1991 I first saw Chetnik insignias on bearded young thugs peddling
chauvinist cassettes and blood-curdling pamphlets. This was a sign
that the old system was breaking down; for much less than what
those thugs were doing, the student newspaper *Student* had been
banned the previous year at the insistence of Slobodan Milošević
himself. The young nationalist thugs looked like caricatures of Chetniks from the Second World War. This was not surprising. The only
models the young had were from the war movies that glorified the
Communist partisans and treated the Chetniks as collaborators, rap-
ists, looters, and killers. That, of course, was precisely what had
made the Chetniks attractive to the new converts! They were a Serbian folk version of the skinheads and young neo-Nazis in the West.
Similar cultural blends in the Croatian paramilitaries mixed Ustaše
symbols with heavy-metal, skinhead, and Rambo images, sometimes
topped off with Catholic prayer beads and a cross. These were the
groups that would do some of the fighting and commit most of
atrocities in the wars that started that summer.

I remember being amazed in the spring of 1991 that no one
seemed shocked at their aggressive seizure of public space in the very
center of Belgrade. I was amazed that no veterans of the partisan war,
with their experiences of Chetnik crimes and collaboration, contested
the space or protested. They did not, and the reason was shocking:
all allies were apparently now acceptable in the fight against Albanian "separatists" and Croat "Ustaše." A united front of the old
Communist hard-liners and neofascist Chetniks was visibly on the
way. The chickens came home to roost in the elections in Serbia in

December 1992 when to the shock of the Belgrade political public Šešelj's vicious neofascist party won over 25 percent of the vote. Serbia had produced the highest neofascist vote in all of Europe, East or West! This truly traumatized my friends in the opposition in Belgrade who had still desperately clung to the idea that somehow Serbia, because of its (somewhat mythified) democratic tradition, would be better than Croatia. This simply was not the case — the Croat neofascists got less than one-quarter of the vote their Serbian equivalents had gotten. This rise of national socialism in Serbia would separate friends and relatives in the next two years, much as the rise of the Nazis had earlier.

The Swedish Institute of the Workers' Movement (later renamed the Olof Palme Center) had given me a modest grant to try to help democrats and social democrats in Yugoslavia through a project optimistically called "Transitions to Democracy in a World Perspective."[1] The grant made it possible for me to provide minimal material aid — like fax machines and the means to produce a newsletter (in English) — to the democratic left in a disintegrating Yugoslavia. We also organized meetings with new independent unionists in the media and shipyards and among teachers in Croatia and Serbia. During this period, I spent most of my time in Croatia.

From Democratic to Social-Democratic Opposition

As the war spread in the late summer of 1991, the UJDI became an anachronism. Most of our members turned to organizing social-democratic parties in their respective republics. If Yugoslavia was to come apart, we wanted to make sure that our new states were democratic, had reasonable social programs, and were open to cooperation across the new borders. Most of us believed that this could best be done by organizing new social-democratic parties and unions because that would be the only way to organize broadly and compete against authoritarian populism and nationalism. Most of my friends in Macedonia and Slovenia remained in the reformed former Communist parties, which in those two states had evolved into genuine social-democratic organizations.[2] Because of their profound suspicions of politics and political organizations, many of the younger intellectuals preferred to work with social movements, which in practice meant ecological, women's, and peace groups. An important group in Belgrade around the Democratic Reformist party, led by Vesna Pešić, argued that it was premature to raise leftist political issues in Serbia because the most urgent goal was to establish peace, minimal democratic norms, a law-abiding state, and human rights.[3] The advocates of these various views continue to cooperate amicably to this day. I joined the Croatian Social Democratic Union (SDU), which was the result of a merger of the Reformist party established by the last Yugoslav premier Ante Marković, UJDI activists, and some independents. The SDU was led by Branko Horvat, arguably the leading democratic-socialist economist in Eastern Europe.

My personal position became even more uncomfortable after the right-wing nationalists won the first pluralist elections in Croatia. I was not only a Serb, but to make things worse, I was also an active and prominent participant in left-wing Croatian politics. However, this did not stop my political activities, and with some trepidation I ran as a candidate on the SDU list in the summer of 1992. Carrying a gun or having bodyguards seemed increasingly necessary during this time.

Paramilitary groups of urban lumpen types were increasingly visible on the streets of Zagreb and Belgrade during the spring of 1991. And it soon became a genuine issue whether or not to carry licensed arms. My friends and even a few friendly policemen on Brač recommended that I carry a gun when I was away from the island or speaking in small industrial towns and rougher neighborhoods. That would have been unimaginable during the long Titoist twilight.

The War in Croatia and the Media

By the fall of 1991 armed conflict in Croatia evolved from the local revolt by the Serbian minority into a brutal war of aggression by the Yugoslav army and the Serbian government. Communications between Croatia and Serbia were cut; travel and phone messages between eastern and western parts of former Yugoslavia now had to go through Hungary or Bosnia. As the war in Croatia accelerated, the democratic opposition from the various republics still continued to organize roundtable meetings of the federal government and opposition, mostly in Sarajevo where we had mass support.

My own project pulled together a conference near the Hungarian border that fall with participants from the democratic opposition and some independent intellectuals, as well as democratic socialists from Western Europe, Russia, and Eastern Europe. We tried to make sense of what was happening and to work out some joint proposals. These were modest efforts to keep some kind of nonnationalist and democratic leftist community together. Old personal ties and friendships crumbled as many of the intellectuals I knew, as well as friends and family members, rallied to the defense of their own nation. The pressure to do so was immense.

Revived images in the media of the genocidal massacres of the Serbs in Croatia during the Second World War traumatized people who had seemed immune to nationalism. My Croatian friends were bombarded with pictures of burning cities, including Dubrovnik, which is a cultural icon, and the massive destruction of churches and monuments. Large numbers of refugees in both Croatia and Serbia made the suffering visible and immediate. Television on both sides has repeatedly shown horrendous pictures of massacred and mutilated bodies in vivid color. This reached a point where child psychologists in Belgrade and Ljubljana protested that children were showing massive war neuroses and fears. By the spring of 1992 television in Belgrade and Zagreb had become quite unbearable to watch, and the war had spread to Bosnia, where the relatively objective station run by the federal government from Sarajevo was an early casualty of the war.

The War in Bosnia and Politics in Croatia

The second Croatian elections took place in August 1992 while the new and even more brutal war in Bosnia had been raging for months. The ruling Croatian right-wing nationalists imposed an electoral law grossly tilted in their favor, but some of us still tried to negotiate a general coalition with other democratic leftists and the regional parties from Istria and Dalmatia in time for the election. The best that we could do was to have a joint democratic-socialist candidate for president who got a respectable 4.7 percent of the vote in a field of sixteen. We also helped elect five members from the regional parties in a parliament of 137.

We managed to campaign in the teeth of wartime nationalist hysteria and get a respectable hearing and very high visibility. Branko Horvat, Nikola Visković (a popular gadfly member of the outgoing parliament), and I campaigned in the media, temporarily accessible during the elections, and before grim audiences of unemployed workers and veterans from the Slavonian front. We received a surprisingly respectful hearing. I remember getting tremendous applause when I attacked President Tudjman of Croatia as a puffed-up provincial authoritarian, a former Communist general who had all of Tito's vices and not a single one of his virtues. There were innumerable threatening phone calls and depressingly much hate mail. But there were also warm letters from pensioners, school teachers, ordinary workers, and members of the traumatized Serbian minority who were grateful for the campaign.

A larger unified party of the democratic left should emerge soon in Croatia because much of what we predicted about the economy and politics unfortunately did happen. The economy continues going into a tailspin; there are endless financial scandals — more and more white Mercedes and BMWs move through streets that are full of the young unemployed, miserable pensioners, and abandoned veterans.

During the campaign the Croat government emphasized its support of an independent Bosnia against Serbian aggression. Yet it soon became obvious to all that the Croat authorities were involved in a scandalous plan to set up a separate Croat state in Bosnia and demand the partition of Bosnia on ethnic lines, much as the Serbs had done. However, the major aggressors have been the Serb nationalists and their paramilitaries; they have committed massive and well-documented atrocities and rape in order to drive Muslims and Croats from the parts of Bosnia they intend to annex. Nevertheless, Croat troops have also occupied large parts of Bosnia and have often fought the by now mostly Muslim troops of the Bosnian government. In 1993 fighting broke out between Muslims and Croats in Bosnia; the fighting was accompanied by atrocities on both sides.

Renewed attacks by the Croatian troops against the Serb rebels in the UN-protected zone have helped the regime tighten its stranglehold over the media. However, those attacks are also a warning about the fragility both of the Vance-Owen plan for Bosnia and of that plan's successor, the Owen-Stoltenberg plan. The new fighting in Croatia broke out because the Vance plan in Croatia was hardly worth the paper it is written on. The plan in Croatia presumed that after the UN guaranteed minority Serbian rights, the militias would be disbanded and disarmed and replaced by civilian police that would reflect the ethnic makeup of the area *before* ethnic cleansing. That is an absurdity. Without substantial international protection Croat policemen in the Serbian Kraina areas would be under attack the minute they left the police stations. Alternately, they would at best treat the local population the way the Israeli forces treat the hostile Arab majority in the Gaza Strip and West Bank. The difference is that these locals are armed. Neither alternative is a promising proposition for peace. The plan also assumed that the refugees would return to their homes safely — that is, the homes they have been burned out of and driven away from, often by their own neighbors — and that the major highways and railroads would be opened. Nothing of the sort was carried out, and the Croats finally lost patience and tried to open up the highways and free the hydroelectric dam.

The partition of Bosnia as proposed by the Vance-Owen and the Owen-Stoltenberg plans — a partition accepted shamefully by the Security Council and more ambiguously by the Clinton administration — will surely end in similar built-in provocations if no effective enforcement mechanism is proposed. Further, the partition is grossly unjust to the Muslims. Although they are 44 percent of the population and the Croats are only 16 percent and the Serbs 32 percent, the Muslims are given the same number of provinces (3) as the other groups. Large Muslim minorities are given to Catholic Croat nationalists and Orthodox Serb nationalists to administer. The reverse is not the case although the Bosnian Muslims have a far better record in treating minorities than either the Croats or Serbs.

As noted earlier, no provision has been made for the large number of people who chose not to join any of the three tribes, who described themselves as Yugoslavs, who are secular cosmopolitans, or who are children from secular mixed marriages. These were the dominant populations of the cities. The Vance-Owen proposals were a shamefully unjust approach to the problems caused by the murder of the viable multiethnic political community of Bosnia. The revised Owen-Stoltenberg proposal, offered in the summer of 1993, was, if anything, worse.

The Bosnian Muslim leaders have insisted on a unified multiethnic

Bosnian state belonging to all of its citizens. In that they have had the support of the leftist and democratic groups in the Serbian and Croatian communities. That democratic project has now been drowned in blood and atrocities that the chauvinist Serbian and Croatian barbarians claim reveal that people of different ethnic or, as in this case, religious backgrounds cannot live together. Western Europe and the United States stood by and let Bosnia be devoured by murderous nationalist authoritarians, thereby giving a signal to all such in Eastern Europe and the former Soviet Union that they can do likewise and get away with it. The new Owen-Stoltenberg proposals simply proposed to legalize the rape of Bosnia.

Both Serbian and Croatian nationalist myths emphasize the centuries of wars against the Ottoman Turks. Muslim Slavs, ethnically and linguistically identical to the Croats and Serbs, are somehow transformed into the legendary Turkish enemy and made to pay for the years of Turkish dominance. Given that most urban "Muslims" are secular and culturally indistinguishable from their Serbian and Croatian neighbors, I find this hard to understand.

Unlike most North American intellectuals, most Europeans, especially East Europeans, do not accept a multicultural and multiethnic environment as normal; only consciously internationalist and cosmopolitan Europeans do. Internationalism was always very fragile in the socialist movement: the Communists turned into a caricature of Soviet patriotism in the countries of Eastern Europe. Writers like E. P. Thompson have long stressed the intimate link between communitarian localism and class consciousness. And yet during the years I have lived and worked in Yugoslavia, it had seemed that a new, heterogeneous, popular culture was emerging among the young and among the urban workers. Multiethnic Sarajevo was the major source of popular music and culture. The current wave of nationalism strikes me as the revenge of provincial language and history teachers and all who insist that they must preserve that which is specific to their nation. The war in Bosnia is obviously also an urbicide — cities have been relentlessly bombed into shambles. This is the revenge of the local red-necks who have always hated the cities. The cities are where massive intermarriage and denationalization take place, where various national groups mix and make friends, where women enter professions, where the young reject tradition. They are seats of political authority and the source of modernity. The villagers have always hated and envied the cities, and this war permits the destruction of these dangerous places.

The major responsibility for the destruction of Yugoslavia clearly lies with the Communist leadership of Serbia, which rather than face democratization, which became all but inevitable in the late 1980s, turned to mobilization of national chauvinism in order to create a new post-Communist popular base for their authoritarian rule. The Serbian mobilization of nationalist passion through mass rallies and absolute control of the mass media destroyed Yugoslavia because it drove the other national groups into the arms of their own nationalist leaders. Rather than stay in a Yugoslavia ruled by Serbia, the other republics chose independence. Rather than accept the independence of Croatia and Bosnia with substantial Serbian minorities, the Serbian regime chose war in order to redraw the political boundaries. Its demand that all Serbs live in one state is absurd given how intermixed the populations are. In this day and age it is also anachronistic — I have never heard a reasonable German complain about the fact that Germans live in Austria, Switzerland, and Luxembourg. It would be reasonable for the Serbian leaders to demand international guarantees that their fellow nationals be treated decently and be given full civic and citizenship rights in non-Serbian states. Unfortunately the Serbian leadership cannot do this because it is not ready to extend the same rights to its own large and restless Albanian minority. An election in Serbia in December 1992 gave almost 30 percent of the vote to an openly chauvinist and fascist party and its allies. All of this simply underlines how essential for democracy and human rights it is that states be defined as states of all of their citizens rather than as national states of the dominant national group.

Being a citizen of Yugoslavia had meant to me being a member of a very heterogeneous community, an interesting community that permitted a wide range of ways of being a citizen. The new identities we are now forced to assume are so much narrower, more parochial, and less flexible. A bridge between the old and new civic identities is only partially created by the intentional community of the democratic-socialist movement. I now feel personally poorer, and I believe many citizens of former Yugoslavia feel the same.

Postscript:
Fall 1993

ETHNIC NATIONALISM
AS IT REALLY EXISTS

Those of us who are by origin from the general area of the Balkans
(that is, Balkanites) are often irritated when the historical divides between Europe and Byzantium or between Catholicism and Islam are
invoked by "Western" commentators to explain the crimes, furies,
and carnage released by ethnic nationalism in Bosnia or the atrocities
committed during the conflict in Croatia. That is an easy and irresponsible way to blame the victims of the scandalous role that the
European Community and the United States have played in the death
of Yugoslavia and the murder of Bosnia. Some of us even consider
ourselves to be more Western, in terms of political and cultural values, than these commentators. And we believe ourselves to be more
Western in that specific sense than, let us say, the National Fronters
in England, Basque ETAers, IRA and Protestant extremist killers in
Ulster, and neo-Nazis and racists in the United States, not to mention
various chauvinist, quasi-fascist nationalist parties, movements, and
grouplets in Western Europe and the United States. It all depends on
what one considers to be the genuine values of Western political culture in this day and age. The West, indeed, has an ambiguous history
and tradition in this respect.

186

Ethnic Chauvinism: Not an East European Product

One could easily argue that racism and ethnic chauvinism have historical roots in the Western tradition. That rootage is one of the major reasons (reflexive anti-Communism being the other) there was so much understanding and tolerance for the vicious chauvinism of the anti-Communist, right-wing exiles and for the nationalist, post-Communist regimes that arose in the ruins of former Yugoslavia and the former Soviet Union.

"Scientific" (or better, "scientistic") racism and ethnic chauvinism are genuine Western European products and a part of the major current of the development of social and political ideas. Racial or ethnic theories of nationalism are relatively recent. They are not to be confused with the explicitly racist theories of Gobineau and Chamberlain or the more benign, romantically inspired ideas of Herder and the brothers Grimm, with their celebration of the folk. *Nationalism,* as distinct from patriotism, has its roots in the nineteenth century and did not really become a major force until the end of that century. One can argue that its course of development parallels and interacts with that of the mass socialist movement.

Nationalism, as Benedict Anderson argues, posits the centrality of *imagined communities,*[1] or rather, as he cogently put it, "imagined political community — and imagined as both inherently limited and sovereign."[2] His point, which is similar to the one made by Ernest Gellner and others, stresses that the national community in question is subjectively imagined in ways that have little to do with objective history or real attributes. Such an imagined community, again following Anderson, is *limited* because outside that community lie other nations; it is *sovereign* because it strives for the freedom of the nation to be realized in a sovereign state. But this makes nationalism a modern category, no older than the notion of the sovereignty of a people as distinct from the legitimacy of hereditary dynastic rule. After all, dynastic rule was more often than not nonnational, as was the feudal system itself. Nationalism, when ethnically defined, ascribes boundaries that designate who is and who is not a member of the *political* nation, the political community to which sovereignty belongs. Once it does so it *may* also define broader or narrower rights for those who are not members of that national community but who reside within the borders of the national state belonging to the political nation.

Such rights for resident foreigners have a long and varied history, but one thing is clear: they cannot be equal with those of the citizens who are members of the political nation.

Racism and ethnic chauvinism in the history of political thought in the United States and Western Europe are well documented (books on American racism have been a minor industry for decades). It takes little effort to dig up endless quotations, laws, and works that reveal that in the not very distant past this racism and ethnic chauvinism were even quite "politically correct" in the United States and Western Europe. Racism and ethnic chauvinism were also found on the left: Jack London left the Socialist party because it objected to his explicit notion that socialism was for the white workingman only. He was not alone: many trade unions were openly racist; most supported racist, anti-Chinese laws at the beginning of this century; many remain racially exclusionary to this day. It is hardly necessary to emphasize here that Hitler came to power in Germany, a nation celebrated for its contributions to Western culture.

Racial chauvinism was quite explicit in both Theodore Roosevelt's neo-Darwinian imperialism and Woodrow Wilson's treatment of African Americans. Under the former, the last African-American fighting unit of the U.S. Army was ignominiously dissolved. Under the latter, racial segregation in the nation's capital reached new lows. More to the point, there was no outcry in either case from an outraged public. A public holding truly democratic and ethnically egalitarian principles hardly existed at all and was rare even on the left. Most social scientists and the educated public took it for granted that mass intelligence testing of U.S. Army draftees during the First World War *proved,* scientifically no less, that Italians, Greeks, Latin Americans, East Europeans, and Jews were intellectually inferior to Americans from northwestern Europe. The inferiority of African Americans was simply assumed. In New England, French speakers and Portuguese were numerous enough to constitute an ethnic "other" and were also widely defined as stupid, dirty, and unreliable. Ethnic chauvinism played an explicit role in the sentencing of Sacco and Vanzetti — the sentencing judge even said so, using a vulgar chauvinist epithet. Ironically enough, today theories of racial and ethnic specificity or "mentalities" are openly propounded by "essentialists" in African-American studies.

Mass violence and brutality against others do not, however, have to be based on notions of ethnic nationalism or historical grievances. The outsider can be defined in other than ethnic ways. There is little evidence, for instance, that the images Serbs, Croats, and Muslim Slavs have of each other attribute racial or ethnic inferiority to those whom they are fighting or persecuting. After all, they are all of the same ethnic origin and use the same language. No one denies that the ancestors of the Muslim Slavs were either Serbs or Croats before they converted to Islam. Ethnic chauvinism is no more or less present among groups of British soccer fans fighting one another than it is in Croatia, Bosnia, or Serbia. In fact, the first armed paramilitary groups formed in the Yugoslav states were recruited from the soccer fans who already had a history of fighting all and sundry, not too different from the British soccer club fans. The difference was that in former Yugoslavia the new political elites (post-Communist former Communists) who chose to mobilize support with nationalist legitimation *armed* their thugs. Most of these were as little "historically shaped" as most individual British soccer gang members, whom they matched in loutish illiteracy. Intellectuals, or at least semi-intellectuals, particularly those local historians, ethnographers, journalists, novelists, and poets whose turf was defined by the boundaries of their national language or a specific local variant of a language, were generally the real believers and spreaders of the nationalist myths. Such beliefs are hardly uppermost for the combatants in the civil wars, who are often quite open about their own motives for fighting, which are similar to those of postdisaster looters. That is, their motives are greed, settling real or imagined accounts, and wielding, for once in their alienated lives, some visible and frightening power over unarmed, helpless others.

No Winners in Former Yugoslavia

Rebecca West's flawed masterpiece, *Black Lamb and Grey Falcon,* seems to continue to fascinate a host of Western authors writing about the present-day Yugoslav tragedy. But West wrote from a point of view that was almost completely pro-Serbian and strongly pro-Yugoslav. That is, her guide, "Constantine," was Vinaver, a brilliant Serbian nationalist of Jewish origin who managed to convince her that Islam had been an unalloyed catastrophe in the Balkans. He also helped convince her that the Croats were hopelessly corrupted by years of culturally shallow and morally bankrupt Austrian rule, and that only the Serbs, rooted in a vibrant Byzantine and pristine national tradition, could save a Yugoslavia that would represent a barrier to the pernicious eastward march of Germanic culture, commerce, and power. This march presumably threatened the Western European liberal democracies and had to be opposed.[3] (Echoes of this idea are heard among lovers of conspiracy theories even today.) This notion of the Serbs as a bulwark against such threats was what made saving Yugoslavia important for some people. It was also dangerous nonsense, for it was Serbian hard-fisted domination of the first Yugoslav state that made it an all-too-ready victim of Nazi Germany and fascist Italy.

Serbian centralist rule also helped foster a vicious, defensive Croatian chauvinism and native fascism that make the creation of a democratic Croatian state today so difficult. Tom Nairn and others to the contrary, a large majority of Serbs in Croatia today do not live anywhere near the old military frontier (the Kraina). They are, therefore, quite sensibly frightened of becoming second-class citizens in a Croatian state run by right-wing nationalists and leavened by returned fascist exiles and young semieducated ultras who combine body building and skinhead viciousness with a nostalgia for a distorted Ustaše past. For the Serbs in Croatia, then, there are only three possible solutions: immigration into a desperately poor and increasingly less hospitable Serbia; moving to a Kraina that is run by political thugs and whose political future is very much in doubt; or the victory of nonnationalist democratic forces in Croatia.

The first two are *personal* solutions, and they are enthusiastically encouraged by Croatian right-wingers because the result would be a Croatia ethnically cleansed of Serbs. The last solution requires the self-mobilization of Croatian nonnationalist democrats on the basis that it is in their own interest to live in a decent country that can call on the patriotism of all of its citizens irrespective of ethnic origin. In such a civic state both individual and collective human rights would be protected, including broad cultural autonomy for those members of the minorities who seek it. But that most desirable outcome is one to which Serbs in Croatia can contribute in only a minor way, for such an outcome depends on the problematic prospects of democracy in Croatia.

Contemporary ethnic chauvinism insists that individual citizens are not responsible for solely their own actions; rather, individual citizens are seen as existing essentially as members of "real" — that is to say, "ethnic" — national communities and thus share in collective responsibility for the actions of the leaders or sections of that community.[4] Therefore, it becomes completely logical for some Croats to persecute peaceful Serbian citizens of Croatia for what their rebellious fellow nationals have done to other Croats. This was even explicitly stated by the *zupan* (governor) of Zupania, an eastern Croatian district. "It is intolerable that there are Serbs who are living quite normally in Croatia today," he pronounced. Presumably he believes something should be done about that intolerable situation, and many superpatriotic Croat nationalists will presumably see to it. But this local politician was not alone. Alas, he is all too typical of the new little men whom the post-Communist nationalist wave has tossed into power. His type will be found throughout the states that have emerged from the wreckage of Yugoslavia, and for that matter throughout the former Soviet Union.

The Croatian people are clearly major losers in the destruction of Yugoslavia. This is a taboo topic in Croatia because the gain of national independence (a "thousand-year dream") is supposed to be so great an achievement that it is unpatriotic to question the price. The price, however, has been paid on many levels. In terms of economics, the way independence was achieved and the war that inevitably followed created a financial catastrophe for all but a small band of speculators, black marketers, and people with political connections to the ruling party and the right-wing émigré community. Incomes have dropped to a fraction (perhaps a quarter) of what they were before the war. An immense amount of industrial and tourist capacity was destroyed by the war of aggression of the Yugoslav army, and probably even more was destroyed by the criminal process of "privatization" that shamelessly robbed Croatia of much of its industrial wealth. To compound the trouble, hundreds of thousands of refugees, who will never be able to return home because their homes no longer exist, will be a massive burden on the economy for decades. They will also be an irredentist factor skewing Croatian politics to the right for a long time. In terms of politics, independence has relegitimated fascist and near-fascist political forces reveling in nostalgia and symbols of the 1941–45 period. This permeates and corrupts po-

litical and cultural life and is so uncontrolled that it has resulted in
Croatia losing almost all the international sympathy it had earned
as the victim of the savage destruction of Vukovar and the bombing
of Dubrovnik. The barbarism of Croatian troops in Bosnia, the destruction of Mostar, concentration camps, and ethnic cleansing have
equated the Croat political establishment in Croatia and above all in
Bosnia with the much more massive crimes committed by the Serbian
regime and its Bosnian surrogate. It will take decades before Croatia
recovers from the poison fruits of independence obtained within the
framework of an ethnically national state. There was nothing whatsoever inevitable about this. This is a catastrophe created by human
beings, and the first Croatian president, Franjo Tudjman, will not be
treated kindly by future Croatian historians.

As I have said above, there is no question but that Yugoslavia,
particularly the Yugoslavia of the almost confederal constitution of
1974, had been a much lesser evil. That semiconfederal Yugoslavia,
however, was no longer on offer by 1988–89 because of the destructive mobilization of massive Serbian chauvinism by Serbia's present
president, Slobodan Milošević.

Milošević will go down as a highly successful and cunning politician who brought untold misery and destruction to the Croats,
repression to the Albanians in Kosovo, and near genocide to the
Bosnian Muslims. He did all this while destroying Yugoslavia. It is
already clear, however, that the greatest damage he has done has
been to the Serbs themselves. The Serbs in Serbia and in the other
states of former Yugoslavia will be paying for decades for their murderous nationalist and chauvinist celebration and disgraceful love
affair with Milošević and fascist killers and war criminals like Vojislav Šešelj, Arkan, and the Bosnian Serbian junta. Both the innocent
and guilty will be paying, but the innocent will be paying more because many of the guilty have looted all there was to loot in Serbia
and Bosnia and have prepared retreats in friendly places like Greece
and Cyprus. Under Milošević the Serbian economy became a basket
case. Per capita wages and pensions dropped from some place around
$4000 to $120! Tens of thousands of talented young people have
left the universities, institutes, and research centers and will probably never return. The reputation of Serbia as the center of liberal and
democratic thinking in old Titoist Yugoslavia has been completely
obliterated by an unprecedented level of conformist compliance with

the nationalist celebration of primitive xenophobic fantasies. The Serbian intelligentsia proved unable to organize even a minimally effective opposition to the repression in Kosovo and mass slaughter and rape in Bosnia. The shame for the failure of the opposition has driven most intellectuals out of politics completely and will poison political life in Serbia for decades, making the work of those few courageous enough to attempt to build a decent antinationalist opposition even harder.

Milošević has succeeded in impoverishing his nation and making it the pariah of Europe and the world community. The tragedy did not result, however, simply because Milošević was more skilled than his opponents in the brutal game of Balkan politics and deceit. This skill of his has, indeed, been a curse for Serbia, and it will not recover for generations. And yet, others are also at fault: this tragedy could have been prevented with early and energetic intervention from the European Community and the United States.

Most contemporary Bosnians are urbanites on whom the primacy of national identity was forced by a bankrupt political class, first Communist and then post-Communist. By voting for the social-democratic reformists or for the former Communists, 28 percent of Bosnians voted against all nationalist parties. The reformists won the elections in Tuzla and the center of Sarajevo. They still hold power in Tuzla. More than 25 percent did not vote at all, and a substantial number who did vote for the Serbian, Croatian, and Muslim parties did not expect their vote to result in either a partition or a civil war. Huge demonstrations for peace took place in Sarajevo just before the Serbian aggression began the war. A few Serbian sniper mercenaries shot at the demonstrators.

Why on earth, then, do so many — like U.S. Secretary of State Warren Christopher, the spokespersons for the UN, and Vance, Owen, and Stoltenberg — keep insisting that the various ethnic nationalist leaders represent a majority of the Bosnian population? There is absolutely no hard evidence to prove that proposition. A great deal of evidence exists to the contrary. Could it be that the existence of a substantial body of citizens who did not fit neatly into the three tribal flocks would be inconvenient because they would make the partition of Bosnia an obvious outrage? This is, indeed, the very outrage that the entire international community, led by the United States, seems bound and determined to impose on the hapless citizens and government of Bosnia. Presumably this plan is supposed to make the world forget the genocide of the Muslim Slavs as a viable community. Of course that is a delusion — the problem will not be that easily disposed of. Not only will over three million of these miserable refugees haunt Western Europe and the world community, but almost certainly a bitter terrorist war of revenge will keep the Bosnian issue alive well into the twenty-first century. At a time when there appears to be some hope that the Palestinian problem might move toward a solution in the Middle East, Europe and the United States have helped create a similar problem right in the Middle of Europe.

No group will come out of the Bosnian catastrophe with its honor intact. The mass murderers of the Serbian and Yugoslav government and armed forces, their Croatian accomplices, and the local Bosnian surrogates of Belgrade and Zagreb are obvious culprits. Their policies of mass murder, "ethnic cleansing," and rape have been documented all too well. By 1993, reports of Croats massacring Muslims and driving them into concentration camps made it clear that morally there was little to chose from between the Serbian and Croatian aggressors, in Bosnia at least. The Bosnian government contributed its little bit through its incompetence and lack of clear goals, but it was obviously primarily the victim. What are we to say about a U.S. policy, in both the Bush and Clinton administrations, that, on the one hand, encouraged the Bosnians to keep fighting and dying, dangling promises of aid, and, on the other hand, cravenly escaped taking any steps that might actually have stopped the carnage? How about the European Community that piously kept insisting that every means, short of force, should be used to get food, fuel, and medicine to cities suffering medieval siege in the heart of Europe?

By November 1993, Senator Robert Dole was calling for an investigation of the increasingly well-documented claim that UN food and fuel aid was being manipulated to pressure the Bosnian government to accept a partition of Bosnia, a scenario in which the results of Serbian and Croatian aggression would be recognized not only by the world community, but also by the victims.[5] In particular, the charge was that the UN was deliberately not stockpiling food, medicine, and fuel in Sarajevo and other Bosnian cities, this in order to make it clear to the Bosnian forces that they could not survive another winter of sieges without catastrophic casualties. The UN thus became an accomplice in the murder of Bosnia. Most of the food was provided by the United States, yet U.S. officials not only did not protest UN efforts to prevent the Bosnian government from stockpiling food and other supplies for the winter; those officials also classified the relevant documents to provide a cover-up. Further, Fikret Abdic's rebels, who are fighting against the Bosnian government in the Bihac area, were supplied with fuel and food.[6] The French troops within the UN forces even built a pipeline to ensure delivery of such supplies. All this to pressure the Bosnian government to sign its own death warrant.

The UN — which gave its peace-keeping forces an impossibly limited mandate that prevented them from shooting back when shot at and forbade them to defend the civilian victims of mass rape and murder — did not cover itself with honor in this mission. This failure to develop an effective UN role in Bosnia and Croatia, despite the great cost involved, will set back the development of genuine international peace-keeping forces for decades.

There were many alternative policies that the UN, the United States, and the European Community could have pursued. And here we must remind ourselves that the limitation of the powers of the UN forces is mostly the result of U.S. and West European policies, just as the passivity of the European Community and NATO is in good part, although not exclusively, the result of the absence of an energetic and clear U.S. policy. Arms could have been made available to the legitimate government of Bosnia to enable it to fight against the aggressors. There could have been air attacks on the Serbian artillery positions from which Sarajevo has been shelled for almost two years. Even if all the positions had not been taken out, the air attacks still would have been a clear message to both the aggressors and victims. Croatia could have been threatened with sanctions if it did not stop carving an independent state of "Herzeg-Bosna" out of Bosnia. Above all, the United States could have mobilized its own powers and those of its West European allies to stop the war. That would have been a message to all — and there are many — who want to use the Bosnian "method" to deal with inconvenient demographic facts.[7]

Nationalism: Delusions and Realities

Many Western liberal or even leftist analysts seem still to believe that nationalism (*their* decent and democratic nationalism to be sure —

not the existing, ugly, bloody, soiled, and real-life thing) represents authentic democracy. They have not gotten over their sentimental and uncritical love affair with the national liberation movements in the Third World or the nationalists of the "submerged" nations of Western Europe.[8] This spurs them to write all manner of god-awful stuff. For instance, in an article entitled "We Are All Bosnians Now," Thomas Nairn writes: "Democracy is people power. And in this region people are primarily communities, the democratic impulse is strong but also collective, ethnic rather than individual or abstract."[9] But democracy, as we should know by now, must be more than the untrammeled rule of a mob. It must, certainly, include the right of individuals to organize collectively along class or national lines. But it must also include individual rights and the right to choose not to be a part of a collectivity; and, in particular, it must include the right of individuals and minorities not to be a part of the national collectivity, particularly the national collectivity as defined by the momentary nationalist leaders. Individual freedom and rights of minorities are threatened even further when national and religious identities are combined, as secularists in Ireland and Israel know all too well. In the case of Israel, the religious establishment defines who is and is not a Jew and thus who is and is not a full citizen of the state. This should be intolerable in a democracy and in a situation where in reality a large proportion of the Jews are secular. The minority has in this case been allowed to tyrannize the majority.

It is the failure to understand this principle that has made a settlement in Northern Ireland so difficult. Does being Irish necessarily have to mean being Catholic or subject to explicitly Catholic laws on matters like divorce, abortion, and the place of religion in schools? Can one today be a full *citizen* of Croatia and not be a Croat? Can a non-Muslim be an equal citizen in an Islamic state? How about someone who is an atheist but is of Muslim origin? Can non-Serbs (who constitute over 30 percent of the population of Serbia) be equal citizens with Serbs in a state that defines itself as the national state of the Serbs and uses the exclusive, emotion-laden symbols of Serbian history (often a version concocted by the nationalists themselves) and the Serbian Orthodox church in public institutions and schools? Those types of issues, not in the least bit specific to former Yugoslavia, make the revival of ethnic nationalism as a major factor in mass politics so problematic and dangerous to democracy today.

Further, there is the problem of defining present-day, really existing nationalism. It will not do to invoke Mazzini and the liberal nationalism of the nineteenth century[10] or for that matter the nationalism of the national liberation movements. Those movements in the Third World also had problems with concepts of democracy, but those problems were of a different sort. Present-day nationalism, particularly in Eastern Europe and the former Soviet Union, stresses the centrality of the imagined national community to political mobilization and action. It is not about cultural autonomy, the right to a national identity, or equal rights. More often than not it is about imposing a view, very often a minority view, of what the proper national (or religious) identity and language of all citizens living in a given territory must be. The imposition can be done administratively or even by force and terror. The IRA and Basque ETA are good examples of the latter. So are Muslim fundamentalists in many countries today.

In a world in which more and more people must live and work in countries where they were not born and where they constitute a national or ethnic minority, this new ethnic nationalism is an obvious threat to democracy. For one thing, it defines the citizens of the polity *ethnically* and therefore drives all others to become second-class citizens, or at best to assimilate. In most, though not all, cases, new ethnic nationalists do not permit just anyone to become a part of the politically dominant nation. Membership is open only to those who are born into it. Clearly this is incompatible with any notion of democracy that includes personal rights and freedom. But I will not cheat: it is not on those extreme examples that I base my basic argument that *today*, in an increasingly integrated and cosmopolitan world, ethnic nationalism is hostile to democracy and pluralist societies. Contemporary ethnic nationalism represents, in Benjamin Barber's phrase, a "jihad against McWorld." It is antimodern and antidemocratic in its basic impulse, and that is why it is attractive to the present postmodernist academic obscurantists. Decent democrats do not really belong in that company.

Ethnic nationalism today is the form of communitarian politics that is explicitly opposed to liberal-democratic concepts of *individual* rights. The ethnic community is defined as the only relevant unit when it comes to rights, grievances that need to be addressed, and representation. The ethnic group (sometimes a religious community), in counterposition to *intentional associations* (that is, communities that individuals associate with voluntarily, such as social and political movements, which make up the base of a civil society), is defined as the most relevant community, certainly the most *politically* relevant community. Therefore, modern nationalism in the form that it actually (not ideally) takes in most countries today represents a problem for democratic politics in a great number of places beside the post-Communist societies.

Confronting the Realities of Present-day Nationalisms

There are many who would claim that the above cases represent perversions of true nationalism and that *their* nationalism is a far better and nobler thing. That sort of caveat reminds me of Leszek Kolakowski's bitter prose poem *What Is Socialism?* (written when Kolakowski was still a socialist), which begins: "We will tell you what socialism is. But first we must tell you what socialism is not. . . . " After listing all that socialism is not, he ends: "That was the first part. But now listen attentively, we will tell you what socialism is: Well, then, socialism is a good thing."[11] Such was Kolakowski's way of adding to the debate on socialism.

In the United States today, there is widespread debate about the politics of cultural pluralism. On the left of that debate, there are many advocates of nationalism and politics of ethnic identity who are unaware of the real-life history and role of the concept of national identity. Too many go around saying that "their" nationalism — or at least the nationalism of oppressed groups — is a good thing. Like Kolakowski and "his" socialism, they are ready to explain what "their" nationalism is not. Their nationalism, of course, is not the nasty, real-life stuff practiced by new national states that have emerged out of the debris of late Communism; it is not the nationalism of the Croat regime that represses all independent press and massively denies citizenship to non-Croats; it is not the nationalism of the Latvian regime, or the Estonian regime, or the Georgian, Armenian, and Azerbaijanian regimes, all of which yearn for ethnically pure — or at least much purer — homelands and set about obtaining them by hook or by crook, bureaucratic repression or violence. The list — at each step undermining abstract notions of a good and pure nationalism — continues.

We have Russian and Serbian nationalisms, which are even more dangerous because they have more subject peoples and because the Russians and Serbs are far stronger militarily than their neighbors. The nationalists of both larger and smaller nations demand the right to deal with their own minorities the way they consider just. A grim reality here is that many of these "minorities" were only relatively recently transformed into minorities in lands where their ancestors have lived for centuries; these transformations have been accomplished administratively through the creation of new national states or by new policies adopted by the dominant national group. This is the case with Russians in the Ukraine, particularly in Crimea (which never was a part of the Ukraine until Khrushchev generously "gave" it to the Ukraine in the early 1960s); with Serbs in Croatia; with Muslims in Bulgaria; with various Transcaucasian peoples who found themselves on the wrong side of a previously "soft" frontier; with Russian and Ukrainian speakers born in Latvia and Estonia; and so on.

The right of self-determination in real life poses many complicated questions about national rights and the rights of fragments of nations distributed among many states. An example is the long-suffering Roms (Gypsies). Then, of course, there is the not so minor issue that the right of self-determination in sub-Saharan Africa could create dozens and dozens of new "nation-states," all of which would also have historical grievances, often against other peoples living among them.

The memory of the fate of Asians in East Africa, who for the most part had no other national home, should sober some of the advocates of unlimited self-determination for all. Then we have the nasty fact that India, Sri Lanka, Pakistan, Afghanistan, and Burma all have the potential for endless fragmentation into the many ethno-national groups of which they now consist. There is no possible consensus about frontiers or mutual responsibility for infrastructural assets that were jointly built. Do we favor the breakup of these states into new *imagined* national states? I write "imagined" because many are too small to survive except as some kind of Bantustan, and many are hopelessly ethnically mixed, no matter what their nationalists claim.

There are at least two additional problems. One is when the claim is for territories that used to be populated by the people in ques-

tion but that have in recent times changed demographically. This
applies, for example, to the Native American claims for parts of
the United States; to Basque claims for territories that are held by
Spanish-speaking peoples; to claims of Baltic nationalists against descendants of Russian post-1945 settlers; to the clashing claims for
Palestine; and to the "historical" claims of Serb, Hungarian, Croatian, German, and Polish nationalists. A second problem — seemingly
somewhat eclipsed for the moment — has to do with "submerged"
nationalisms. In the 1960s it was fashionable to back these nationalisms — that is, nationalisms that probably no longer had the support
of the majority of the people involved but were nevertheless passionately advocated (sometimes violently) by romantic minorities, often
including poets, linguists, and historians. Maoists had a weakness
for that sort of thing. These nationalisms may not be as much to the
forefront as they once were, but they continue to loom as problems.

Nationalism Jettisoning Democracy

In some of the richer regions of national — or multiethnic — states,
there is a "nationalism" based on resentments that "we" are being
unfairly taxed for "them," who usually breed too much and work
too little. An excellent example, mentioned earlier, is the case of the
Lombard Leagues, which want to stop paying for the south of Italy
and use an increasingly racist and nationalist language to insist on the
differences between the north and the south. There was a good bit of
that sort of thing in the language of the right-wing nationalist separatists in Slovenia and Croatia. I nevertheless believe that what really
broke up Yugoslavia was the aggressive national populism of Slobodan Milošević's Serbian regime with the help of the federal army. I
believe that until Milošević began his nationalist rampage in 1987,
no national group was repressed or exploited as a national group,
except the Albanians.

Today, after two aggressive wars — one waged against Croatia and the other against Bosnia — Yugoslavia is effectively dead.
However, it is not at all clear why a fight for separate states was
more logical than a fight for a democratic, multiethnic confederation
that might have avoided the worst of the carnage *and* provided a
sounder base for future development. The problem is that the sepa-

ratist minorities that took over Slovenia and Croatia wanted separate national states no matter what, and were not too concerned with democratic practices or legitimacy.[12] This poses a question: What if tomorrow, or ten years from now, a new narrow majority voted to reunite with other Yugoslav states? Why would that be a less legitimate decision? But clearly one cannot build and break up states at each election; therefore, one is constrained to ask: Should not constitutions make the act of separation a weighty and serious act that requires, let us say, two-thirds of the vote? But nothing of the sort happened in either the violent breakup of Yugoslavia or the nonviolent breakup of Czechoslovakia. In the latter case it was clear that large *majorities* on both sides of the new national divide were against breaking up the unified state, and yet an irresponsible political establishment was able to force the breakup. In what sense was this an advance for democracy?

Nationalism of Internal Oppressed Minorities

Another type of nationalist language and grievances is advanced by internal minorities like the African Americans, Native Americans, and Latin Americans in the United States. Some people on the left seem to assume automatically that this process is unquestionably good and involves sound demands leading to effective tactics. I think otherwise. I believe that broad civic solidarity — involving support by the majority of the population — is necessary in order to bring about the massive economic transformation necessary to establish minimal economic equality. To achieve that the most powerful claim is that of common citizenship in a common polity, that which we have in common not that which separates us. Without massive economic transfers and full-employment policies, which cannot be won without the support of majorities, competing ethnic claims become a deadly zero-sum game that the weaker and less numerous will almost always lose. And if for some reason they do not lose, a massive backlash of resentments can do long-range damage to any possibility of building majority-minority coalitions capable of maintaining economic justice.

The notion of historical grievances — often harbored by internal, oppressed minorities — leads us back to the post-Communist scenarios. There, the dangers of concentrating on historical grievances are pronounced. In chapter 5, I used the example of Transcaucasia, where one of the first effects of Gorbachev's glasnost was that for the first time in decades the expression of pent-up, age-old hatreds and grievances was permitted. These grievances were nursed by dissident intellectuals who were catapulted into power with the unanticipatedly rapid collapse of Communism. They represented the only non-Communist elites, and as such they had a totally disproportionate influence on the media and public opinion in the first post-Communist years. These intellectuals legitimated a renewed or reinvented ethnic nationalism and revived its traditional language of historical grievances. Because past wrongs cannot be righted, what has remained is vengeance.

Transcending Nationalism

The tragic death of Yugoslavia has shown that the existing international institutions, traditional diplomacy, and mechanical respect for national sovereignty are inadequate when it comes to dealing with the new post-Communist realities in Eastern Europe and the former Soviet Union. They do not really work in most of the world. They cannot stop civil wars and massacres. They were always inadequate. The end of the Cold War, however, creates an opportunity to begin imagining these forces in new and different ways. Given the situation in former Yugoslavia, one is particularly drawn to imagining a new and different UN. This would be a UN that began to develop its own armed and police forces capable of preventing the kind of catastrophes that occurred in Yugoslavia. This means a genuine international police force, a foreign legion in blue berets. When such peace forces moved into an area, like Bosnia, they would establish safe zones in all major cities, disarm the competing armies, and, after establishing minimal preconditions for this, hold supervised free elections. The newly elected officials would have gradually expanding authority backed up by a blue-beret force increasingly composed of locally recruited but UN-trained and UN-equipped police. The country would retain UN supervision of courts and police for a limited period, and then the UN presence would, like the proverbial Cheshire Cat, gradually vanish.

After an effective UN international police force was created, pressure for the disarmament of all national armies would increase because their purpose would no longer be clear. The UN force based on career professionals recruited for long-term service could be financed with a part of the savings from the reduction of armed forces of individual nation-states.

Historically, the left and nationalists competed for the same voters and supporters. But the left is today wounded and in a moral crisis. The tribes are mobilizing, and this is not a process that seems limited to any particular area of the globe. It is now at its most acute stage in Eastern Europe and the former Soviet Union. This mobilization is a dangerous and hollow substitute for democracy. It is also extremely dangerous for regional peace.

In order to fight this danger effectively it is essential to develop new notions of community: the community must be understood as being constituted by all citizens within the polity, and these citizens must be bound by some concept of common good. This kind of community cannot be created and maintained if a society is flooded with messages that stress a ruthless struggle for personal advancement and enrichment regardless of social costs. It cannot be created and maintained in a society in which social and economic differences are expanded and in which an increasing number of citizens are destined for permanent unemployment or marginal employment that keeps them below the poverty level, no matter how defined. It cannot be created and maintained in a society in which ever-larger numbers of the homeless become nonpersons, as we are told that it is not possible for the state to do anything for these fellow citizens in desperate need, and that to try to do something will only make things worse. In short, neo-Darwinian "cold" values stressing market egoism militate against building a democratic community of equal citizens. One cannot create a community bound by common universalist values if the stress is on consumerist values that define an ever-growing portion of the society as surplus outsiders. For an effective community to exist, some minimal notions of social equality are necessary. That means not only abolishing all discrimination based on socially defined ascribed characteristics, such as gender, race, or ethnicity, but also minimizing the social distance created by excessive differences in wealth and opportunity. Thus just as modern nationalism and socialism developed simultaneously and in interaction with each other, overcoming the imagined exclusive national communities requires creating an alternate voluntary community based on democracy and social justice. That remains the supreme democratic project for the twenty-first century.

NOTES

Introduction
The Relevance of the Death of Yugoslavia

1. Although the leaders of Serbia and its allied microstate of Montenegro claim to be the heirs of the old Yugoslav federation, it is reasonably clear that the present state calling itself "Yugoslavia" is a rump of the old one. All non-Serb republics — Slovenia, Croatia, Macedonia, and Bosnia-Herzegovina — have declared their independence and with the exception of Macedonia have been recognized by the international community and are members of the UN. Rump "Yugoslavia" now rules over the previously autonomous provinces of Kosovo and Vojvodina with only dubious legality, having abolished their autonomies. Practically speaking, "Yugoslavia" is only the extension of Serbia at this time.

2. *Kraina,* the Slavic word for the frontier, is also the basis for the name Ukraine (U-kraina), in its own language.

3. In fairness I should state that I had favored armed intervention against Serbian aggression as early as fall 1991. I argued at that time and since that had there been an early UN intervention the war would not have spread; Vukovar would not have been annihilated; and the war in Bosnia would never have taken place.

Chapter 1
Essential Background on Yugoslavia

1. The Serbian nobility — such as it was — had adapted very easily either by converting or by becoming "Uniate Catholics" — that is, Catholics who were allowed to keep the Orthodox Slavonic forms of the Mass and married priests in exchange for accepting the supremacy of the pope. There were recurrent efforts to force the Orthodox population in the empire as well as in the

Venetian possessions to convert to Uniate Catholicism. It took a great deal of stubborn resistance on the part of Serbian frontiersmen to keep their traditional religion, and because they were hardly theologically sophisticated, they clearly kept it in good part as a matter of communal identity.

2. External guarantees are needed because leaders of the new independent states that have arisen out of Yugoslavia, particularly Serbia and Croatia, lie without shame or measure when it comes to human and minority rights within their own borders. In this they are helped by a mostly tame press and opposition, which show almost no spine when it comes to criticism of their own nation's human rights record. This is particularly the case when minority rights are in question. Serbia is clearly more aggressive; Croatia equally clearly has even less free media.

3. *Yugoslav Survey* (Belgrade: Statistički Zavod, spring 1982), reporting on the 1981 census.

4. The republics and provinces are very uneven in size and population and not at all homogeneous in national makeup. In the following census figures from 1981, population figures are given in thousands; ethnic makeup figures, in parentheses, are percentages. Note that the Republic of Serbia includes the previously autonomous provinces of Vojvodina and Kosovo.

Republic/Province	Population	Ethnic Breakdown by Percentage
Bosnia-Herzegovina	3,941	Muslim (40); Serb (37); Croat (20); Other (3)
Montenegro	565	Montenegrin (67); Muslim (13); Serb (8); Albanian (7); Other (6)
Croatia	4,391	Croat (79); Serb (14); Other (7)
Macedonia	1,808	Macedonian (69); Albanian (18); Turk (6); Other (7)
Slovenia	1,838	Slovene (92); Croat (3); Other (5)
Serbia (with Provinces)	9,005	
Serbia, alone	5,491	Serb (89); Muslim (3); Albanian (3); Other (6)
Vojvodina	1,969	Serb (56); Hungarian (22); Croat (7); Other (14)
Kosovo	1,545	Albanian (85); Serb (9); Montenegrin (2); Other (4)

In Macedonia minorities were pressured to declare for the majority nationality. As usual, Gypsies are underreported. The complexity of the ethnic breakdown shows just how hard it was to even attempt to achieve any kind of "fair" distribution of posts by national criteria. This was a problem both on the federal level and in the individual republics.

5. From Vladimir Žjerjavić, *Gubici Stanovništva Jugoslavije u Drugom Svjetskom Ratu* (Population losses of Yugoslavia during the Second World War)

(Zagreb, 1941). I accept these as reliable figures. Žjerjavić's figures have been independently confirmed by a Serbian émigré demographer and by my own doctoral research in 1973.

6. A large bibliography on the Yugoslav war and revolution and on the collaboration and massacres exists. A good beginning would be with Jozo Tomaševich, *War and Revolution in Yugoslavia: The Chetniks* (Stanford, Calif.: Stanford Univ. Press, 1975), as well as his *War and Revolution in Yugoslavia: The Ustashe* (Stanford, Calif.: Stanford Univ. Press, 1978). Another useful source for that period is Robert Lee Wolff, *The Balkans in Our Time* (New York: Norton, 1956).

7. To be sure, both Serbs and Croats are fighting in Bosnia. Although the Croats' official claim is that they are fighting as allies of the independent Bosnian government, the fact remains that they fight under their own command and have created Croatian civil authorities and extended the use of Croatian currency to the area they control, roughly 32 percent of Bosnia. (They numbered around 17 percent of the population in 1992.) The Serbs are more clearly the aggressors and make no pretense to be operating under the authority of the Bosnian government. They control roughly 65 percent of the territory while representing only 33 percent of the population. The losers are clearly the Muslims (who are 42 percent of the population) and all urban dwellers who prefer to continue living in the historically ethnically mixed cities.

8. The European Free Trade Association (EFTA) consisted of some (mostly neutral) European countries that were not in the European Economic Community (EEC). The major countries in EFTA were Sweden, Switzerland, and Austria. EFTA was a perfect halfway house to the European Community. It was criminal vanity on the part of the Yugoslav Communist leaders and their gross overestimation of the importance of the nonaligned movement that kept Yugoslavia out of EFTA.

9. Probably the most balanced work in English on the recent history of East European nationalism is Ivo Lederer and Peter Sugar, eds., *Nationalism in Eastern Europe* (Seattle: Univ. of Washington Press, 1969). A more contentious work is Ivo Banac's *The National Question in Yugoslavia: Origins, History, Politics,* 2d ed. (Ithaca, N.Y.: Cornell Univ. Press, 1992); the first edition (1978) was (somewhat surprisingly, at the time) translated into Croato-Serbian by Globus in Zagreb (1986). On post–Second World War Yugoslavia, the soundest, though dated, work is George Hoffman and Fred Neal, *Yugoslavia and the New Communism* (New York: Twentieth Century Fund, 1962). Other works are Dennison Rusinow, *The Crisis in Croatia* (New York: American Universities Field Staff, 1972), and his more recent works such as "Unfinished Business: Yugoslav National Questions in the Tito Era and Beyond," in *American University Field Staff Reports* (New York: American Universities Field Staff, 1981). For other valuable information one should consult Ruza Petrović, "National Composition of the Population," *Yugoslav Survey* 24, no. 3 (August 1983); two works by Stipe Šuvar in Croato-Serbian, *Nacije* (Zagreb: Naše Teme, 1970) and *Medjunacijonalni Odnosi* (Zagreb: Naše Teme, 1970); and also Šuvar's collection of essays on the national question, *Nacije i Medjunacijonalni Odnosi* (Zagreb: Naše Teme, 1988). This all too brief list does gross injustices to many other worthy works, but will do for a start.

Chapter 2
What Happens When Ethnos Becomes Demos

1. By far the best study of the mass national movement in Croatia and its intricate and ambivalent relationship to the general problems of liberalization of Yugoslav-wide economic policies is Dennison Rusinow, *Yugoslav Experiment* (Berkeley: Univ. of California Press, 1974).

Chapter 3
Troubled Transitions:
Post-Communist Societies in Crisis

1. In Hungary, national populists have already begun attacking "cosmopolitan" (read Jewish, big-city) liberals over that precise issue. Similar national populist attacks on economic reforms, and on pluralistic democracy, with or without anti-Semitic subtexts, can be expected in Poland, Romania, and the Republic of Serbia in Yugoslavia.

2. Alec Nove's modest and reasonable book, *The Economics of Feasible Socialism* (London: George Allen and Unwin, 1983), represents an excellent antidote for the usual dogmas about the role of the plan and market in modern mixed economies.

3. Marxists have had real problems understanding the persistence of nationalisms. Tom Bottomore is right when he argues that "Marxists have contributed little in the way of analysis and research into these phenomena, and have indeed tended to ignore or dismiss them as being of minor significance" ("Sociology," in David McLelland, ed., *Marx: The First 100 Years* [London: Fontana, 1983], 140). Very good books are Ronald Munck, *The Difficult Dialogue: Marxism and Nationalism* (London: Zed Books, 1986); and Eric Hobsbawm's instant classic, *Nations and Nationalism since Seventeen Eighty: Programme, Myth, and Reality* (Cambridge: Cambridge Univ. Press, 1990).

4. This, for example, was the position of Hungarian nationalists throughout the nineteenth century: the Magyars were the "state people," and all others were only tolerated. To be sure, the Hungarians encouraged others to join the state people by becoming "Magyarized" — that is, by adopting the language and culture of the state people.

5. French historians made a useful distinction between *pays réel* (or the real country — the country of traditions, customs, folklore, local vernacular, and customary law, which is what people feel emotionally attached to) and *pays légal* (the legal country, or country of laws, which is the invented, formal, legal-rational state with its laws, official language, and bureaucratic, as against traditional, authority).

6. See Nove, *Economics of Feasible Socialism.*

7. Cited in *New York Times,* 13 December 1991, sec. D, p. 2.

8. Cited in *New York Times,* 18 December 1991, p. 20.

Chapter 4
Nationalism as the Nemesis of Democratic Alternatives

1. The areas inhabited by Albanians in Kosovo, southern Serbia, and Macedonia were conquered by Serbia during the Balkan War against Turkey in 1912, were reconquered in 1918, and were conquered once again in 1945. The large Albanian majority in Kosovo had opposed these conquests and had backed Turkey, Austria, and Italy in turn against Serbia and Yugoslavia. Application of the principle of self-determination would dictate that that area should have seceded long ago. Unfortunately for the Albanians, Kosovo is associated with the high points of Serbian medieval history and is the site of a number of important cultural moments and monasteries. Kosovo is therefore an icon of Serbian nationalism, despite the fact that less than 10 percent of the population is now Serb or Montenegrin.

2. The great exceptions were some of the Serbian nationalists who were for a Yugoslavia, but only one dominated by Serbia. This would have required an authoritarian regime because the Serbs, while the most numerous group, still constituted a minority in Yugoslavia even if the Montenegrins were included. This explains why there were endless arguments about the validity of the census and about whether or not the Muslims were a nation or simply Serbs suffering from false consciousness.

3. The Bulgarians do not recognize Macedonians as a national group in Bulgaria, which is consistent with their repression of the much larger Turkish minority as well. Macedonian is closely related to Bulgarian, almost like Serbian and Croatian, which always makes for trouble since "almost," it seems, is never enough. Greece has denied the Macedonians' existence as a national group and has suppressed the use of their language. It also denies visas to Yugoslav citizens who have been born in Aegean Macedonia. The fate of the Macedonian minority in Albania is grim, as is that of everyone else in Albania.

4. Whereas the membership of the LCY in Croatia as a whole for those over sixteen was 7.4 percent, the 15 percent Serbian minority accounted for 24 percent of the Croatian LCY membership. Incidentally, when the LCY was still in power, its membership varied sharply by republic for the over-sixteen population, thus: Kosovo: 5.6 percent; Slovenia: 6.5 percent; Macedonia: 7.2 percent; Croatia: 7.4 percent; Bosnia: 8.9 percent; Serbia: 9.5 percent; Vojvodina: 10.7 percent; and Montenegro: 12.4 percent. Source: *Statistical Herald of Yugoslavia* (Belgrade: Statistički Zavod, 1985).

5. So-called Muslim fundamentalists were a minor and marginal phenomenon, which did not stop the Bosnian courts from dealing out sentences in the early 1980s that should have outraged human rights advocates. Few human rights advocates in Serbia, Croatia, or Slovenia were heard from, although more vocal protest was heard when nationalist Catholic and Orthodox priests fell foul of the same laws. There was a double standard among Yugoslav human rights advocates when Muslims were in question.

6. The very influential work by Arend Lijhart, "Consociational Democracy," in Kenneth McRae, ed., *Consociational Democracy* (Toronto: McClelland and Stewart, 1974), stressed that fragmentation of a polity makes stability

and consensus possible because there is no possibility of majorities imposing their will on the rest. That may be a very desirable system for some under some circumstances, but democracy is hardly the name for such a system.

7. Regional differences in income per worker were increasingly in favor of Slovenia over the years. Thus the per capita gross national product (GNP) of Kosovo was 48 percent of the Yugoslav average in 1954, 33 percent in 1975, and 27.8 percent in 1980. The GNP of Slovenia was 188 percent of the Yugoslav average in 1954 and 201 percent in 1975. In short, by 1975 the Slovenian GNP was more than six times that of Kosovo or Macedonia.

8. For centuries the Turks recognized only religious groups as collective representatives of their subjects. These were given considerable autonomy but were not equal. The Muslims were at the top of the caste system. Orthodox Christians and Jews had a secure place within the empire. Catholics were suspect because Turkey warred for centuries with the Catholic Powers, and in any case the pope represented a hostile power.

9. For more specialized information and a general history, see Barbara Jelavić, *History of the Balkans*, 2 vols. (Cambridge: Cambridge Univ. Press, 1983). Even better is Rebecca West, *Black Lamb and Grey Falcon* (New York: Viking, 1940), although it suffers from a pro-Serbian slant.

10. Their Zagreb counterparts continued fighting Croatian nationalism to the end, sometimes almost single-handedly.

Chapter 5
No Democracy without Both Universalism and Modernity

1. To be sure, there are also democratic nonparliamentary means of mobilizing public opinion and changing laws: demonstrations, sit-ins, strikes, and hunger strikes all come to mind.

2. The best source on Ukrainian nationalism remains John A. Armstrong, *Ukrainian Nationalism* (New York: Columbia Univ. Press, 1963).

Chapter 6
Nationalism, Globalism, and Democracy

1. Of course not all are equally affected by the economic disaster that has overtaken most of former Yugoslavia, as has been pointed out by Mika Tripalo, who has said that while the people of Croatia have been reduced to the level of the population of Biafra, their leaders live like Emperor Bokassa (quoted from *Danas*, 24 March 1992).

2. *Relatively* is the key word here — that is, relative to the rest of Eastern Europe.

3. Benjamin Barber, "Jihad against McWorld," *Atlantic Monthly* (March 1992).

4. Witch-hunts against former Communists have been legislated in a number of East European states. An atmosphere hostile to former Communists and above all to the tradition of the partisan war of liberation has been encouraged by politicians and the mass media in many of the Yugoslav republics, sometimes by former Communists (who are now nationalists) still in power under very thin disguise.

5. The pathological suspicion and hatred of Muslim Slavs — who in no other respect except religious and cultural identity differ from their Serb, Montenegrin, and Croat neighbors — is worth a study in itself. It is close in character to anti-Semitism in countries where the Jews were culturally and linguistically assimilated to the majority (Germany and Austria). It also is rooted in the five hundred years of Turkish Muslim domination in the region and the centuries of near-genocidal war of *reconquisada* that was sanctioned by the Catholic and Orthodox churches and was mythologized through heroic epic poems and legends. It was an atavistic sentiment all too easy to mobilize among Serbs and Montenegrins. Repeated anti-Muslim statements by the Croat press and President Tudjman show that this sentiment is also present among the Croats. The victims, alas, are probably the most secularized Muslim population in the world.

6. That hostility was quite real in many social circles, but it nevertheless must not be forgotten that the Yugoslav Communists did respectably well in the first free elections in 1990 in *all* the republics, winning in three (Serbia, Montenegro, and Macedonia) and being the largest opposition party in two. Thus they did better than East European Communist parties on the whole. To be sure, continued evolution of the Serbian party turned it into a party that rejected the positive heritage of Yugoslav Communism while keeping only the link with the political police and the tendency to repressiveness.

7. For the life of me I cannot understand why the term *Byzantine* should be insulting. After all, through most of its history the Byzantine Empire was far more civilized, humane, and cosmopolitan than the contemporary "West," which was in its own barbaric Dark Ages during the flowering of Byzantine culture. In any case, through most of their independent history — that is, until they were conquered by the Hungarians — the Croats had intimate ties with Byzantium. The word probably became a term of abuse when used by the Catholic "Frankish" crusaders to justify their looting of Constantinople during the Fourth Crusade. Its reappearance in Croato-Serbian polemics is weird.

8. This information is based on my own lengthy interviews and conversations with former cabinet ministers and ambassadors of the federal government of Ante Marković. Through cross-checking I am convinced that it is true. Both the prime minister and the secretary for international affairs were among the first targets of the military "hards," during the first half of 1991.

9. A powerful argument to that effect is found in Barber, "Jihad against McWorld."

Chapter 7
A Personal Summary

1. The "world perspective" was initially provided by the Mexican and Egyptian institutes, which wanted to see what they could learn from the problems of transition to democracy in Yugoslavia and Eastern Europe. This formula also enabled West European social democrats to participate in some of our activities.

2. In both Slovenia and Macedonia these social-democratic former reform-Communist parties are now in coalition governments.

3. Vesna Pešić is now a major leader of the citizens' group that unites the leading opposition to Milošević's regime and provides backing for the more moderate federal prime minister Panić (a dual U.S.-Yugoslav citizen) and federal president Ćosić. The situation in Serbia is close to an internal civil war. It may still end with an army coup.

Postscript: Fall 1993
Ethnic Nationalism as It Really Exists

1. Benedict Anderson, *Imagined Communities,* 2d ed. (London: Verso, 1993). This is one of the absolutely indispensable books about modern nationalism. Others are: Ernest Gellner, *Thought and Change* (London: Weidenfeld and Nicolson, n.d.); Hans Kohn, *The Age of Nationalism* (New York: Harper and Row, 1962); and Hugh Seton-Watson, *Nations and States: An Enquiry into the Origins of Nations and the Politics of Nationalism* (Boulder, Colo.: Westview, 1977).

2. Anderson, *Imagined Communities,* 6.

3. Germany's clumsy diplomatic strong-arming of its West European partners for early recognition of Croatia seemed to confirm this long-lived conspiracy theory.

4. This is not at all limited to Eastern Europe. Nor is it limited to majorities in multiethnic societies. The assumption by many African-American nationalists that *all* whites are racists or that they are *all* responsible for racism is an illustration of this view. Clearly, "gender" exclusivists who argue that all males are sexists who long to rape are of a piece with that stereotyping mind-set. Catharine MacKinnon is a good example of the latter.

5. *News from Bob Dole, U.S. Senator from Kansas, Senate Republican Leader,* bulletin dated 4 November 1993.

6. See *Christian Science Monitor,* 8 October 1993.

7. An example is the Abkhasian "independence movement," which claims territories in Georgia, where the Abkhasians are only 17 percent of the population. The members of the movement apparently intend to "correct" this demographic inconvenience through "ethnic cleansing," Bosnian-Serb style.

8. The left had a great deal of uncritical sympathy for the Welsh, Scots, Breton, Occidant, Basque, Irish, and Catalan nationalisms in the 1960s. Some

of that is still around. The assumption was that these nationalisms represented the wishes of the local peoples; however, that assumption often had no foundation in fact. In that case, we were told that the people suffered from a false consciousness imposed on them by their colonizers.

9. Thomas Nairn, "We Are All Bosnians Now," *Dissent* (fall 1993).

10. This was a state-building, nonethnic nationalism that was mostly secular. This is why Jews could and did play such a major role in the national unification of Italy and why the Vatican opposed that unification.

11. Leszek Kolakowski, *What Is Socialism?* (n.p., 1956).

12. All opinion polls had shown that a minority was for secession in both Slovenia and Croatia before the war began. Even after the war, the ruling party in Croatia had only a plurality. It is an open question how much support the nationalists would have if peace were signed and they no longer had a monopoly of the media.

SELECT BIBLIOGRAPHY

Allworth, Edward, ed. *Ethnic Russia: The Dilemma of Dominance*. New York: Pergamon, 1980.

Anderson, Benedict. *Imagined Communities*. 2d ed. London: Verso, 1993.

Anderson, M. S. *The Eastern Question*. London: Macmillan, 1966.

Armstrong, John A. *Ukrainian Nationalism*. New York: Columbia Univ. Press, 1963.

Arnaud, Nicole, and Jacques Dofny. *Nationalism and the National Question*. Montreal: Black Rose Books, 1977.

Ash, Timothy Garson. *The Uses of Adversity: Essays on the Fate of Central Europe*. New York: Random House, 1989.

Banac, Ivo. *Eastern Europe in Revolution*. Ithaca, N.Y.: Cornell Univ. Press, 1992.

———. *The National Question in Yugoslavia: Origins, History, Politics*. 2d ed. Ithaca, N.Y.: Cornell Univ. Press, 1992.

Barton, Allen, Bogdan Denitch, and Charles Kadushin, eds. *The Opinion Making Elites of Yugoslavia*. New York: Praeger, 1973.

Bilandjić, Dušan. *Jugoslavija Poslije Tita*. Zagreb: Globus, 1986.

Bottomore, Tom. "Sociology." In David McLelland, ed., *Marx: The First 100 Years*. London: Fontana, 1983.

Burbank, Jane. *Intelligentsia and Revolution*. Oxford and New York: Oxford Univ. Press, 1986.

Burg, Steven I. *Conflict and Cohesion in Socialist Yugoslavia: Political Decision Making since 1966*. Princeton, N.J.: Princeton Univ. Press, 1983.

Carter, April. *Democratic Reform in Yugoslavia: The Changing Role of the Party*. Princeton, N.J.: Princeton Univ. Press, 1982.

Chirot, Daniel. *Social Change in the Twentieth Century*. New York: Academic Press, 1977.

———, ed. *The Crisis of Leninism and the Decline of the Left: The Revolutions of 1989*. Seattle: Univ. of Washington Press, 1991.

Cohen, R. S., and Mihailo Marković. *The Rise and Fall of Socialist Humanism*. Nottingham: Spokesman Books, 1975.

Dahl, Robert. *Democracy and Its Critics.* New Haven: Yale Univ. Press, 1989.

Denitch, Bogdan. *After the Flood: Politics and Democracy in the Wake of Communism.* Hanover, N.H., and London: Wesleyan Univ. Press, 1992.

———. "The Evolution of Yugoslav Federalism." *Publius* 7 (Fall 1977): 107–18.

———. *Legitimation of a Revolution: The Yugoslav Case.* New Haven: Yale Univ. Press, 1975.

———. *Limits and Possibilities: The Crisis of Yugoslav Socialism and State Socialist Systems.* Minneapolis: Univ. of Minnesota Press, 1990.

———. "Stability and Succession in Yugoslavia." *Journal of International Affairs* (Winter 1979): 223–38.

Di Palma, Giuseppe. *To Craft Democracies.* Berkeley: Univ. of California Press, 1990.

Djordjević, Dimitrije, and Stephen Fischer-Galati. *The Balkan Revolutionary Tradition.* New York: Columbia Univ. Press, 1981.

Drulović, Milojko. *Self-Management on Trial.* Nottingham: Spokesman Books, 1978.

Feher, Ferenc, and Agnes Heller. *Eastern Left and Western Left: Totalitarianism, Freedom, and Democracy.* New York: Humanities, 1987.

Feher, Ferenc, Agnes Heller, and George Marcus. *Dictatorship over Needs.* Oxford: Basil Blackwell, 1983.

Foucault, Michel. *Language, Counter-Memory, Practice.* Edited by Donald Bouchard. Ithaca, N.Y.: Cornell Univ. Press, 1971.

Giddens, Anthony, and David Held. *Classes, Power, and Conflict.* Berkeley: Univ. of California Press, 1982.

Glenny, Misha. *The Fall of Yugoslavia: The Third Balkan War.* London: Penguin, 1992.

Helsinki Watch. *War Crimes in Bosnia-Hercegovina.* New York: HRW, 1992.

Hobsbawm, Eric. *Nations and Nationalism since Seventeen Eighty: Programme, Myth, Reality.* Cambridge: Cambridge Univ. Press, 1990.

Hoffman, George, and Fred Neal. *Yugoslavia and the New Communism.* New York: Twentieth Century Fund, 1962.

Horvat, Branko. *ABC Yugoslovenskog Socijalizma.* Zagreb: Globus, 1989.

———. *Kosovsko Pitanje.* Zagreb: Globus, 1988.

———. *The Political Economy of Socialism.* Armonk, N.Y.: M.E. Sharpe, 1983.

Jackson, Richard. *The Nonaligned, the UN and the Superpowers.* New York: Praeger, 1983.

Jelavić, Barbara. *History of the Balkans.* 2 vols. Cambridge: Cambridge Univ. Press, 1983.

Kamenka, Eugene. *Nationalism.* Canberra: Australian Univ. Press, 1973.

Keane, John. *The Civil Society and the State.* London: New European Perspectives, 1988.

Kedourie, Elie. *Nationalism.* London: Hutchinson, 1960.

Kohn, Hans. *The Idea of Nationalism.* New York: Macmillan, 1945.

Konrad, George, and Ivan Szelenyi. *Intellectuals on the Road to State Power.* New York: Harcourt Brace Jovanovich, 1979.

Korač, Miladin. *Socijalisticki Samoupravni Sistem Proizvodnje*. Belgrade: Komunist, 1980.

Lederer, Ivo, and Peter Sugar, eds. *Nationalism in Eastern Europe*. Seattle: Univ. of Washington Press, 1969.

Lefebre, Henri. *De L'état*. Vol. 3 of *Mode de Production Étatique*. Paris: Éditions Inedit, 1978.

Lehmbruch, Gerard, and Phillipe Schmitter, eds. *Trends toward Corporatist Intermediation*. Beverly Hills, Calif.: Sage Publications, 1979.

LeoGrande, William. "Evolution of the Nonaligned Movement." *Problems of Communism* 29 (1980): 21–26.

Lerotić, Zvonko. *Nacela Federalizma Visenacionalne Države*. Zagreb: Globus, 1985.

Lewis, Paul. *Eastern Europe: Political Crisis and Legitimation*. New York: St. Martin's, 1984.

Lijhart, Arend. "Consociational Democracy." In Kenneth McRae, ed., *Consociational Democracy*. Toronto: McClelland and Stewart, 1974.

Lowenthal, Richard. *Social Change and Cultural Crisis*. New York: Columbia Univ. Press, 1984.

Magaš, Branka. "The Destruction of Bosnia," *New Left Review* 196 (1992).

———. *The Destruction of Yugoslavia: Tracing the Break Up, 1980–1992*. London: Verso, 1992.

Marković, Mihailo. *Democratic Socialism: Theory and Practice*. New York: St. Martin's, 1982.

Maurer, Paul. *United States–Yugoslav Relations: A Marriage of Convenience*. Bern: SOI Sonderdruck, 1985.

Milenković, Deborah. *Plan and Market in Yugoslav Economic Thought*. New Haven: Yale Univ. Press, 1972.

Miller, Norman, and Roderick Aya. *National Liberation*. New York: Macmillan, 1971.

Munck, Ronald. *The Difficult Dialogue: Marxism and Nationalism*. London: Zed Books, 1986.

Nord, Lars. *Nonalignment and Socialism: Yugoslav Foreign Policy in Theory and Practice*. Stockholm: Rabén and Sjögren, 1972.

Nove, Alec. *The Economics of Feasible Socialism*. London: George Allen and Unwin, 1983.

Palmer, John. *Europe without America: The Crisis in Atlantic Relations*. New York: Oxford Univ. Press, 1987.

Palmer, R. R. *The World of the French Revolution*. New York: Harper, 1971.

Pearson, Raymond. *National Minorities in Eastern Europe 1884–1945*. London: Macmillan, 1983.

Petrović, Ruza. "National Composition of the Population." *Yugoslav Survey* 24, no. 3 (August 1983): 18–26.

Ramet, Pedro, ed. *Yugoslavia in the 1980's*. New York: Westview, 1985.

Rosenau, Pauline Marie. *Post-modernism and the Social Sciences*. Princeton, N.J.: Princeton Univ. Press, 1992.

Rusinow, Dennison. *The Crisis in Croatia*. New York: American Universities Field Staff, 1972.

————. "Unfinished Business: Yugoslav National Questions in the Tito Era and Beyond." In *American Universities Field Staff Reports.* New York: American Universities Field Staff, 1981.

————. *Yugoslav Experiment.* Berkeley: Univ. of California Press, 1974.

Schmitter, Phillipe. "Still the Century of Corporatism?" *Review of Politics* (January 1974).

Seton-Watson, Hugh. *The East European Revolutions.* New York: Praeger, 1955.

Sher, Gerson S. *Praxis.* Bloomington: Indiana Univ. Press, 1977.

————, ed. *Marxist Humanism and Praxis.* Buffalo: Prometheus Books, 1978.

Stojanović, Traian. *A Study in Balkan Civilization.* New York: Alfred Knopf, 1967.

Šuvar, Stipe. *Medjunacijonalni Odnosi.* Zagreb: Naše Teme, 1970.

————. *Nacije.* Zagreb: Naše Teme, 1970.

————. *Nacije i Medjunacijonalni Odnosi.* Zagreb: Naše Teme, 1988.

Szelenyi, Ivan. "The Prospects and Limits of the East European New Class Project." *Politics and Society* 15, no. 2 (1986–87).

Talmon, J. L. *Romanticism and Revolt: Europe 1815–1848.* London: Thames and Hudson, 1967.

Taylor, A. J. P. *The Hapsburg Monarchy.* London: Hamish Hamilton, 1948.

Thompson, Mark. *A Paper House: The Destruction of Yugoslavia.* New York: Viking, 1992.

Tihany, Leslie C. *A History of Middle Europe.* New Brunswick, N.J.: Rutgers Univ. Press, 1976.

Tismaneanu, Vladimir. *The Crisis of Marxist Ideology in Eastern Europe.* London: Routledge, 1988.

Tomaševich, Jozo. *War and Revolution in Yugoslavia: The Chetniks.* Stanford, Calif.: Stanford Univ. Press, 1975.

————. *War and Revolution in Yugoslavia: The Ustashe.* Stanford, Calif.: Stanford Univ. Press, 1978.

Tomc, Georg. "Regional Differences and Income Stratification in Yugoslavia." Paper presented at Woodrow Wilson Conference, Washington, D.C., 1986.

Triska, Jan, and Charles Gati, eds. *Blue Collar Workers in Eastern Europe.* London: George Allen and Unwin, 1981.

Ward, Barbara. *Nationalism and Ideology.* New York: Norton, 1967.

West, Rebecca. *Black Lamb and Grey Falcon.* New York: Viking, 1940.

Willet, Peter. *The Nonaligned in Havana.* New York: St. Martin's, 1981.

Wolff, Robert Lee. *The Balkans in Our Time.* New York: Norton, 1956.

Woodward, Susan. "Corporatist Authoritarianism versus Socialist Authoritarianism in Yugoslavia." Paper presented at a meeting of the Political Science Association, New York, 1981.

INDEX

Abdic, Fikret, 195
Abkhazia, 212 n. 7
abortion, 78, 133, 144
Academy of Sciences. *See* Croatian Academy of Sciences; Serbian Academy of Sciences
Afghanistan, 199
African Americans, 83, 137, 188, 201, 212 n. 4
African-American Studies, 137, 188
African Studies, 137
aid: Eastern Europe's need for, 89, 92; linking human rights to, 146–47; political manipulation of, 194–95; prerequisites of, 99
Albania, 119, 162, 209 n. 3. *See also* Albanians
Albanians: grievances of, 26; in Kosovo, 106, 116, 117–18, 118–19, 209 n. 1; in Macedonia, 103; Milošević's tactics and, 60, 61; nationalist myths of, 137; number of, in Yugoslav republics following the Second World War, 26; rape and, 121; resistance to Serbs in Kosovo, 119–20; Serbs' attitude toward, 115; short-term prospects for, 162; treatment of, in second Yugoslavia, 100–101; women's rights among, 121; Yugoslav census figures for (1981), 29, 30. *See also* Albania
Algeria, 129, 130
Anderson, Benedict, 187, 212 n. 1

anti-Semitism, 75, 84, 146, 208 n. 1, 211 n. 5
Arkan, 69, 192
Armenia, 133
Army. *See* Yugoslav National Army
Arrow Cross party, 142
atrocities. *See* concentration camps; ethnic cleansing; massacres; rape
Austria: role of, in the disintegration of Yugoslavia, 12, 51–52, 53; support of Croatian independence, 31; ultranationalists in, 138, 139; wartime massacres and, 33
Austria-Hungary, 22, 24, 40
Austrian Empire, 22
Azerbaijan, 3

Bakunin, Mikhail, 23
Balkan wars, 102, 114, 209 n. 1
Bangladesh, 52
Barber, Benjamin, 152, 197
Basques, 86, 151, 186, 197, 200
Battle of Kosovo (1389), 72, 113–14
Belgium, 37
Benelux, 166, 169
Biafra, 86, 210 n. 1
birth control, 118, 122, 133
Black Hand, the, 174
Black Lamb and Grey Falcon (West), 53, 189
Black Studies, 137. *See also* African-American Studies
blockades, 163
Bokassa, Emperor, 134
Bolsheviks, 35

in, 81, 145; nationalists in, 159;
Native Americans in, 200; neo-
Nazis in, 186; politics as theater in,
154; politics of identity in, 159–60,
198; problems of multiethnicity in,
172; racism and ethnic chauvinism
in, 188; responsibility for death
of Yugoslavia, 186; trends in
universities in, 17
Unity of Death, 174
universities: African-American history
and U.S., 137; attitudes toward
Eastern Europe in U.S., 17
Ustaše, 41, 73, 83, 104, 142,
178; massacres by, 30, 62, 107;
massacres of, 31

Vance, Cyrus, 193
Vance-Owen agreement (for Bosnia),
182, 183; provisions of, 6–7
Vance plan (for Croatia): provisions
of, 5; weaknesses of, 182–83
Vanzetti, Bartolomeo, 188
Visković, Nikola, 182
Vojvodina: Austria-Hungary's influence on, 24; borders of, 25, 26;
census figures (1981) for, 206
n. 4; economic policies of former
Yugoslavia toward, 71; Milošević's
tactics and, 60; in second Yugoslavia, 100; Serbia and, 106; written
language in, 28
Vukovar, 4, 192, 205 n. 3
Vyzhutovich, Valery, 93

Walesa, Lech, 47
war-crimes trials, 8
welfare states, 80, 81, 86, 93, 94,
148
West, Rebecca, 53, 189
West Bank, the, 84
Western Europe: Bosnia as a threat to
stability in, 2; different models of

market economies in, 94; Eastern
Europe's need for aid from, 89;
failure to act in Bosnia, 184;
nationalism and xenophobia in
parliaments of, 138; nationalism
of "submerged" nations of, 196;
nationalists in, 159; neo-Nazis
in, 186; politics of identity in,
160; roots of racism and ethnic
chauvinism in, 187, 188; youth
culture in, 73
Wilson, Woodrow, 24, 188
women's rights, 78–79, 118, 129,
130; in Kosovo, 120–22; in
Macedonia, 122
workers' councils, 64
World Bank, 12, 160
World War I. *See* First World War
World War II. *See* Second World War

Young Turks, 142
Yugoslav National Army: decay of,
106; events in Kosovo and, 123;
explanation of rogue character
of, 163–65; invasion of Slovenia,
43; massacres by, 31; nationalism
and devolution of, 39; national
makeup of, 40–42; responsibility
for destruction of Yugoslavia,
8–10, 63, 149–50
Yugoslav National Liberation Army,
35
Yugoslavia, former: borders after
Second World War, 25; ethnic
balance in, 36–40; ethnic makeup
of, 28–30; history of formation of,
22–25; responsibility for breakup
of, 51–53, 69–72; settlement of
national disputes in, 100–101

Zadar, 25, 26, 41
Zionism, 82
Žjerjavić, Vladimir, 206–7 n. 5

Bogdan Denitch, currently professor of sociology at the CUNY Graduate Center, is the author of several books, including *After the Flood: Politics and Democracy in the Wake of Communism* (1992); *The End of the Cold War* (Minnesota, 1990); *Limits and Possibilities: The Crisis of Yugoslav Socialism* (Minnesota, 1990); and *The Socialist Debate: Beyond the Red and the Green* (1990). He has written articles on nationalism, multiethnic societies, U.S. foreign policy, social movements, and various topics on Europe in transition. He is also an editor of *Dissent*.